TRUST ME,
I KNOW
WHAT
I'M DOING

TRUST ME, I KNOW WHAT I'M DOING

100 More Mistakes That Lost Elections,
Ended Empires, and Made the World
What It Is Today

BILL FAWCETT

Berkley Books, New York

THE BERKLEY PUBLISHING GROUP
Published by the Penguin Group
Penguin Group (USA) Inc.
375 Hudson Street, New York, New York 10014, USA

Penguin Group (Canada), 90 Eglinton Avenue East, Suite 700, Toronto, Ontario M4P 2Y3, Canada
(a division of Pearson Penguin Canada Inc.) • Penguin Books Ltd., 80 Strand, London WC2R 0RL,
England • Penguin Ireland, 25 St. Stephen's Green, Dublin 2, Ireland (a division of Penguin
Books Ltd.) • Penguin Group (Australia), 707 Collins Street, Melbourne, Victoria 3008, Australia
(a division of Pearson Australia Group Pty. Ltd.) • Penguin Books India Pvt. Ltd., 11 Community
Centre, Panchsheel Park, New Delhi—110 017, India • Penguin Group (NZ), 67 Apollo Drive,
Rosedale, Auckland 0632, New Zealand (a division of Pearson New Zealand Ltd.) • Penguin Books,
Rosebank Office Park, 181 Jan Smuts Avenue, Parktown North 2193, South Africa • Penguin China,
B7 Jaiming Center, 27 East Third Ring Road North, Chaoyang District, Beijing 100020, China

Penguin Books Ltd., Registered Offices: 80 Strand, London WC2R 0RL, England

This is an original publication of The Berkley Publishing Group.

The publisher does not have any control over and does not assume any
responsibility for author or third-party websites or their content.

Copyright © 2012 by Bill Fawcett & Associates Inc.
Interior maps created by David Cherry. Maps copyright © 2012 by Bill Fawcett & Associates Inc.
Cover illustrations by Dave Hopkins / American Artists.
Cover design by Danielle Abbiate.

PUBLISHING HISTORY
Berkley trade paperback edition / December 2012

Library of Congress Cataloging-in-Publication Data

Fawcett, Bill.
Trust me, I know what I'm doing : 100 more mistakes that lost elections,
ended empires, and made the world what it is today / Bill Fawcett.
p.   cm.
ISBN 978-0-425-25736-4
1. History—Miscellanea.   2. History—Errors, inventions, etc.   I. Title.
D10.F37 2012
909—dc23
2012025593

PRINTED IN THE UNITED STATES OF AMERICA

10   9   8   7   6   5   4   3   2   1

To Susan Allison

INTRODUCTION

Here you have the story of some of the world's most powerful men making absolutely horrible decisions and obvious mistakes. Any good cynic will immediately ask how to narrow the choices down to just one hundred through all of history. Certainly there were a lot of mistakes to choose from. Those included here are some of the most interesting and outrageous errors that generals, kings, and presidents have made. Some dramatically changed everything, some are fun to read about, and many will make you marvel that they happened at all. These mistakes, bad decisions, and the occasional scandal all affected how you live your life today. When we look at the past, it becomes obvious that the march of history is often a stumble. How you live, work, and love today are as much the result of mistakes as they are the result of some brilliant plans or an inspired leader's guidance. Take a good look around, and then read the headlines. Really, did you think things got this way on purpose?

||||||||||||||||||||||||||||||||||||||||||||||||||||||||||||||||||||||||||

LOSING IT ALL

Immortality

259 BCE, CHINA

||||||||||||||||||||||||||||||||||||||||||||||||||||||||||||||||||||||||||

I n a look at the mistakes and failures of leaders all through history it seems appropriate to begin with a man who changed half the world but failed himself and his dynasty. Most certainly, the young prince Ying Zheng became the most successful ruler of his time, yet he ended his reign as perhaps the greatest failure.

Qin Shi Huang is often called the first emperor of China. In fact, that is what he called himself, and it is the literal translation of his name and title, Qin Shi Huang (pronounced *chin shuh huang*). In the West, Qin is often phonetically spelled "Chin," as in "China." This is not because he was the first person to rule a large part of China. For generations before Qin Shi Huang was born, northern China was controlled by the Zhou dynasty. But the Zhou were merely the most dominant of many, almost independent, warlords. Qin Shi Huang became something new and different.

Empires had risen in China where two or more of the many warring states had been conquered for a few years or even a few generations. For almost three centuries before the rise of Qin Shi Huang, the nations of China were simply, and appropriately, referred to as the "warring states." These nations were Qi, Wei, Yan, Zhao, Han, Chu, and Qin. By the time Qin Shi Huang took the throne, the last remnants of Zhou control over the seven feudal nations were gone, and warfare among them was common. His era was also the time period that gave rise to the study and science of war, including Sun Tzu's famous book *The Art of War*.

So if there were earlier "emperors," why is Qin Shi Huang universally recognized as being the first emperor of China? The eastern Zhou and those others who had tried to dominate the heartland of China had ruled through the local nobles and princes. The earlier emperors were basically just the most dominant feudal lords, controlling, through the local lords, various parts of China. Qin Shi Huang took a different route and became the ruler of something that was new at the time. The empire he created was not just another collection of feudal loyalties; Qin Shi Huang instead created a centralized administration and culturally uniform state. Qin Shi Huang was the first emperor of China as we think of that nation today. He may have failed in many ways, but he left behind a land with awareness of its unique and shared identity.

While the young Qin Shi Huang did begin his life as a prince, his early years were hardly idyllic. To begin with, the young prince Ying Zheng was likely not his father's child. His mother may have originally been the wife of, or was at least the lover of, a rich merchant named Lü Buwei. This merchant had also become the friend of a young Qin prince. When Zhoa Ji became pregnant, Lü arranged for her to become the prince's concubine. In 259 BCE, she gave birth in Hanan to Ying Zheng, whom the prince believed to be his own son.

When the future emperor was only thirteen years old, his father, the ruler of Qin, died. Ying Zheng was too young to rule in such turbulent times, so Lü Buwei acted as his regent. Yep, the same man who may well also have been his father. This worked at first, but as Ying Zheng got older, he began to make his own decisions. This does not seem to have gone over well with his regent.

In 240, Zheng was nineteen and trying to take full control of

Qin. His regent and possible father, Lü Buwei, plotted with the king of Wei to take over Qin while the young king was away from the capital. His mother also joined the plot. By that time, she had borne two children, potential rivals for his throne, by a general named Loa Ai. Her son may have been a king, but her personal habits certainly were not noble. Their armed revolt failed. Both his mother and Lü Buwei were banished. The dowager queen spent the rest of her life living isolated on an estate in a far corner of Qin. The former regent, whom some historians suspect was also Zheng's father, was said to have become so obsessed waiting for further punishment that two years later he drank poison.

The young king learned quickly, and this time he surrounded himself with wise advisers. The administration of Qin and the Qin army was dramatically improved. The economy of Qin boomed, and he hired the best professionals to train and lead his armies. By his mid-twenties, Ying Zheng ruled the most powerful of the seven warring kingdoms.

Ying Zheng became feared, and with good cause, by his weaker neighbors. Outright war was only one of the ways that the warring states' kings attacked each other. In 227 BCE, the king of Yan sent two very skillful assassins who penetrated all of Zheng's defenses. The young ruler literally fought them off himself, using his personal sword until help arrived. Later, a musician entertaining his court almost succeeded in assassinating the Qin king with a lead-weighted flute. More attempts failed, but they did seem to have given the young ruler an understandable obsession with staying alive. He was not paranoid; rather, a lot of people were trying to kill him. This was the turbulent era in which the classic Chinese movies such as *Crouching Tiger, Hidden Dragon* and *Hero* were set. In fact, the hit movie *Hero* is the story of an assassin from one of the conquered warring states. Seeking revenge, he set out to kill Qin Shi Huang, but when he shared the vision of a united China, the emperor was spared.

In the next ten years Ying Zheng became Qin Shi Huang by conquering all six of the rival states. The last to fall were Yan and

Zhao in 222 BCE. All through this time there were likely more as-sassination attempts. At least one, again sent by the Yan king, al-most succeeded. With northern China under his control, Qin Shi Huang continued throughout the next decade to expand his rule south even as far as today's Vietnam.

The emperor had seen how the earlier attempts to build a last-ing empire on a feudal foundation had failed. So he remade his administration using appointed officials. The former nobles were either neutralized or invited (in the way you cannot refuse) to leave their home provinces and live near the capital. This sepa-rated them from their former lands and any support, and isolated China's former nobility in a place where they could be easily watched. Qin Shi Huang then simplified the written language and forced its use all through the kingdom. He issued new money, standardized weights, and created (using forced peasant labor) a vast network of roads.

The first emperor had both united and given a common iden-tity to an area easily equal to the land conquered later by Europe's greatest empire, Rome. At this same time in Europe, Rome was an Italian power that was still digesting conquered Etruscan cities. When Qin Shi Huang conquered the last of the warring states, Rome was a central Italian power that was desperately fighting off a Gaulic horde that almost destroyed the city before its empire got started. Although it was not ruled by his descendants, Qin Shi Huang created the basis for the Chinese empire that survived more than a thousand years longer than Rome.

But there was a much darker side to Qin Shi Huang's rule as well. Having decided on Confucianism as the basis for his bureau-cracy, he banned all other philosophies. This ban did not just keep other viewpoints out of textbooks. He ordered that all non-Confucian books and those not directly related to his new laws be burned. In 212 BCE, a group of scholars had the audacity to dis-agree with the emperor, so he had 460 of them buried alive. Then he had another 700 stoned to death. It is not surprising that after all that, there was a lack of public questioning of his laws or decisions. To unite China, Qin Shi Huang became one of the most oppressive and hated rulers in history.

It seems that most leaders who rule great empires cannot resist building on a grand scale. Qin Shi Huang did this, erecting palaces and the Lingqu Canal. This canal was a commercial success, linking the Yangtze and Pearl River networks. It allowed trade (and taxes) to expand greatly once completed. It also cost the lives of thousands of laborers who were literally worked to death. Not only did Qin Shi Huang demand all war prisoners and convicts work themselves to death on his massive government projects, but he also forced every male in China to spend a year working on them without pay. It was a policy designed to antagonize virtually every family, and it did.

The greatest construction project in the world was also begun by Qin Shi Huang. Even a unified China was not powerful enough to stop massive raids by the horsemen of the steppes. At the time these horsemen were called the Xiongnu. Several hundred years later, these same tribes became known as the Huns. So the emperor ordered a series of fortifications joined by a wall or bank. Literally hundreds of thousands of laborers were forced to work on this defensive line, and tens of thousands, some say hundreds of thousands, died brutally while building it. These were the first sections of what we today call the Great Wall of China.

But the mistake that Qin Shi Huang made was not of overbuilding, nor was it a poor philosophical decision. It was a personal mistake. He wanted his empire to last forever and eventually decided the best way to do that was to seek immortality. The first emperor of China became obsessed with finding a potion or magic item that would grant him that immortality.

Much of the emperor's efforts were spent not ruling but seeking an elixir of eternal life. To accomplish this, he financed all sorts of magicians and charlatans. Much of his time was spent traveling to the far corners of the empire on this search. But Qin Shi Huang did not travel alone. He was always accompanied by a good portion of his court, hundreds of servants, and about sixty thousand soldiers. While doing this, he tended to be a less effective ruler. When this caused a problem, he simply became more brutal, torturing and killing any discontents.

There was also a second problem with Qin Shi Huang's decision to become immortal. If you are going to live forever, then you do not need to worry about your successor. The emperor had an heir, but spent no time teaching him to rule and generally kept him isolated so he could not become a threat to his father.

Now, Qin Shi Huang was provided by his many alchemists and magicians with potions that were to make him immortal. Perhaps some of these men even believed in what they fed their emperor. Unfortunately for Qin Shi Huang, the base ingredient in many of these immortality potions was mercury (the liquid metal). Mercury is highly toxic and a nerve poison. Long before exposure to mercury kills you, it affects the brain. Hat makers in Europe once used mercury to make felt, and it was also used when they chewed the felt cloth, softening it as part of the process. Almost every man who chewed on the mercury-soaked cloth went mad. This result became the source of the phrase, still used today, as being *mad as a hatter*. Eventually, Qin Shi Huang himself became mad as a hatter. So China had an absolute and notoriously brutal emperor who was also going insane. He still demanded that his every command be instantly obeyed, even if those commands were irrational. Although it is likely that no one pointed that out to him. Life in a traveling court must have been nerve wracking and was often fatal.

It was on a journey searching for yet another rumored magic item that could make his immortality potion work that Qin Shi Huang died near the seashore. Shortly after his death, the inadequately prepared first son and heir committed suicide, tricked into it by his prime minister who installed and controlled Qin Shi Huang's second son as emperor.

With the repressive and extravagant emperor's death, the resentment of just about everyone erupted into revolt. The nobles saw a hope of regaining their former position (but most eventually failed in this), and peasant revolts became commonplace. Three years later, in 207 BCE, an army of rebels defeated the Qin army and Qin Shi Huang's dynasty ended. Ironically, some of those rebels were likely armed with weapons looted from the now-famous terra-cotta figures who were meant to guard Qin Shi Huang after his death.

The first emperor of China succeeded in creating a unified nation. And that nation was truly the first of its kind. But because of his obsession with immortality, his own dynasty lasted less than two years after his death. Qin Shi Huang united China and then died early, losing it all by foolishly trying to live and rule forever.

‖‖‖

PERSONAL AMBITION

The War Lover, Alcibiades

431 BCE, GREECE AND SICILY

‖‖‖

This is a classic example of how the ambition and greed of one politician brought down an entire nation.

In 431 BCE, a twenty-seven-year war began between Athens and Sparta. This was called the Peloponnesian War, named after the lower peninsula of Greece, the Peloponnese, where most of it was fought. The war began well for Athens, even though Sparta invaded their land. Knowing that they could not defeat the Spartans in a land battle, the Athenians were sold on a plan by their leader, Pericles. The plan was initially successful, and the Greeks retreated into their city, which was protected by high walls. Because there was no real siege equipment yet, there was nothing the Spartans could do but burn down the farmhouses around the city and wait outside the walls. But Athens was also connected by a long fortification to their nearby port, and so it could not be starved out and even continued to be a major trade center during this time.

For the next year, the Spartan army sat outside those high walls, and the Athenians used their superior fleet to cause their rival Greek city-state and its allies problems elsewhere. The eventual drawback came during the siege. The population of Athens more than tripled and inevitably plague, probably the bubonic, arose in the crowded city. In the next months, Athens lost almost a quarter of its citizens, and many who survived were weakened. Athens's foresighted leader, Pericles, died in this plague and Cleon took over. Cleon and the Athenian army, who were transported by their fleet of triremes, actually managed to defeat the Spartans on land at Sphacteria. But the Spartans countered with a successful campaign against the Athenian allies in northeastern Greece. More battles ensued in 422 BCE, and both Cleon and the Spartan leader Brasidas were killed.

After nine years of war, both sides were tired. So the leader of the peace faction, Nicias, took charge of Athens. A treaty with Sparta was signed in 421, over the objections of Alcibiades and the faction we would today call Athens's "hawks." There was a chance for Athens to recover and rebuild, with most of her dominance in Greece intact. But the ambitious and charismatic Alcibiades was not satisfied with peace. If there were peace, the assembly would have no reason to put him in power, and there would be no glory from victories to add to his prestige. So the ambitious Athenian noble soon found a way to restart the war. The opportunity came when a group of nobles, who had been displaced from a small Sicilian city run by their rival city Syracuse, came to Athens, silver in hand.

Early in the spring of the following summer the Athenian envoys arrived from Sicily, and the Egestaeans with them, bringing sixty talents of uncoined silver, as a month's pay for sixty ships, which they were to ask to have sent them. The Athenians held an assembly and, after hearing from the Egestaeans and their own envoys a report, as attractive as it was untrue, upon the state of affairs generally, and in particular as to the money, of which, it was said, there was abundance in the temples and the treasury, voted to send sixty ships to Sic-

ily, under the command of Alcibiades, son of Clinias, Nicias, son of Niceratus, and Lamachus, son of Xenophanes, who were appointed with full powers; they were to help the Egestaeans against the Selinuntines, to restore Leontini upon gaining any advantage in the war, and to order all other matters in Sicily as they should deem best for the interests of Athens.

Thucydides, *The History of the Peloponnesian War*

Anxious for glory, Alcibiades and his allies saw the invitation to assist the Sicilian city as a pretext to lead the Athenian army in a takeover of the entire island. Sicily was one of the richest areas in the Mediterranean and, like Greece, was divided between competing cities. These cities had begun as Greek colonies and shared both the Greek language and culture. They had little involvement in the Peloponnesian War so far, though what little assistance Syracuse had once given Sparta was also used to gain support for Alcibiades's invasion. The decision was classic realpolitik. The war party saw a way to enhance its own standing and gain a new colony for Athens. And they took it.

Greed and ambition brought about this decision in an Athens that was still recovering from plague and a war with Sparta. This was a war that had ended only by a truce, and it was far from settled. Sparta was likely to, and later did, start the war again. But that didn't matter, because a successful war would make Alcibiades and his followers supreme in Athens. The assembly voted to invade a distant and powerful island. There seemed little motive beyond politics and greed. There was no threat to Athens, and there were no great philosophical differences. The real irony was that Syracuse, the major city in Sicily, was also the other most active democracy of all the Greek states. They were governed in the same manner as Athens, not by elected kings, such as those who ruled Sparta, or hereditary emperors, such as in Persia. Syracuse was, in its way, politically more like Athens than almost any other Greek colony. Located on the tip of Sicily, Syracuse was, also like Athens, a major center for trade and commerce. For no more reason than that they could, and in what proved to be the middle of their war with Sparta, Athens chose to attack a powerful and distant city-state that was similar to them in almost every way.

Politics was vicious in Athens. Before the expedition left, Alcibiades, its chief proponent and likely military commander among the three leading the expedition, found himself accused of sacrilege. The penalty was death, and it is probable the charge was trumped up by his political enemies. The timing was just too good. If he stayed and fought the charge, the fleet and most of his supporters would be gone. If he left, Alcibiades could be called back at any time and the assembly would still be controlled by the opposition. He tried to get the trial to happen before the fleet sailed for Syracuse, but he failed to do so. He chose to accompany his men. This put extra pressure on him to find a quick victory. If he returned a hero, the charges would just disappear.

At first the battle went well, and the Athenians defeated Syracuse's army in a traditional battle. But when the Syracusian army retreated into their city and things settled down to a siege, everything went wrong. The Athenians were not in a similar position as that of the Spartans when they were warring before. The one hopeful difference was that they had a fleet and could at least have a chance of isolating Syracuse. But this required the Athenians to keep their fleet near Syracuse, and there were few nearby protected harbors. This meant that the Athenian fleet would be vulnerable to storms.

Then Alcibiades was recalled to Athens without a success to save him. Because all of his allies were camped outside Syracuse, he knew the results of the trial were foregone. Such trials were by popular vote, and his supporters would not be there. Alcibiades, Athenian noble, chose discretion over valor, fled to Sparta, and took service with their kings.

Outside the walls of Syracuse, with the Athenians' most competent commander, Alcibiades, gone, things went from bad to worse. Nicias, who had opposed the entire invasion, became a rather indecisive commander. Reinforcements arrived, but the

Greeks could not take the city. Then, with most of the triremes with them, a large part of the entire Athenian fleet was lost in a storm. Eventually, the entire expedition, including all its reinforcements, was forced to surrender. Thousands of hoplites, the best in the Athenian army, and the majority of its fleet and sailors were gone, lost far from home while losing a war there had been no reason to start. The few thousand Athenian survivors spent the rest of their lives at hard labor in Sicily's quarries. Virtually no one returned home to Athens.

The result of Athens's decision to attack Syracuse on little more than a pretext was its eventual doom. It was not a rapid thing, and fortunes in the war that soon restarted between Athens and Sparta changed more than once. Even Alcibiades eventually found himself back in Athens and commanding another army for a short time. The Athenian army, their navy, and their wealth never recovered from the losses on Sicily. Sparta restarted the war, and after twenty-seven years, they finally defeated Athens. Athens lost the Peloponnesian War not in battle against Sparta, but because of an unneeded and ill-fated war they chose to start against fellow Greeks on an island far from their city.

The man who persuaded Athens to mount the expedition against Syracuse that cost the city-state so much was Alcibiades. He was considered one of the best-looking and most charismatic men in Athens. A member of an old, noble family, Alcibiades was smart, charming, a good speaker, and rich. Among those who sang his praises was Socrates. Yes, that Socrates, master of philosophy and famed hemlock drinker, was a fan of Alcibiades'.

Alcibiades was the leader of the faction in Athens that disliked Nicias's treaty with Sparta and wished to continue with the war. They got their wish, but only in the worst possible way. It is definitely ironic that his leadership decisions to attack Syracuse put Athens in a position in which it would eventually lose the very war he desired to restart and win.

When it became apparent he was going to be convicted of the crime of mutilating dozens of statues of Hermes, messenger of the gods, which were spread along many streets throughout the city, he was forced to change sides. The statues were thought to bring the city good luck, and the myth was that their destruction doomed Athens to bad luck. (Hmm, perhaps they were right.) The penalty for this sacrilege was death. When recalled for what was a certain conviction, Alcibiades chose instead to run to Sparta and offer his services against Athens. Alcibiades finally had the war he had agitated for, but he was now fighting against Athens and for Sparta.

For a while Alcibiades's arrangement with Sparta worked, but while leading Spartans in assisting the city of Chios in revolting against Athenian control, the former Athenian leader was warned that he was to be assassinated. It seems that Alcibiades had se-duced the wife of the Spartan king, Agis II, and the man wanted revenge. In fact most of Sparta suspected that the king's new son was actually Alcibiades's offspring. Thus the Athenian had to flee once more. Alcibiades was now unwelcome in both Sparta and Athens. This pretty much ruled out his living in any Greek city in the world because, after two decades of near constant war, they were by now all allied to one side or the other. So Alcibiades fled to the protection of the capital of the Persian satrap (governor) Tissaphernes. Tissaphernes was in charge of dealing with Greece for the Persian Empire and, to date, had supported Sparta with gold and supplies. It was traditional for Persia to play one Greek city-state against the other. They had been doing it for generations. There Alcibiades persuaded the satrap to stop supporting Sparta and instead support Athens.

Bringing with him Persian support, and more important Per-sian gold, Alcibiades was once more welcomed in Athens. He returned to the city and was eventually put in charge of their army. The position didn't last very long because one of his chosen commanders, Antiochus, was badly defeated, and Alcibiades took the blame for appointing the loser. Alcibiades continued to be active in Athenian politics but found his advice on military ac-tions ignored. When the city fell to Sparta in 404 BCE, he was no longer safe anywhere in Greece and began a journey to Persia. Alcibiades never made it. His party was attacked on the road, and he was killed. The Spartans were suspected because Alcibiades would have been the logical focus of any Athenian revolt. But others thought he died at the hands of the brothers of a Persian noblewoman he had seduced.

3, 4, 5, and 6

LACK OF PLANNING

Why There Was No Alexandrian Empire

356 BCE, MACEDONIA
AND PERSIA

There is no question that Alexander III of Macedon, known to most people as Alexander the Great, was one of the greatest commanders of history. He never lost a battle or failed to subdue a city he besieged. He won battles fought from Thrace and Greece to India. What this conqueror of half the world never accomplished was to leave behind a lasting empire. Because of Alexander's mistakes, the son of the woman he loved, and his heir, died young and a captive.

Born in 356 BCE, Alexander was the son of Philip of Macedon. Philip was first the undisputed king of the militarily powerful kingdom of Macedonia, and later he was the effective ruler of all of Greece. When Alexander was born, Greece and the Persian Empire had effectively been at war, hot or cold, for several generations.

Philip was a war leader. He was a man who took what was a rather backwater kingdom, Macedonia, and turned it into the most powerful state on the Greek peninsula. Philip developed a professional army with new weapons and tactics that would serve Alexander well. While Philip was hardly an ideal parent and often a judgmental taskmaster to his son, there was no question that he spared no effort to prepare Alexander to be the leader of a united Greece and assist him in his dream of taking revenge on Persia. From the ages of thirteen to sixteen, Alexander studied philosophy, medicine, and the scientific method with Aristotle. Aristotle cultivated the young prince's inquisitive mind. All his life, Alexander valued knowledge, and it is not by mistake that the greatest library in history was located in Alexandria.

Alexander's first experience at independent command came when he was sixteen, the age of adulthood in Bronze Age Greece. Alexander was left in charge of Macedonia in 340, while his father attacked and conquered a Greek area known as Byzantium. With Philip away, the Maedi, a Thracian mountain tribe in the northern part of Macedonia, chose to revolt. They likely felt that with Philip's young and still-unknown son in charge, they had an advantage. Alexander and the forces he raised in Macedonia crushed the Maedi.

Two years later Alexander was entrusted with command of the entire left wing of the Macedonian army in the battle that gave Philip undisputed control of all of Greece. In a final bid for independence, a number of Greek states had allied together and challenged Philip's rule. The battle was hard fought until Alexander saw a gap open in the Greek line and led a courageous cavalry charge to it and against the flank of a sacred band of Thebes. This broke the cohesion of the Greek phalanxes and won the day. This victory was probably the high point of the relationship between Philip II and his son, Alexander III.

A few years later, Philip chose to divorce Alexander's mother, Olympia, who seemed to have been a rather difficult person, at best. She tended to mysticism and meddling in court politics. The divorce freed Philip to pursue a much younger beauty. This threatened Alexander's position as heir. Should the new wife have a son, he would be considered just as eligible to replace Philip as Alexander. He did not take this well and insulted Philip publicly at the wedding feast. Alexander and his mother were forced to flee to Epirus, but Alexander was able to fairly quickly reconcile with his father. His mother, Olympia, remained away from the Macedonian court until Philip died.

Macedonia was not really part of Greece and was considered by Greeks to be an uncultured barbarian land with ambitions of being Greek. This was pretty much what it was until Philip II put it on the military and political map. There is nothing like a convert, and Philip strove to be seen as the protector, not the dictator, of Greece. Alexander was raised to be a true believer in the superiority of Greek culture and philosophy. Perhaps because he was considered by some Greeks to be an outsider, the young prince, like many who try to fit in from outside, was also fanatical about being a champion for Greece. Or at least he was until he found himself conqueror of all of Persia. (But that mistake we will discuss a little later.) Also his father, Aristotle, and all of the Greek philosophers and leaders imbued Alexander with a sense of both the Greek military superiority and the need to defeat a Persian Empire that continued to threaten its independence.

Twice Persia had nearly succeeded in conquering all of Greece, and this left a lasting animosity between both sides. Persia also had annexed all of the Greek colonies on the eastern shore of the Aegean Sea. Greece, having at most a small fraction of the population and wealth of Persia, also unquestionably had a very great chip on its collective shoulder. Persians made no secret of the fact that they saw Greeks as being rough and uncultured. From his first days, it was Alexander's ambition to defeat Persia and spread "his" Greek culture, establishing a lasting empire in which Greece would be secure. It is this goal that dominated Alexander's life, but because of his leadership style and lapses in judgment, he was doomed to fail.

ALEXANDER'S ARMY

The Macedonian army, which because of Alexander's invasion of Persia contained troops from all over Greece, was the most powerful and effective military force of its day. Beyond defeating two attacks by the much wealthier and more populous Persian Empire, the Greek phalanx was recognized as superior to any unit the Persians could put in the field. In fact, many Greek men, coming from relative poverty and limited opportunity, chose to become mercenaries and often found employment in Persia. Greek mercenaries were often hired by the Persian satraps (governors) and often formed the core of any Persian army. Greek mercenaries fought for the Persian emperor Darius III even in his final defeat at Arbela.

In 401 BCE, a force of about ten thousand Greek mercenaries was hired by Cyrus the Younger in his attempt to overthrow his brother, Artaxerxes II, the Persian emperor. Cyrus's army met Artaxerxes's and defeated it, but Cyrus was killed during the battle. His army fell apart, the Persian units disappearing into the countryside or changing allegiance. This left ten thousand Greek mercenaries deep within Persia with no employer or paymaster and on the losing side of a revolt. The local satrap then made matters worse when he tricked and killed all of the Greek commanders. This demonstrated the power and sheer intimidating strength of the Greek warriors: The ten thousand Greek soldiers were still able to walk out of the heart of Persia intact. Their story was told in *Anabasis*, and the account was written in 401 BCE by Xenophon, who was one of the three men who took charge when their officers were killed. The account would have been read by Alexander, and its lessons were not lost on him. Such military feats were likely what encouraged first Philip, and then Alexander, to think he could defeat an empire with many times the population of his own and massively greater wealth.

Infantry battles in this era tended to resemble a rugby scrimmage. Both sides pushed and killed until one side gave way. The most effective unit for pushing and stabbing was the Greek phalanx. It was composed of from as few as eight to as many as twenty-four or even more lines of pike-armed soldiers. These pikes were often well over twenty feet long. In reality, only the men in the first few lines could use their pikes. The majority of the men in the rear simply pushed forward on the men in front of them. This kept the formation moving forward or at least prevented them from being pushed back. Because the phalanx could remain intact only when the men were standing or moving forward, being pushed back could mean defeat.

A phalanx, on flat terrain and moving forward, was nearly unstoppable except by anything but another phalanx. The real problem with the phalanx as a formation was its inflexibility. It was incredibly powerful at its front but was unable to respond to flank attacks. Nor was it effective on rough terrain or once it had lost cohesion.

Among the innovations introduced by Philip II and Alexander was the use of the sarissa, a shorter type of pike that was about sixteen feet long. Their infantry was trained not only to fight in the traditional square formation of the phalanx but also to form long lines only a few men deep or create wedged or triangular formations with the point facing their opponents. This flexibility, when tied to a much superior use of cavalry, gave Alexander's armies a decisive superiority.

To understand the mistakes he made, you have to remember that Alexander's goals were to unite his known world under one empire. This would not only eliminate any threat to Greece but lead to universal peace and prosperity. His means to do this was to conquer everyone and anyone. It was, to steal a quote, to be the war to end all war. The reason we call Philip's son Alexander "The Great" is because he basically succeeded in the conquering part. For over a decade and a half, Alexander won every siege and defeated every army he fought, even when badly outnumbered. Unquestionably, he was the greatest military mind of his time, if not all times. But when you look at the long-term results, you see that there he was far less successful.

3: Leading from the Front

Philip II had already put his plan to invade Persia into motion when he was assassinated. He had a son by his new wife, but the boy was still a baby. There had always been some question about whether Alexander had anything to do with the murder. It was committed by one of his friends, and the killer was slain immediately by Alexander's personal retinue. With the only other heir very young and a war virtually started, there was no choice but to make Alexander king of Macedonia. Olympia, Alexander's mother, returned and took over the court. Philip's new wife and infant son did not fare well or last long.

Alexander was not able to begin the attack on Persia right away. First an alliance of Greek cities decided it was once again a good time to regain their independence. He hurried south and dealt with them. Then a number of those same Thracian tribes he had battled at age sixteen revolted again. While the new Macedonian king was putting down that uprising, a number of Greek cities heard a rumor that Alexander had died. They revolted again. Alexander had to rush his army all the way across Macedonia, but in a week they were approaching Athens, the center of resistance. The city took one look at who led the large army approaching and "welcomed" him into the city. This crushed the Greek's second revolt and established Alexander as Philip's heir. Alexander was in complete control and was finally ready to move against Persia. He should have learned a lesson from all this about succession and chaos, but in the very end, he didn't.

With his kingdom secure, Alexander was ready to lead his new army into Persia. Landing with about forty thousand soldiers, the Macedonians were soon met by forces raised by the local satrap. They fought with the Persians in their favorite situation, lined up with the Granicus River in their front and forcing any attack to cross it.

Alexander formed his army with a dense formation of infantry in the center and his cavalry on both sides. When the Persians saw Alexander commanded the cavalry on the right side, they reinforced that part of their army, knowing he would lead the decisive attack. They were right about Alexander leading the attack but not where it would fall. The battle opened with one of Alexander's best generals, Parmenion, attacking Persia on the left with horsemen backed by infantry. He had some success, and the Persians reacted by moving what remained of their reserves and some of the soldiers from the center of their position. They succeeded in stopping Parmenion's horsemen and infantry. Then, just as the new Persian troops were forcing the Macedonian left back, Alexander led his horsemen across the front of the rest of his unengaged infantry and tore into the weakened Persian center. The new Macedonian king rode at the point of a giant cavalry wedge, which cut deeply through the Persian heavy cavalry fronting their line and then easily through the lighter infantry behind. The charge then turned and drove toward where the Persian satrap commanded.

Being in the front of the battle, Alexander soon was in a melee with the commanding Persian noble's bodyguards. If the official accounts are to be believed, he personally killed a number of them. Then one of the Persians, Spithridates, stunned the Macedonian king with a blow from his battle-ax. The mounted Persian was himself killed just before he was able to deal a deathblow. Alexander recovered and was soon able to show himself to the army, maintaining morale.

With its center shattered and its commander threatened, the entire Persian army broke and was scattered. The mounted Persian units fled and left eighteen thousand Greek mercenaries standing in the open to be mercilessly slaughtered. Alexander considered them to be traitors, and all but two thousand were killed. The survivors were all condemned to hard labor. It was a time when heroes were revered and personal courage was at a premium. Leading from the front, Alexander inspired his men, but at the cost of putting the one man who united them at risk. Perhaps at this point, when he was establishing his reputation with his father's army, this made sense. Later this courageous habit cost him dearly.

Moving south down the eastern Mediterranean coast, Alexander conquered all of the ports, one after the other. A few cities held out and took months and an engineering wonder to defeat. But eventually he controlled them all. This neutralized the powerful Persian navy without a battle. No ports, no port in a storm, and more important no food. Most of the ships and crews changed sides or were abandoned. Alexander then moved into Egypt, which welcomed him, in the tradition of the pharaohs, as being the son of a god.

Awakening to the full extent of the threat, the Persian emperor, Darius, gathered with him what should have been an overwhelming force. Alexander marched back up the coast to meet him. The two armies met on the banks of the Pinarus River, near the city of Issus. Even though Darius had far superior numbers, he took a defensive position. Alexander again feinted against one side of the Persian line and then pinned most of the rest with his infantry. Then he personally led the Companions, his best cavalry unit, and others horsemen against the Persian left, breaking through it. Alexander kept his successful horsemen in check and swung the wedge around to charge directly against the spot where Darius was commanding the battle from an ornate chariot.

The Persian emperor's personal guard, including his brother, moved forward to stop the charge and slay Alexander. Most of them died, and when Darius was unable to maintain control of his chariot after a second chariot driver died, he fled the battle-field. With their emperor in retreat, the Persian army panicked and broke up. Alexander was badly wounded in the thigh in the final stages of attacking Darius.

So who was the wiser commander? The king who led the charge and was nearly killed . . . again . . . or the emperor who fled and lost the battle but was unharmed? Alexander's first continu-ing mistake, and one that probably cost him his life, was that he led from the front and was often the first man over the wall during a siege. In one case, this habit of being first over a city wall left him alone for several minutes, wounded, surrounded by enemies, and barely saved, until, at the last second, some of his Companions arrived. Plutarch lists seven major wounds that Alexander sus-tained, the last being dealt in India, where the emperor insisted on leading the key attacks.

Plutarch's list of Alexander's major wounds is as follows:

He was wounded in the head by a sling stone and then his neck was smashed with a club while fighting in Illyria just after Philip died.

At Granicus, Alexander was badly wounded in the head by a dagger.

At the Battle of Issus, there was that sword wound to his thigh while charging at Darius.

At Gaza, Alexander was first shot in the ankle with an arrow and then had his shoulder badly dislocated.

At the battle of Maracanda, an arrow struck his leg so hard that it split the bone.

When fighting the Aspasians, he was struck deeply by another arrow in the shoulder.

Attacking the Gandridae, Alexander was once more badly wounded in one leg by an arrow.

All in all, there are historical references to Alexander being wounded at least two dozen times. The last blow was to the chest and lung while in India.

It has to be noted that many of the wounds came after the Battle of Gaugamela, when Alexander had already conquered Persia and was himself the sole emperor. If he wanted a stable empire, he could have stayed in the capital and ruled it. But he could not resist the call of war. He moved on to conquer today's Afghanistan, Bactria (where he met the love of his life, Roxanne), and eventually India. These many victories certainly won him the title of perhaps the world's greatest commander, but they were in a way without meaning. He won the wars, but he never united the empire those victories created. The many wounds he received showing his heroism almost certainly hastened his death at a young age.

So that was Alexander's first mistake: He could not stop leading from the front. He was a hero, and eventually that took its toll. The greatest general of history died at the age of thirty-three, worn out from campaigning and very much debilitated by his many wounds. He never had the chance to come back and ensure that his conquests would create the universal and lasting empire that was his vision.

4: Too Much Time Spent Fighting, Not Enough Ruling

Rather than sending out his generals to deal with any revolts after defeating Darius, Alexander spent most of the next two years leading his army over the far parts of Persia and beyond, eliminating all opposition. Because of this, there is a phrase historians

THE FACE OF ALEXANDER

Entire libraries can be filled with books that speculate on the appearance or the mind of Alexander the Great. We know he was the son of one of the other great military commanders of his era. Or we do unless we believe what his mother often maintained. She claimed that the night he was conceived she mated with a giant snake that appeared from nowhere in her bed. The snake was known as a common ploy by the god Zeus, Olympus's most notorious seducer. This meant that Alexander was the son of Zeus and a demigod. How much he himself believed this is unknown. Certainly, he used his mythical origins to ensure his welcome in such places as Egypt. It was there that the oracle at Siwa declared the Macedonian a god, and so this was accepted by many in Egypt and beyond. Perhaps the thought he was facing a demigod can help explain the otherwise courageous Darius III's behavior both times he personally faced Alexander.

Certainly as a young man Alexander looked little like his father, Philip. But then by the time of Alexander's birth, Philip's face was badly scarred and he was missing an eye. The empty socket was said to become infected often. Alexander himself was said to be well formed and very handsome. His image on coins and frescoes reflects this.

While Alexander the Great is often portrayed with blond hair, that is inaccurate. His hair was light brown, not blond, although it was often bleached by the sun during his years of campaigning. Many descriptions of Alexander also record that each of his eyes was a different color. This is a real condition but it does not affect vision. While Alexander was badly wounded several times, his face was unscarred, and he retained his good looks.

never use: *the Alexandrian Empire*. This is because there never really was one. Within months of Alexander's death, his conquests had been broken up and divided between his former generals. Years of warfare followed as each tried to conquer the other.

There was another immediate reason for this breakup as well, but we will get to that mistake soon. More than a decade after he conquered Persia, Alexander the Great spent far less than half his time actually running the empire. He took many steps that spread Greek culture and fused it with Persian, but he simply was not at the center of power and did not live long enough to bring about a true cultural change or give everyone a sense of one unified empire such as the Romans later had. Alexander never lost a battle, he was truly a great general, but in a sense he lost the war. He never managed to merge the cultures fully enough to ensure the future continuity of the empire he created. There is no question he tried, but history says in this he failed. In some ways he was more like a warlord, not an emperor, because his empire did not long survive his death.

5: Losing Empathy with His Soldiers

No one thought more of his soldiers than Alexander, and normally the men returned the feeling. But one of the things a commander has to do is understand the needs of his soldiers. Now, Alexander initially did this very well. If nothing else, leading from the front and taking the same risks as your men does help morale. But Alexander also had a greater plan, or perhaps he just got blinded by his own success, nearly losing command of his army not once, but twice.

At his greatest victory, Gaugamela, Alexander defeated the last and largest Persian army raised by Darius. Or perhaps it is more accurate to say he brilliantly created a situation in which Darius could and did make his own massive mistake and defeat himself. Having effectively taken the capital, and with it control of virtually all of the Persian Empire, Alexander soon began dressing and acting like an eastern potentate. This included wearing the ornate robes of a Persian noble, taking over the harem, partaking in extensive feasts, and the rest. He also began making his Greek commanders and soldiers not just bow to him but prostrate themselves on the floor in front of his throne. Perhaps he needed this to win over the Persian nobles and bureaucrats, but it upset many of his troops and officers. As a way to integrate the two worlds, he ordered eighty of his top commanders to take Persian brides. The discontent his behavior caused among the normally much more egalitarian Greeks and Macedonians was so bad that Alexander had to speak to the men and make a real effort to win them back. Even then he had to reluctantly allow a number of his veterans to return to Macedonia with their plunder.

But perhaps Alexander did not take the lesson to heart. As he prepared to move into India, after spending most of the last seven years campaigning, his army effectively revolted. Alexander the Great was able to regain his control by handling them masterfully and appealing to their pride and reminding them of the successes they had gained under his command. As a result, Alexander had to send back a portion of this army and move on with a smaller and more mobile force.

After his victory at the Battle of the Hydaspes, Alexander again showed how his own desires blinded him to the feelings of his soldiers. They were deep in India, having just won a difficult battle, and Alexander wanted to march east to find and conquer everything to the end of the world. For a third time, the army refused to follow. They were worn out. But this time the commanders and army were united and would not relent. Eventually Alexander agreed instead that they would travel down the Ganges to the sea and would return home from there.

So the arguably most successful commander in history three times showed he had completely lost both empathy with and the support of his army. Alexander the Great's army was fiercely loyal, but not blindly so. It was an army he never failed to lead into victory, but Alexander seemed to have failed to understand the limits of what he could demand of his remarkable force.

6: Failing to Name an Heir

Alexander's final mistake not only doomed the empire he had created but also his beloved wife and newborn son. In his years as emperor, Alexander, for reasons unknown, never officially designated a successor or even named a regent for his newborn son. He did make it clear he expected his son to rule after him, but he made no other arrangements. A younger Alexander had fought three wars just to establish his position on the throne immediately after the death of his father, Philip of Macedon. So it is hard to say that he did not understand the problems caused by there being no clear heir to the empire he wanted to last forever. But even though he spent the entire last two years of his life in the empire's Persian capital, Alexander never stated who should rule if he died.

There is no question that Alexander the Great wanted to leave behind a permanent empire. He saw an empire that merged both Greek and Asian cultures. He established over twenty cities, all named Alexandria, to support this vision of planting Greek culture throughout Persia. The most famous of these cities sits at the mouth of the Nile and is still called Alexandria more than two thousand years later. Nor is there any question that he loved his wife and cherished their son. But no matter what his intentions, leaving the succession undefined without a mechanism for transition guaranteed disaster.

The classic story, probably not true, is that when asked as he died who should rule next, Alexander answered "to the strongest." Considering he was dying of what appears to have been West Nile virus complicated by the cumulative effect of his wounds and hard living, it is more likely that by that point he was unconscious. The effect was the same. His goal of a lasting empire and cultural unity was lost. Quickly the Macedonian commanders began fighting among themselves and dividing up the empire. Roxanne and his son were taken to Macedonia by Antipater, who claimed to be protecting them until the boy was old enough to rule for himself. Seven years later, Antipater poisoned them both. Within a few months, the empire was divided into "successor states," which were at near-constant war with each other.

Never in ancient times were even the lands of the Persian Empire again united. Instead of his legacy of a cross-cultural empire, Alexander's lack of dealing with his own mortality doomed the lands he once ruled to decades of war, while taking the family he loved to imprisonment and then death.

||||||||||||||||||||||||||||||||||||||||||||||||||||||||||||||||||||

7

COWARDICE

How to Lose an Empire in
Ten Seconds

331 BCE, PERSIA

||||||||||||||||||||||||||||||||||||||||||||||||||||||||||||||||||||

The first time Darius III, Persian emperor, met Alexander the Great in the Battle of Issus, things did not go as he planned. He had placed his army in a strong position, with the steep banks of the Pinarus River in front of them and hills to one side and ocean on the other. He could not be flanked, and any attacking Macedonian would have to fight while climbing up the riverbank.

Darius was correct in that the position could not be flanked, but the rest of his plan was for the Macedonian army to be slaughtered by his armored cavalry and infantry at the top of the riverbank, as the attackers lost cohesion crossing the shallow river. Alexander did not try to force the position, but instead he ordered his infantry to attack up to the bank and then hold. With his army pinned by the left side of Alexander's infantry, Darius was unable to reach the rest of the Macedonians and had lost control of the battlefield despite his numerical superiority. Then a wedge, formed by the Companion cavalry—his elite armored horsemen—and with Alexander himself leading at the point, smashed through his line along the river and turned to attack the Persian emperor. As his noble bodyguards and even his charioteer died around him, Darius withdrew and then kept on retreating. With their emperor fleeing, the Persian line collapsed, and those who could not flee were slaughtered.

The Battle of Gaugamela, sometimes called Arbela, was the second and last time these two commanders met in battle. Darius was now fighting within a few days' march on his own capital, and he had spent weeks preparing the battlefield. He was determined to not make the same mistakes as he had at Issus. He was fighting near his source of supply, on a battlefield of his choice, and he had assembled a much larger army, while adding a number of weapon systems unavailable to the Macedonians.

Darius had raised troops from all over his empire. Among them were not only all forms of cavalry but also chariots with scythe blades attached to their wheels. He planned on these breaking up the Macedonian infantry formation. Mercenaries hired from distant India had even brought with them fifteen war elephants. The armored elephants were not only an imposing sight but their smell alone was often enough to frighten cavalry horses. The mere presence of elephants could render entire cavalry units unable to charge or even to flee. To maximize the effect of all of these mobile forces, the Persians had literally leveled the terrain until it was playing-field smooth.

The Persian emperor then made sure that he had a great superiority in infantry and heavy cavalry and placed them both in a long formation that had the flanks anchored. He even recruited thousands of Greek mercenaries to form phalanxes and ordered them to support key parts of his line. Having been beaten when on the defensive, this army was prepared to advance, not just to stand as they had at Issus. Heavy cavalry units were deployed throughout the massive formation to allow Darius to respond to any movement by the Macedonian horsemen.

Finally, to protect himself from another charge, the emperor surrounded his throne not only with his personal and noble guards but also with thousands of his best infantry, the Immortals.

When Alexander appeared late in the day, he camped in the hills near this well-prepared killing ground. Darius was understandably nervous about a night attack. Indeed many of Alexander's commanders suggested just that. They were badly outnumbered, perhaps as much as five to one or more, and darkness would make organization on both sides difficult and so assist the smaller side. Alexander refused, stating he would not "steal" an empire. Darius was unaware of the decision and so made his first small mistake and kept his massive army in place and in formation all night while the Macedonians rested.

With the dawn, Alexander's army marched onto the far side and the flat open field. He would fight on the Persian emperor's prepared battlefield. Almost immediately, Darius ordered his scythed chariots to attack. The horses pulling these proved highly vulnerable to the Macedonian's arrows and javelins. When a few chariots did reach the enemy's line, the more mobile Macedonian infantry opened corridors that the horses instinctively ran through, exposing the drivers to javelin fire from both sides. Rather than disrupt Alexander's cavalry, a charge by Darius's elephants met a similar fate. Only a few even reached the Macedonian formations.

Alexander then began to move his army forward, angling back the right side of his formation so that his stronger left side, commanded by the able Parmenion, came first into contact. Darius, having learned at Issus to just sit on the defensive and give up the initiative, ordered his own right flank, consisting of at least twice as many soldiers as they faced, forward. The fighting was almost immediately fierce.

Alexander then led his best horsemen, including the Companions, on a ride from the center of the battlefield toward Persia's left flank. Darius began ordering his cavalry and even infantry units to move with this threat so that whenever Alexander attacked, he would be met with overwhelming resistance. He had seen this at Issus and was determined to not allow Alexander to find a weak portion of his formation. This weakened the Persian center, but that must have seemed to be of little concern because the Macedonian infantry opposite it was not yet close enough to be in position to attack.

Picture the Persian emperor on his raised and elegant throne, surrounded by messengers, while his commanders watched his unpredictable opponent's best horsemen riding away toward his right flank. All the time the Persians must have wondered when Alexander would turn and slam into whatever forces he was in front of, yet never knowing when he would actually do this. Darius ordered unit after unit to bolster that part of the line so that wherever the Macedonians struck it would be strong enough to hold. After all, he had many times the men that the Greeks had, and he could afford to be strong all along the left side of his army. All this time Parmenion and the best of the Macedonian infantry were loudly engaged, without either side seeming to gain an advantage and with nearly half their armies to their right.

Then Alexander did what he so often did, something his opponent did not expect. Turning his Companions completely around, he led all of his cavalry back across the Persian front until it was nearly at the center of the battlefield again. There he joined up with of the slower moving Macedonian infantry to form his classic wedge formation with himself and his armored Companion cavalry at the point and his infantry along both sides. The much larger Persian army simply could not react quickly enough. There would have been a flurry of runners sent by Darius to recall the units but no time for those forces to turn around and hurry back.

The wedge struck, and the heavy horsemen tore through a thinned line of cavalry and infantry. Within minutes, the Macedonian wedge was cutting through the elite but lightly armored Immortals. The wedge itself was aimed directly at Darius on his throne. And here is where Darius made the mistake that lost his empire and changed history.

The Persian emperor panicked and ran.

Yes, again, just as he had at Issus. Darius saw himself in danger and fled. Leaving the throne, he mounted a horse and ordered all the nearby units to follow or stand and slow any pursuit.

The right half of Darius's army was engaged and holding its own against Parmenion. In fact, it was beginning to win and was pushing back the Macedonians. Things were so bad that once Darius had fled, Alexander did not pursue. He was compelled to swing his entire cavalry force and save that half of his army. A large part of the Persian army still had never even been engaged in the fighting. That remaining half alone outnumbered Alexander's entire army. But Darius did not go and rally them or join the men fighting Parmenion. He simply rode off the field and away. Over thirty thousand men, a force still strong enough to turn the battle, left with him. When it became apparent he was abandoning his army, many of them melted away. Hearing that Darius had totally deserted his men, the units not already fighting broke apart or retreated.

Weeks later, after fleeing to the far reaches of his former empire, Darius was killed by his own remaining commanders. This left Alexander free to deal with the Persian right wing, save Parmenion and his infantry, and win both the battle and the empire.

Speculation is always dangerous in history. But it is hard not to wonder what would have happened if Darius had not lost his courage. Had Darius not panicked but instead simply moved to command the tens of thousands of unengaged soldiers on his left, Alexander would have had to follow him. The Macedonian might well have fought his way through to Darius again, but it would have taken time and hard fighting. During that time the units under Parmenion, which were still badly outnumbered and being forced back, could have broken. That would have cost Alexander some of the best units in his army, and Arbela would have been at most a draw. But Darius did flee, even though his remaining army far outnumbered Alexander's. The battle and empire were lost not only because of Alexander the Great's brilliance but as the result of Darius's cowardice . . . again.

DARIUS III

The Persian emperor Darius III was likely not a descendant of Darius the Great, though he claimed to be. This was almost for sure just propaganda, because the emperor he replaced, Artaxerxes, went to great lengths to have killed every male relative he had, even cousins. (This was not uncommon in Persia. Politics were a real matter of life and death.) Relatives of any Persian emperor were almost always rallying points for rebels and usurpers. There was simply no uncle of Artaxerxes's left alive to produce him as a son. Note that the ten thousand Greek mercenary infantrymen chronicled in *Anabasis* were in the employ of the emperor's rebelling brother.

It was the lack of relatives that opened the way for Darius to the throne. Without a designated heir to throne, those who wanted to rule used every means to gain power. Darius III was the last man standing when all his rivals had been assassinated. His real name was Codomannus, and he had the reputation of being a competent and courageous commander. In fact, he rose quickly in the Persian army due to his battlefield courage. A marriage to a rich and influential Persian, from an important, noble family, also assisted him in his rise.

None of this gives insight into his behavior at the battles of Issus and Arbela. Perhaps being the absolute emperor of the greatest empire of its time changed or softened Darius. Or it might simply have been the case that almost being killed by the charismatic and supposedly godlike Alexander III was more than he could handle.

8

||||||||||||||||||||||||||||||||||||||||||||||||||||||||||||||||||||||

PRIDE OVER SURVIVAL

Carthago Delenda Est

||||||||||||||||||||||||||||||||||||||||||||||||||||||||||||||||||||||

The Punic Wars lasted over a century, from 264 to 146 BCE. The three wars were really one extended conflict between the two most powerful nations in the western Mediterranean: Rome and Carthage. They were fought to see who would dominate that part of the world, both politically and economically. The first Punic War was started in 264 BCE by the Greek colonies on the Italian side of Sicily asking Rome to assist them against Syracuse and the other independent cities on the eastern side of the island. Those cities were supported by Carthage. Rome agreed, and their success in capturing Messina from its Carthaginian garrison provoked a greater conflict, which would last over a century.

In Sicily, the Roman army dominated, capturing many cities, but they could not finalize the win. This was because the Carthaginian navy was able to land soldiers anywhere along the island's shore and even raided Italy itself. No one could win because the two forces tended to balance each other out.

A stalemate forced the Romans for the first time to begin

building a fleet. Before the First Punic War, Rome had no navy at all. If they needed to move soldiers by sea, they hired merchant ships. They went about creating a navy in a typically Roman way by simply copying a Carthaginian ship that had run aground during one of their raids on Italy. Becoming a naval power was not easy, and Rome lost whole fleets to weather and war, but they persisted. With their secret weapon, the corvus, they defeated the main Carthaginian fleet and shocked a Carthage whose naval superiority had been uncontested for generations. This forced Carthage to accept a treaty that cost them many of their holdings and an indemnity payment to Rome.

SECRET WEAPON

The corvus was simply a narrow drawbridge that was installed on the first Roman ships used in the Punic Wars. It was hinged at its base so that it could be raised and then dropped forcefully onto the deck of any nearby ship. A spike or beak at the end of the corvus would then dig into the enemy ship's deck, locking the two ships together. *Corvus* translates as "crow" or "raven" in Latin. Roman soldiers could then rush over and effectively turn a sea battle into a series of little land battles at sea.

Before the corvus, the main tactic in naval warfare had, for centuries, been to ram your enemy and sink them. This favored the experienced and efficient Carthaginian crews. Rome could not match them as sailors, but they had the best infantry. By using the corvus, Rome was able to engage where it was strong and nullify the Carthaginians' skill. The corvus was also awkward, and crossing against determined resistance was costly. Once Rome's sailors gained experience, it was no longer used.

After Carthage lost the First Punic War, Rome controlled virtually all of the islands in the western Mediterranean and had forced the city to pay massive amounts of gold and silver. To compensate for the territorial losses, the African city began to actively conquer and control much of Spain. Commanding in Spain was the Barca family who, for three generations, commanded Carthage's mercenary armies there.

The grandson of the first Barca in Spain was the famous Hannibal. He dominated what is now called the Second Punic War, taking the battle to Italy in 217 BCE. He defeated two large Roman armies in the first two years, the second with the classic double envelopment at Cannae. Still Hannibal was unable to exploit his early successes or force a peace. Rome was also unable to defeat him, and for over thirteen years Hannibal's army rampaged through Italy. It was unable to defeat Rome or take any of the peninsula's major cities, but it did massive and traumatic damage to the countryside and the Roman psyche. Finally Rome landed an army near Carthage under the command of Scipio Africanus. Hannibal rushed back to defend the home city, but he was defeated in 203 BCE at Zama.

The terms imposed by the second treaty were extremely onerous and painful for Carthage. The city was no longer allowed to have any army and only a token navy. It was not to engage in its own foreign policy or to declare war without Roman permission. Any disputes were to be determined by Rome, and Carthage had to accept Rome's decision. There was also an indemnity so great that many Romans felt it would never be paid off.

It took the Carthaginians almost fifty years to pay off that indemnity, but they did. Eventually the city again prospered as a commercial center. During most of this time, Carthage also had a problem with its former allies and source of mercenaries, Numidia. Carthaginian territory was being constantly raided, and because they were left nearly helpless by the Roman ban on their having any army, there was nothing they could do to defend themselves. Numidia, having changed sides before Zama, was a favored

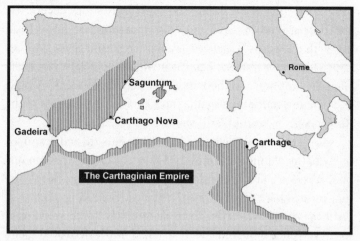

The Carthaginian Empire

ally of Rome. Rarely did the Romans, who claimed the treaty right to settle such conflicts, find against their allies and in favor of their former foes.

But once the indemnity was paid, Carthaginians felt they were no longer under the restrictions of the treaty signed after Zama. They felt prosperous, and because they owed Rome no more indemnities, the city was free to act as it chose. It raised an army and defended itself against the next Numidian attack. In fact, the new army turned the tables and sent raids into Numidia.

Rome disagreed. The generation that was raised while Hannibal spent over a decade pillaging Italy was still alive. The men who had been soldiers back then were now the elders running Rome. A good indicator of how traumatically the Romans remembered the Second Punic War was their name for it, the Hannibalic War. It had been too costly and too close for a proud and cautious republic to forgive or forget.

But here's where Carthage made a mistake. After four decades of peace, Carthage again challenged Rome. But Rome had not forgotten how it had once been nearly defeated by them. Having visited the revitalized Carthage, Cato the Elder began to agitate in the Senate even before Rome had other causes for concern. He ended every speech, even those on plumbing and horse trading, with the words "*Carthago delenda est.*" Carthage must be destroyed. A close modern equivalent would be if Japan in 1980, when its economy was booming, had decided to form an army and invade South Korea again. Think how all the veterans of the Korean War or World War II would have reacted.

Carthage not only defended herself but pursued and destroyed many of the Numidian camps. In 146 BCE, Carthage had no real navy, a very small army, and no overseas possessions. But at first they pushed back when Rome threatened. The ruling families of Carthage must have very badly misjudged how Rome would react to a resurgence by an old enemy that had nearly destroyed them. It was a mistake the city would never recover from. Rome first replied by sending Carthage ever more onerous demands. Suddenly reality dawned, and the Carthaginians tried everything to meet them. So the Romans simply sent more and more difficult demands. The one Carthage finally had to ignore was an order to dismantle their entire city and move it miles inland.

Rome sent an army.

The siege of Carthage was long and bloody and its defense valiant. All quarter of a million Carthaginians rallied to defend their city when the Roman army appeared. All metal was given up and shaped into weapons. Women cut their hair, and this was used to power catapults. Anyone capable of fighting, of any age or sex, stood to the city walls. The Romans found that they could not take Carthage. They could put it under siege and did. Food ran out and still the city fought off every attack. When it finally surrendered, most of the fifty thousand Carthaginians still alive were simply too weak to resist.

Cato the Elder got his wish. Carthage was destroyed. All of the survivors were sold into slavery. The city walls, which had thwarted the Roman army for over a year, were torn down and the city inside them burned. The Roman Senate then forbade anyone

THE CITY

Carthage was a city-state located on the coast of North Africa. It was founded by the Phoenician merchants several centuries earlier than Rome. The Romans still regarded them as Phoenicians, and this gave the three wars their name: *Phoenician* is "punicus" in Latin. The core of their empire was the city of Carthage itself. Though at the time of the First and Second Punic Wars, the Carthaginians controlled first many islands and then a good portion of southern Spain.

Carthage was ruled by a king, but much of the power was in the hands of wealthy merchant families. The city was, in effect, really an oligarchy. It was always a city founded by and run by merchants. Trade was its most important consideration. Most of what is commonly known about Carthage is based on what their enemy, Rome, said. Rome won the wars, so Romans wrote the histories. This led to the Roman propaganda often being accepted as truth. To begin with there was no real proof Carthaginians sacrificed babies to Baal. Nor did they tend to oppress areas they controlled. That would have been bad for business. Aristotle actually thought very highly of the city and its government:

> The Carthaginians are also considered to have an excellent form of government, which differs from that of any other state in several respects, though it is in some very like the Spartan. Indeed, all three states—the Spartan, the Cretan, and the Carthaginian—nearly resemble one another, and are very different from any others. Many of the Carthaginian institutions are excellent. The superiority of their constitution is proved by the fact that the common people

> remain loyal to the constitution. The Carthaginians have never had any rebellion worth speaking of, and have never been under the rule of a tyrant.
>
> . . . The government of the Carthaginians is oligarchical, but they successfully escape the evils of oligarchy by enriching one portion of the people after another by sending them to their colonies. This is their panacea and the means by which they give stability to the state.
>
> —*On the Constitution of Carthage*, Aristotle (340 BCE)

Unlike Rome, Carthage had no real army. Armies are expensive to maintain, so the city, made up of shrewd merchants, rented its army by hiring mercenaries. The men came from all over the western Mediterranean, but Numidians and Spaniards formed the core of armies, such as the one with which Hannibal crossed the Alps. Carthage did have an excellent navy, which was far more important to its economy. The navy guarded the trade routes and ports that made Carthage the wealthiest city of its time. It was not unusual for common Carthaginians to join the large and highly trained navy. At the start of the First Punic War, the Carthaginian navy was uncontested in its control of the western Mediterranean. Rome literally had no fleet at all.

from living on the former site, forever. Even today it remains a thinly populated ruin.

Carthage was an oligarchy. The decisions that sealed the city's fate were made by a few powerful families with the support of the people. The leaders of a resurgent Carthage underestimated and misunderstood how Rome would react. There is a line in a song by Jim Croce, "You don't tug on Superman's cape." Carthage had lost both earlier wars. It must not have understood or lost sight of just how traumatic their greatest successes, Hannibal's victories and years in Italy, had been for the Romans. The Carthaginian leaders must have completely misjudged how the much more powerful Roman republic would respond to any sign that Carthage might ever again be a threat. Rome could not either forgive or forget. For whatever reason, Carthage thought it could once again challenge Rome. This cost them, all quarter of a million Carthaginians, everything.

|||||||||||||||||||||||||||||||||||||||||||||||||||||||||||||||||||||||||||

9

LACK OF PERSPECTIVE

Big Mistake

218 BCE, THE ALPS

|||||||||||||||||||||||||||||||||||||||||||||||||||||||||||||||||||||||||||

One of the greatest military accomplishments in ancient military history was also one of its dumbest mistakes. This was the much celebrated Hannibal Barca's crossing of the Alps with elephants. There is no question that this was a great logistical and even leadership feat. But it was also a totally wasted effort, for which his Carthaginian army paid a high price.

In 218 BCE, Hannibal Barca decided to take the war between Carthage and Rome to Italy. Because Rome had gained control of the seas, he chose to march his army to Italy. This involved moving through hostile Gaul and northern Italy. It is likely that Hannibal did not originally plan to lead his army across the Alps, even in the summer. The peaks and high passes are snowy and frozen all year round.

At first Hannibal did well, outmaneuvering or bluffing away Gaulic attempts to block his passage. By the end of the summer, Hannibal had reached the Rhône River. The Romans finally awoke to the threat and sent an army to block him. To evade that army, Hannibal had to avoid the coast when entering Italy. He thus chose to cross the Alps with his entire army. This amounted to about thirty-eight thousand infantry, eight thousand cavalry, and thirty-seven war elephants. The elephants were the problem.

Because he had not planned to cross the cold passes, the Carthaginian army was not dressed or prepared for the freezing temperatures and slippery paths. Nor were any of the paths through the mountains suitable for an army to march on. The Carthaginians, while fending off the local mountain tribes, would have to cut their way through. This they did with some brilliant improvisation. One tale says that when the route was blocked by a massive boulder that had fallen across the only available path, Hannibal soaked the boulder with vinegar and set it on fire. The rock heated unevenly and split, letting the army pass.

So most of the way across the Alps had to be cut by soldiers who were freezing in their light clothes. And the rest of the army could move only as fast as the first soldiers could create a large enough road for them to use. And they always had to deal with sleet and snow. Later experience has shown that it should have taken Hannibal's army around seven or eight days to cross over the passes. But it took Hannibal over two weeks. One of the key reasons is that he had to cut a road wide enough for elephants. Men and carts can use a pathway that is perhaps four to five feet wide. But the war elephants needed a much wider path and this took extra time to excavate. Perhaps it was as much as an extra week, and his lightly dressed soldiers suffered and died from exposure and hypothermia.

When Hannibal and his army finally reached the warm valleys of northern Italy, there remained only twenty thousand infantry, four thousand cavalry, and a mere handful of the war elephants. Half the army had died in those two weeks. And now there were not enough elephants left to use them in a battle. You have to wonder how many thousands of highly trained Carthaginian soldiers might have survived the trek if it had taken only one week and not two. But like so many leaders from all eras, Hannibal put so much faith in his wonder weapon, the elephants, that he lost sight of what it cost his army to bring the animals with them over the Alps.

‖‖

10

DECEPTION
INSPIRED BY PRIDE

A Sick Caesar Sits

44 BCE, ROME

‖‖

On March 15, 44 BCE, as Julius Caesar walked, unguarded, through a crowd of supporters, a warning note was pressed into his hand. The note told of a plot to kill him that day on the Senate floor. Caesar shrugged the warning off, just as he had done that morning when his wife awoke from a terrible premonitory nightmare, begging him not to leave the house. He had also ignored a warning the night before when his soothsayer said, "Beware the ides of March." When his general and close friend Mark Antony discovered the plot, he rushed to the Senate to warn the ruler. But he was too late. The dictator turned demigod had been stabbed twenty-three times by a group of co-conspirators, one of whom was like a son to him. But was Caesar's mistake traveling without a bodyguard and ignoring the plot to kill him or was it the fact that he had remained seated two months earlier during an important meeting with key senators?

In many ways Julius Caesar deserved the mythical status conferred on him by the Roman people. He was an exceptionally skilled military strategist, never losing a major battle. He was also a shrewd politician and a leader who implemented many populist policies that endeared him to the public. He was a gifted writer and propagandist, penning one of the most accomplished Latin works in history, *The Gaulic Wars*. And as head of the Roman republic, he adopted measures that led to permanent changes across Europe, including creating a monthly calendar based on the solar year, which was the basis of the calendar used today.

Caesar's lifelong goal was to obtain complete control over a Roman republic. He wanted this because there were many problems that were not being solved, including recent civil wars, class warfare, a changing economy, the loss of the small farmer, and external threats from the Parthians, among others. A strong hand was needed, and he was sure it should be his. So Julius Caesar began to amass powers typically reserved for royalty. But the last time Rome had known a king, he was a Targquin, a family whose deadly and despotic ways were still remembered.

Julius Caesar also had an affair with the queen of Egypt, Cleopatra, who helped him fund his military invasions and battles. She claimed he fathered her child, whom she called Caesarion. However, Roman law forbade a Roman from marrying a non-Roman, and even if a later marriage were permitted, the Roman aristocracy would have never allowed Caesar to claim that his illegitimate, half-Egyptian son was his rightful heir.

Six months before his death, Caesar secretly changed his will. Because he had no legitimate heir, he adopted his grandnephew, Octavian. In the will, he named the young man his heir to succeed him. He also left every citizen enough money to live on for three months. This virtually guaranteed that he would be adored and revered after his death. It's interesting to note that he also named Brutus as his alternate heir, should Octavian die before Caesar. Caesar suspected Brutus might be his actual son because he had an affair with Brutus's mother around the time of his conception. Caesar certainly treated him as a son.

While he was still wildly popular with the masses of Rome, by

January 44 BCE the Roman ruling aristocracy had come to resent Caesar. He had been named dictator for life, and although he had publicly rejected a crown, some citizens already called him their king. Caesar himself had adopted many royal perks, but was normally careful to at least follow the republican forms. His title was first consul, not king or emperor, though the distinction was by this point only in the name. His face began appearing on Roman coins, an action that was shocking and unprecedented. In spite of Caesar's denials, many Senate members became convinced that Caesar was planning on overthrowing the republic and declaring himself king. He had the support of both the army and the mobs of Rome. In the past, almost every time a man had that kind of support, he had made himself king. In hopes of preserving the republic, which they thought was at risk, a group of senators decided to placate Caesar by offering him deification instead of royalty. But rather than rising in honor to greet the senators when they arrived at his home to officially tell him of this honor, he remained seated. This was a profound insult—only a king sits when senators arrive—and confirmed their suspicions that Caesar did, in fact, consider himself to be king. Yet why would a man so politically astute at handling his enemies refuse to stand and greet the Roman leadership? The senators were there to give him a great honor, and Caesar knew not standing to greet them as equals was the one insult they feared the most.

Many historians agree that Caesar remained seated simply because he wasn't feeling well. Some ancient historians claimed he was suffering from epilepsy and dizzy spells. Julius Caesar was very self-conscious about his seizures, seeing them as a weakness. Caesar had led a hard life in the field with his army for many years and it had taken a toll on his body. But the proud general and consul tried to hide this. Some said that he suffered that day from a migraine. Still others said it was an attack of diarrhea that kept him in his seat. Regardless, the consensus seemed to be that he was physically sick that day.

After that rebuff, more than sixty people from aristocratic families, most of them Senate members, decided that the only way to keep Caesar from becoming king was to assassinate him. The three leaders of the plot were some of the dictator's closest friends, including Brutus. The famous line in Shakespeare's play, "Et tu, Brutus?" refers to what Caesar said to the man he thought was his son at the moment when he was first stabbed.

Caesar was a shrewd general who never lost a battle, and he is considered one of the greatest military strategists of all time. How could a man with that type of genius walk into a trap? He had access to all sorts of intelligence, and he may have heard about the rumored plot to kill him. Nevertheless, he dismissed all his bodyguards right before his murder. He even died with the warning note clutched in his hand.

More recent historians have taken a forensic approach to Caesar's perplexing behavior, attributing it to worsening seizures from a likely epileptic condition. This disease can cause memory lapses and irrational behavior as well as compromised bowel and bladder control. The illness is also a likely explanation for why he remained seated when the senators arrived that fateful day; perhaps that, combined with his ego, caused him to walk into the trap at the Senate.

Within a few years after Caesar's death, every one of the conspirators was dead. But the Roman republic, which the killers were so desperately trying to preserve, basically ended with Caesar's death. As chief heir to Caesar's fortune, Octavian commanded the loyalty of the Roman middle and lower classes, who were outraged by the murder of their champion. Octavian went on to become Rome's first emperor, taking the name Caesar Augustus.

The senators went to Caesar's home to offer him deification, so he was going to be pronounced a god. It could be that Julius Caesar did not feel it was proper for a god to admit to being ill. Whatever the cause, this one action was the turning point and inspiration for the conspiracy that cost him his life. Perhaps if

Caesar had simply apologized to the senators, and told them he wasn't feeling well enough to rise when they entered the room, he could have prevented his own death two months later. Remaining seated may have been the ego-driven mistake that sealed the great Roman's fate.

11

|||||||||||||||||||||||||||||||||||||||||||||||||||||||||||||||||||||||||

LOST HIS
PERSPECTIVE AND
THEN EVERYTHING

Mark Antony's Will

41 BCE, ROME AND EGYPT

|||||||||||||||||||||||||||||||||||||||||||||||||||||||||||||||||||||||||

One of the most famous love stories ever told was that of Antony and Cleopatra. Not only did it have all the ingredients of a Shakespearean tragedy, as William Shakespeare himself surmised when writing their story for the stage, but the doomed affair ultimately changed the course of the Roman Empire.

As mentioned in mistake 10, Mark Antony was a general for Julius Caesar and one of his closest friends. After the murder of Caesar in March 44 BCE, Rome fell into civil war again—in fact, twice. The first time was a civil war between Caesar's supporters—led by Octavian and Antony—and Marcus Brutus and the other senators who had assassinated Julius. Before the fighting started, Caesar's lover, Cleopatra, fled back to Egypt, with her young son, Ptolemy XV Caesar (also known as Caesarion), whom she claimed was Julius Caesar's son. Meanwhile, Caesar's great-nephew and heir, Octavian, aligned with Antony and retained control of Rome. By 42, Octavian and Antony were winning the war, and they crushed the senatorial rebels that October at Philippi. Brutus and most of the remaining leaders of his faction died in the battle or committed suicide. The victors divided the Roman Empire between them, with Octavian taking Rome and Antony taking Egypt. Although Octavian had the homeland, Antony's provinces were by far the wealthier.

Mark Antony had always suspected that Cleopatra had been involved in Caesar's death, and he intended to question her about it. But he also wanted money to conduct a military operation to subdue the Parthian Empire, a goal that Rome strived for almost constantly. He needed the cooperation of the very rich queen of Egypt. In October 41, he summoned her to Tarsus (a city in modern-day Turkey). She initially delayed her response, probably as a power play, to let him know she was very important in her own right and would not be at his beck and call. When she did finally appear, she made what could only be described as a grand entrance. Sailing from Egypt, she traveled on a massive barge covered with flowers and scented with exotic perfumes. As the barge entered the port, she reclined on the deck, dressed as the goddess Venus, adorned in gold and jewels and surrounded by servants who fanned her. He was captivated at once. And like Julius Caesar before him, Mark Antony fell hard and fast for her considerable charms.

Antony was trapped under Cleopatra's spell. He ignored his wife's, Fulvia's, pleas for help back in Rome as she tried to fight Antony's quarrels for him. There Octavian was gathering the strength and support that would leave him the sole leader of the empire. Antony also ignored the Parthian troops who were poised to enter the rich Roman province of Syria. Instead, he went on an extended winter holiday to Alexandria with the queen. She played dice with him, hunted with him, drank with him, and basically didn't let him out of her sight.

While Antony was playing in Egypt with Cleopatra, Roman provinces were being invaded. Trying to entice Antony to leave Cleopatra, Fulvia attacked Octavian in Antony's name, even though the two men were allies at the time. Reluctantly, Antony returned to Rome, but Fulvia died soon after his return. Antony decided to marry Octavian's sister, Octavia, and create a new alliance with his old friend. In December 40 BCE, Cleopatra gave birth to twins fathered by Antony. Just a few weeks after their birth, the queen discovered that Antony had taken a new wife.

In 37, Antony returned to Alexandria to fight the Parthians. He married Cleopatra and publically declared her children as his. The marriage was one of both love and political expediency. He could protect her from an invasion by Rome, and she had the wealth to create and preserve his military might. But he was still married to Octavia at the time, and by leaving his wife in Rome, he destroyed the alliance he had with her brother. As if all that weren't enough, the lovers also portrayed themselves as the earthly versions of two divine couples: the Greek gods Aphrodite and Dionysus and their Egyptian counterparts, Isis and Osiris.

Mark Antony and Cleopatra's relationship infuriated Octavian, and the Roman people became concerned about Cleopatra's influence on Antony. Octavian began waging a propaganda war on the couple in an attempt to win the hearts and the minds of the Roman people so they would support the ouster he was planning. He argued that Antony was a man of low morals for leaving his wife in Rome to be with the promiscuous queen. Antony was summoned back to Rome on several occasions, but he refused to go, choosing to remain with Cleopatra in Alexandria.

In 34 BCE, using Egyptian money, Antony conquered Armenia. Cleopatra and her oldest son, Caesarion, were then crowned co-rulers of Egypt and Cyprus. Her younger children were given titles to preside over other countries. She was also given the title "queen of kings" by Antony, and Caesarion was called "god," "son of god," and "king of kings." But perhaps the most threatening thing for Octavian was that Antony declared Caesarion to be the legitimate son and heir to the Caesar name. Octavian's power base, loyalty, and popularity had come from the fact that Caesar had adopted him and named him heir.

From Egypt, Antony divorced Octavia then accused Octavian

of usurping power and forging the adoption papers signed by Caesar. Octavian returned fire, accusing Antony of treason for ignoring Roman law and illegally keeping property that should be given to other men by lots and waging foreign wars without prior approval by the Senate.

But the proverbial last straw was when Octavian revealed to the Roman people the terms of Antony's will. Antony had divided up pieces of the empire, giving Cleopatra, their children, and even Caesarion, parts of it. Some of the property given away in his will was not even ruled by the Romans at that time. It certainly looked like Antony and Cleopatra had plans to take over Rome as well as other countries.

In 33 BCE, Octavian successfully asked the Senate to strip Antony of his powers and wage war against Egypt. Most of the Roman people supported Octavian's position, no longer trusting Antony to have their best interests at heart. The civil war that followed, between two of Julius Caesar's most powerful men, effectively ended the Roman oligarchy as a governing power.

In 31, Octavian's army and navy battled Antony's Egyptian forces in Greece. Virgil later depicted it as the epic struggle between eastern barbarians and western civilization. The Egyptians sustained huge losses, and Antony and Cleopatra fled back to Alexandria. But within a year that city was filled with Roman soldiers. Rather than be taken as Roman prisoners, the two lovers committed suicide.

After Antony's death, Octavian became the sole ruler of the Roman Empire, which finally included Egypt. By 27 BCE, he was known as Augustus and then held all political and military offices. When he died, all his political powers passed to his son. The Roman Principate had effectively begun.

Antony was insensitive to the Roman people's concerns about his loyalty to Rome and their fears of an Egyptian invasion. When he gifted Roman land to all of Cleopatra's children in his will and even granted them land that was not yet under his control, the public could draw no other conclusion but that Antony and

Cleopatra wanted to invade Italy and conquer Rome for themselves. Antony chose love for a woman over love for his country. And by putting that love in writing as a last will and testament, he changed the history of Rome and ensured he would not be part of it.

12

THE EASY WAY
WASN'T

By Invitation

FIFTH CENTURY CE, BRITAIN

||||||||||||||||||||||||||||||||||||||||||||||||||||||||||||||||||||||||

The early fifth century was very hard on the Western Roman Empire. The empire had been split, and the western half was a mere shadow of its former self. The barbarians had literally already been at the gates of Rome, and there were not enough legions to defend Italy, much less the rest of the empire. Since the emperor was in Italy, it is not surprising that he called the frontier legions home to defend the heart of his empire. The most distant province was Britannia, and when the Suevi, Alans, Vandals, and Burgundians conquered Gaul and went on to threaten the city of Rome itself, the last of the legions were ordered home in 407. This created a problem for those left behind in Britannia. The Romans had been too effective at disarming and keeping the local population peaceful. For over three centuries there had been no other military force allowed in England or Wales beyond the Roman legions stationed there. It had been a crime to even possess weapons in Celtic Britain under Roman rule. But with those legions suddenly gone, there was no one left to defend the prosperous British countryside or cities. There were brave men in Britain, some of whom had served in the legions, but there was no real army. Britain was defenseless.

Almost immediately the Picts and Scots began sending raiding parties past Hadrian's Wall, which was by then only weakly guarded or totally unmanned. The first raids met little resistance and soon the bands of marauding Picts grew in both size and audacity. Their attacks were fearsome and destructive. The raiders often killed or enslaved everyone they could, leaving only devastation behind. The barbarians penetrated deeper and deeper across England and soon threw all of Britain into a panic.

The English king in the mid-fifth century is thought to have

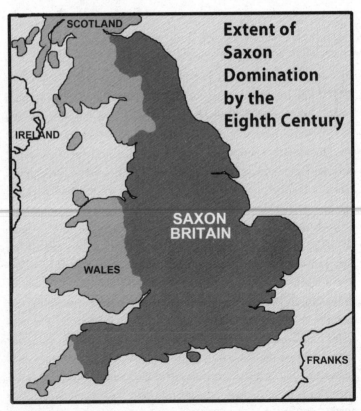

Saxon Britain

been Vortigern, though that may have been his title and not his true name. He called a meeting of the major lords and nobles in 440 with the hope of finding a way to resist the menace from the north. They were unable to find in Britain the military strength needed to defend the land, so Vortigern found another source of trained warriors. He would hire Germanic Saxon mercenaries.

For centuries, the Romans had used German auxiliaries in Britain. Many of these men had come from the German Bight, which ran southwest from the Rhine to northeast of the Elbe. Occupying this Germanic land were the Saxon tribes and the Angles. Over the previous few centuries, the Roman garrison and Britain had to resist raids across the Channel from these tribes, but they often hired Germanic Saxon and Angle warriors to man forts. So employing Germanic mercenaries was not a new concept. Just in this case, it was a really bad one.

The problem was that when Saxons and Angles were recruited by Rome, Roman legions in Britain could restrain the Germanic tribes. But with the legions gone, the German mercenaries soon found they had a near monopoly on organized warfare. At first Vortigern's decision seemed to work. Legend has it that two brothers, Hengist and Horsa, landed with three ships full of Saxon warriors and were welcomed by Vortigern. They were able to drive back the Picts and Scots, but then looked at the situation.

The brothers encouraged more Saxons to cross the Channel, all demanding more pay and land for their families. Their demands became more outrageous and soon could not be met. So the Germanic tribes simply threw out the local Celtic nobles and took over. For the next two hundred years, the Saxons, the Angles, the Chauci, the Jutes, and the Frisians flocked to Britain for the free land and easy pickings. Analyses of DNA and contemporary records have estimated that as many as two hundred thousand Anglo-Saxon warriors and their families crossed into Britain. The British resistance to their inexorable, but slow-moving, invasion is the basis for the tales of King Arthur. Effectively the Anglo-Saxons almost completely dominated Britain from the sixth century up until another invader arrived to supplant them, the Normans under William the Conqueror in 1066.

> *Here Mauricius and Valentinian succeeded to the kingdom and ruled 7 years. And in their days Hengist and Horsa, invited by Vortigern, king of the Britons, sought out Britain in the landing-place which is named Ebba's Creek, at first to help the Britons, but later they fought against them. The king ordered them to fight against the Picts, and they did so and had victory whosesoever they came. They then sent to Angeln and ordered them to send more help, and tell them of the worthlessness of the Britons and of the excellence of the land. They then sent them more help. These men came from three tribes of Germany: from the Old Saxons, from the Angles, from the Jutes came the Cantware and the Wihtware—that is the tribe which now lives on White—and that race in Wessex which they still call the race of the Jutes.*
>
> The Anglo-Saxon Chronicle

Although Vortigern and his nobles thought bringing in the Saxons to fight the Picts was a good idea, as far as all of Celtic Britain was concerned, it most definitely was a tragic and nation-changing mistake. Rather than saving Britain after the Romans left, Vortigern's invitations changed the history of England forever and cost the British Celts their land and culture.

13

SELF OVER
KINGDOM

Harold II

1066, ENGLAND

Harold Godwineson was the last Saxon king of England. He was born in 1022 and was the son of Godwine of Essex. (Yes, that is where you get "Godwineson.") Essex was one of the most powerful and wealthy realms in England. His father had been one of the leaders of the Witan, a council made up of sixty nobles. There was great strife between Godwine of Essex and the king, Edward the Confessor. Part of this was because Edward surrounded himself with Norman advisers and more because of misbehavior and scandals involving members of Godwine's family. One involved Godwine's brother Swegen seducing the abbess of Leominister. With his family threatened by the king, Godwine began to raise an army. The Witan reacted by banishing Godwine and his family. The Godwines were a powerful family but unprepared to take on the entire rest of England and most went to Normandy, though Harold chose to go to Ireland.

A year later, Godwine and sons sailed up the Thames at the head of a fleet of ships and warriors. By then the Witan resented the Normans who advised and dominated Edward. When Godwine made his claim, the nobles voted to support him. Within days the Normans were gone and Godwine was back in charge of Essex and the most powerful earl in Britain.

In 1053, Godwine died and his son Harold succeeded him as Earl of East Anglia, while Harold's brother, Tostig, inherited Northumbria. Together these two brothers subdued Wales and brought it under Edward's control. For a decade things seemed to go smoothly. But in 1064, Harold, still Earl of East Anglia, made a mistake.

He had been shipwrecked on the coast of Normandy. It was also thought by some that Harold, as head of the Godwine family, might have instead gone to Normandy voluntarily to retrieve some family members still there since the banishment. Relations between Britain and Normandy were hardly cordial, and the English earl could have been treated badly or held for ransom by the local lord, William. At this point, the Norman lord was often referred to as William the Bastard. His dad was king; his mom was not the queen. The title was more an identifier than an insult, more a claim of royal blood than a disgrace. Harold was actually given excellent treatment, and while he was there, he was persuaded to pledge his support to William, who claimed the English throne. Harold Godwineson proceeded to swear an oath on sacred relics of a saint, a drastic and powerful pledge in his day. This mistake, which may have seemed good politics and alliance building at the time, enabled William to later declare Harold an oath breaker and gain the pope's support for his invasion in 1066. It was the first of two mistakes that cost the Saxons the land they had ruled for six centuries.

It seemed that Harold was much more popular in Wessex than his brother, Tostig, was in his fiefdom of Northumbria. Tostig had ruled Northumbria harshly, draining it to support his martial ambitions. In 1065, rebels drove Tostig completely out of England. It seemed Harold must have done little to assist his brother because Tostig fled to Normandy and supported William's claim to the throne even after his own brother sat on it. Then before the end of the year, Tostig again changed allegiance, this time allying himself with the Danish Viking king Harald Hardrada.

In 1066, Edward the Confessor died. Harold, who had been his counselor, was at the king's bedside. The popular Harold emerged from the chamber and announced that the king's last words were, "I commend my wife and all my kingdom to your care." The king's wife was also Harold Godwineson's sister, and she supported the claim. The Witan, already filled with Harold's allies, agreed to fulfill the dead king's last wish and voted for him to become king. Harold, as head of the Godwine family, was already the leader of the largest faction in the Witan and one of the most powerful and richest men on the island.

On January 6, 1066, Harold was crowned the king of Britain. This was far from a universal choice, and many rivals waited for the new king to fail. The crowning had been rushed, perhaps to accomplish it before the opposition could organize themselves or their warriors. Harold had no royal blood, and in a time when you ruled by divine right, this was a real problem. No one had to accept him as king by blood, so he had to quickly prove himself worthy of the throne.

William of Normandy immediately made public Harold's oath, but the new king said he had been tricked and was unaware of any relics. Harald Hardrada too publicly demanded the throne and trotted out Tostig to show even Harold's own brother supported his claim's validity. Both William and Hardrada began gathering armies to invade Britain.

At this point, Harold basically summoned large numbers of troops from his nobles and ordered the fryd to assemble. The fryd was a type of militia composed entirely of farmers and craftsmen. Because most Saxon men were trained to use some sort of weapon, this was a real force, not just fodder. Then no one invaded. The trouble with calling up the retainers and the fryd was that once he called the men to service, the king had to feed and support them. Eventually his treasury could not take the strain, and Harold released the fryd and sent most of the army away. The fryd needed to return to their fields because harvest was approaching. Just a few weeks later, Harold got word that Tostig and Hardrada had landed an army near York.

Harold had a choice to make. The Vikings had landed and were marching toward York with his traitorous brother. He had no idea what William of Normandy was doing, except that he was nearly ready to also invade England. The new English king could wait and recall the army. It would take a few weeks to assemble and would give him overwhelming numbers. But the delay would also allow the Vikings to pillage widely and possibly take some of the northern cities. To a man who had to prove himself worthy of being king, those losses were unacceptable. Vikings cutting a swath through his new kingdom would undermine his authority and might even cause the Witan to reverse their decision. More because of his own situation than that of England, Harold Godwineson chose to hurry north.

Fortunately for Harold, he still had at his command his personal retainers, the Huscarls. Numbering nearly three thousand, these professional soldiers were intended to form the core of any British army. Except for those fryd and local retainers that could be gathered as they hurried north, this force made up the army.

Harold and his army traveled quickly, covering the almost two hundred miles in just days. Their arrival on September 20 was unexpected, and it enabled Harold to surprise the normally canny Vikings. When Harold attacked at Stamford Bridge, it was recorded that many of the Vikings did not even have time to put on their armor. The Vikings were smashed and then a quarter of the ships sailed back to Scandinavia. Both Hardrada and Tostig died in the fighting. This loss in 1066 is considered, by many historians, to be the official end of the Viking era.

This is not to say that the Vikings did not put up a good fight. Nearly a third of Harold's elite Huscarls were killed or wounded. All were exhausted by the march, and so the news that William had just landed at Hastings must have been most unwelcome.

At this point, Harold Godwineson, king of England, made the

second mistake that changed the history of England and eventually the world. He still had the same concerns. He could not allow his rivals and enemies in the Witan to be able to show he could not defend the kingdom. If William chose to begin his attack, Hastings would surely fall, and London and most of the more prosperous cities in his kingdom were in danger of falling as well. Again he might have waited, gathered greater numbers, and summoned back thousands of fryd. But the wait might have cost Harold his kingship or crippled it. So again he did what was best for himself and hurriedly dragged his weary Huscarls the 250 miles to where William waited. He gathered a few more men as he rushed toward Hastings but not that many. The only fryd he could count on were those who had formed near Hastings. But regardless, the new king hurried to fight on October 13 at what has since been called Battle Hill.

The Battle of Hastings was a near run thing. The fryd and Huscarls withstood several charges by the Norman horsemen. Eventually Harold's formation broke, and the king himself died when an arrow pierced his eye. It can be easily speculated that had Harold spent even a week gathering his forces, he would have had an army large enough to crush William's. This would have left England in Saxon control, but the delay might have cost the new king his throne. Harold rushed into battle, and every Saxon in England paid for that mistake with Norman rule. Because of Harold's badly given oath and his twice putting his own needs ahead of the defense of Saxon Britain, the country became instead Norman Britain. Because of those two mistakes England was changed forever, and William the Bastard is remembered by history as William the Conqueror.

14

DISDAIN AND EGO

History's Biggest Loser

1216, SAMARKAND

IIIIIIIIIIIIIIIIIIIIIIIIIIIIIIIIIIIIIIIIIIIIIIIIIIIIIIIIIIIIIIIIIIII

This particular diplomatic error is included because it takes the award for one of the single most boneheaded and self-destructive leadership mistakes in this book. The mistake was made in the city of Samarkand, which was the capital of the Khwarezm Empire. In 1215, Khwarezm was perhaps the most prosperous state in the world. Samarkand was known for its culture, its palaces, and its many carefully gardened parks. The empire included what is today Iraq, Iran, Pakistan, and Afghanistan. The Khwarezm army included almost half a million full-time heavy cavalry men. Each man and horse was fully covered in high-quality armor. The court of its emperor, Ala ad-Din Muhammed, was filled with scholars and artists. It was a golden age for literature and the arts.

Much of Khwarezm's wealth came from taxes collected along the Silk Road. Khwarezm controlled part of the only land route between China and Europe. Every merchant paid a fee to use their roads and to be protected by their army.

Bordering Khwarezm to the northeast were the steppes of

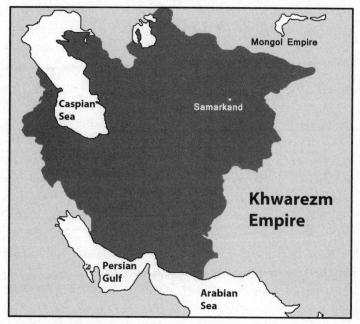

The Khwarezm Empire

Mongolia. At the time of the Ala ad-Din's mistake, the Mongols under Genghis Khan were conquering China. The Silk Road ran through these steppes as well, and the Great Khan also benefited from a wealth of taxes collected from it. With his army busy in China, Genghis Khan made it clear he was interested above all in keeping the lucrative trade routes open. Because of this, he was more than friendly to Ala ad-Din Muhammed, often sending valuable gifts. Both nations did well by this, and if either stopped, trade for both would suffer. The Mongols also went to great lengths to keep the caravans moving along the road. And for a long time, Ala ad-Din Muhammed also made sure that Mongol merchants were well treated as they passed through his lands.

But at some point around 2016, Ala ad-Din Muhammed became suspicious. The Mongols were conquering China much too easily. He suddenly felt threatened, even though there had been no threats or change in his relationship with Genghis Khan. No armies were massing in the western steppes, no invasions seemed to be planned, but Ala ad-Din Muhammed was concerned. It appeared to him that many Mongolian merchant caravans were carrying more than exotic goods. He suspected that they also were bringing in Mongol spies.

So with no provocation he ordered his army to begin raiding the Mongol caravans it had formerly protected. But still Genghis Khan did not threaten or overreact to the insult and losses. Instead he sent a delegation, including an ambassador he appointed, to Samarkand. About fifty important Mongol nobles and scholars were also included in the delegation. Once there, they sought an audience with Ala ad-Din Muhammed, who insultingly stalled the meeting for some weeks. After they finally met, the Mongolian ambassador demanded not only that the attacks stop but that Ala ad-Din Muhammed himself pay reparations for the losses. Again the Khwarezm emperor stalled and then finally called in the Mongolian delegation. His reply was to grab all of the delegates and set their beards on fire. This was said to have greatly amused his court. However, because most Mongol nobles had full beards this also meant they were all badly burned and scarred, and some were blinded. Then to make his point, Ala ad-Din Muhammed personally beheaded the ambassador.

There seems to have been no reason for this calculated insult. Any dispute would disrupt all the trade on the Silk Road. The Mongols had never threatened his empire and had given its merchants special treatment. It is hard to speculate just why the emperor felt he could insult and virtually declare war on a neighbor that was successfully conquering China. Perhaps he felt that the high mountains and narrow passes would discourage any military reaction. Perhaps he felt the war in China would prevent the Mongolians from having enough horsemen to retaliate. Or maybe he just didn't think and showed off for his court at the expense of the less-sophisticated Mongols. For three years there seemed to be few consequences. Ala ad-Din Muhammed kept his army on alert and near the mountain passes that led to Mongolia, but no avenging army appeared.

Whatever the reason, this was arguably the worst diplomatic mistake in all history. It certainly puts all modern blunders (Neville's appeasement of Hitler, the Allies' giveaway at Yalta, and Acheson's not including Korea in a speech listing the areas America would defend from Communism) to shame. In 1219, one hundred thousand Mongolian horsemen (ten Tumens) rode almost unopposed into Khwarezm, through passes hundreds of miles away from where the opposing armies were waiting for them. Within a year, all of Khwarezm's half million armored cavalry were dead or slaves. City after city fell. Many were completely destroyed and every person in them slain or sold into slavery. The entire population of Samarkand was put to death, and that city of gardens and palaces was then also leveled. The Mongols completely crushed the entire empire, eliminating three quarters of its people and leaving those who remained in poverty and hunger. Millions died, and a once-prosperous land turned into a wasteland inhabited by subsistence farmers and herders. This is why Afghanistan is a much poorer and more uncultured place today than it was a thousand years ago. So great was the Mongol destruction that in some ways the area still suffers from it. This incident may well also have been what turned the Mongols' eyes westward. It may have later doomed nations from Turkey and India to Russia and Ukraine to Mongol invasion and domination. This unneeded insult, baiting the most powerful and warlike people of the time, cost millions of lives and changed history in ways that still affect our lives.

As for Ala ad-Din Muhammed? He fled and is said to have died of fright, fleeing to a distant island in the farthest corner of the land he had once ruled, still pursued by twenty thousand Mongols.

Traditions begin for a good reason. In the case of the Mongols, traditions surrounding the death of a great khan were carefully followed. The Mongols were a military state, and their leaders commanded the best soldiers of their day. When Genghis Khan died in 1027, the formerly warring Mongol tribes had been united for only two decades. Electing a new great khan required that all of the leaders agree. If one was not there, he would not be required to recognize a decision he was not part of. So the tradition of the Mongols was for all the leaders to gather and elect their next khan. Considering the stakes and the very nature of those who had gathered, such a meeting would have made a modern political convention look like a tea party. But they met and a unanimous choice was made. This guaranteed their newfound unity and empire.

Genghis Khan's son Ögedei was elected to succeed him, and Genghis's other sons were assigned to command different parts of the empire. This began a second wave of Mongol conquests. By the time Ögedei died in 1241, it was Europe and not the Mongols who benefited the most from this tradition.

After Genghis Khan's death, his son Jöchi became the leader of the Kipchak Khanate, known today as the Golden Horde. When Jöchi died, his son Batu became Kha Khan (Great Leader) of the Golden Horde. Batu and Subotai, who was one of the greatest Mongol commanders, went on to conquer Russia. As usual, the Mongols left the local lords in place and ruled through them. In 1240, they conquered and tore down Kiev, the last major center of resistance east of Poland. This left the Golden Horde free to move deeper into Europe. An unknown Russian poet from Muscovy wrote of the conquest showing the fear and dismay that assisted the Mongols in their conquest.

Yet still did the mountains tremble and our eyes strain across the steppe to find the storm. Then, like the onset of nightfall came the endless shadow of the Horde to blot our lands from view. A numberless multitude swept across the hill crests and like waves of a black ocean did they sweep down upon us. Their arrows fell like clouds of biting flies from the darkened sky. The death screams of our warriors were overwhelmed by

the drumming of infinite hooves so that only the endless thun-
der was heard at the last. Our enemy then struck wide its
wings and eclipsed the sun from Russia's plain forever.

Their first target was Poland and only part of the horde was needed. After pillaging a good part of that nation, they met the Polish army commanded by Włodzimierz of Kraków. The Poles were defeated and those who could flee did. A second battle at Chmielnik sealed Poland's fate. There the more heavily armored, but less disciplined, Polish knights were initially winning. Seeing this, the Mongol commander ordered his whole army to feign retreat. The knights, thinking they were pursuing a defeated enemy, lost all formation as they chased after the Mongol horsemen. When the knights were all spread out and vulnerable, the retreating Mongols turned and reinforcements attacked them from both flanks. Most of the Polish knights died. The king of Bohemia then gathered his army, gathered together the survivors of the two armies that had been defeated, adding them to his own, and moved to relieve Kraków. In a hard-fought battle, he too was defeated. The Bohemian army remained intact, but they were damaged, so they retreated to regroup. With no army left to defend it, Kraków was soon conquered and burned. The Mongols in Poland then turned south and joined the rest of the Golden Horde invading Hungary.

At the start of the thirteenth century, Hungary was one of the most powerful and wealthy of the Christian kingdoms. Subotai and Batu united all the Tumens of the Golden Horde to conquer it. They met the amassed Hungarian army near the town of Muhi, just south of the Sajó River.

Although King Béla of Hungary was concerned and had gathered his army, many of his nobles underestimated the threat the Mongols posed, thinking they faced only a raid by a few thousand horsemen. The battle began very well for the Hungarians. The Templar commander led a good part of the army out in an effort to surprise the Mongols. They managed to find the enemy and

THE MONGOLS

It is a modern misconception to think that the Mongols were some sort of barbarian horde. They were Scythian horsemen and came from the same grasslands the Huns and the Goths had centuries earlier, but they were much more. The Mongol war machine was a refined and highly efficient weapon. At its core was the mounted archer we all think of when *Mongol* is mentioned. But that horseman, hardened to ride days without rest, was not only a fierce but also a highly disciplined soldier. Warfare was life's work for a Mongol warrior. Children played at war, their games training them for battle and their culture valuing them for how well they fought. Perhaps the name that they gave Temüjin, when he united the Mongols, shows it all. The phrase *genghis khan* does not mean "beloved king," "holy emperor," or even "supreme chief." Its translation shows what the Mongols valued the most. He was their "great war leader."

In the thirteenth century most European armies were feudal levies called together for a single battle or war. Their grand tactics almost always consisted of forming three or more battles, with little internal organization, and then charging the enemy. In contrast, the Mongol army was highly organized with permanent units of ten (Arav), one hundred (Zuut), one thousand (Minghan), and ten thousand (Tumen) horsemen. The ten-thousand-man Tumen was the largest permanent unit. Against a large foe several Tumens would work together. Discipline was fierce and brutal, and Mongol warriors were trained from childhood to fearlessly obey any orders given. Promotion was based entirely on merit, and an officer was responsible for both the behavior and the welfare of all the men he commanded.

The combination of highly skilled horsemen, thorough

organization, and harsh discipline created a force that was both flexible and instantly responsive on the battlefield. Rarely did the Mongols outnumber any opponent. They fought battles of movement and tactics. Battles they rarely lost. The Mongols were very much more than barbarian horsemen raiding the steppes. They were the heart and weapon of a world-conquering war machine.

Where the European kings could at best order their masses of troops forward, Mongol commanders using drums and banners could quickly order from ten men to ten thousand to attack, change direction, hold, or fake a retreat. The Mongols conquered from Poland to China and from Siberia to the southern tip of India. At its peak, the Mongol Empire was larger and more populous than that of Rome, China, or Persia. (Since they had, after all, conquered both China and Persia.)

attack while the Mongols were in the process of crossing the Sajó. Thanks to the element of surprise, night, and their crossbows (which came as an unpleasant blow to the Mongols), the Hungarians killed a large number of the raiders, while they were trying to cross the two-hundred-meter-long bridge or swim the river. When the Mongols pulled back, the Hungarians returned to their camp confident they had dealt with the threat.

By the next morning, the Mongols had managed to find another crossing and send a small force across the river. That force, assisted by some stone throwers, cleared the bridge, and the Golden Horde began to cross. When the guards from the bridge rushed into the camp, some of the princes gathered their forces to meet the raiders and retake the bridge. It soon became apparent to the Hungarians that they were facing the entire horde, and they rushed back to gather the rest of the army.

Amazingly confident that his princes could handle the Mongol raiders, Béla had not even begun preparations for a battle. When the princes raised the alarm, it took some time for the main Hungarian force to form. That delay allowed almost all of the Mongols to cross over to the Hungarian side of the Sajó. The two armies met and were evenly matched. Both forces suffered heavy casualties, with Batu losing thirty-five members of his personal bodyguard rank. Only when the late-arriving Subotai crossed the bridge and fell on the Hungarian rear did they retreat into their fortified camp.

Once in the crowded wooden fortification, the Hungarians found they could not effectively sort out their army. Organization failed as fire arrows caused chaos, and morale plunged. The Mongols then left an opening in their lines, and the Hungarian army surged out of the fort hoping to escape. Out of formation and in a panic, they were decimated. Béla and others escaped, but the bulk of the Hungarian soldiers died. The Golden Horde went on to pillage much of Hungary unopposed until what had been a good tradition had a bad result.

There is no question that with Hungary decimated Europe was exposed. The western European kingdoms were at this time much poorer and less populated than the eastern ones Batu had already defeated. It appears that no European nation was capable of defeating the Mongols. The entire French army at the Battle of Bouvines that same year totaled only fifteen thousand.

Ögedei died, and the word went out for all the Mongol lords to return to the capital, more than a thousand miles away, and elect a new great khan. Batu had said he intended to conquer all of Europe as he had Russia. But due to tradition, he felt he had no choice but to return to Mongolia immediately. Because of this, Europe was spared. Had he remained, there is no question that the Mongols would have been in Paris by the spring. But he chose instead to follow his people's customs. It was a mistake for a conqueror, but one that saved Europe.

15

AT SEA WHEN
AT SEA

Kublai Khan's Lost Fleet

1281, JAPAN

Kublai Khan, the Great Khan, ruled one of the largest empires in history, but his thirst for victory also resulted in the worst naval disaster of all time. In 1271 Kublai Khan, grandson of Genghis Khan and self-proclaimed Great Khan of the Mongols, took control of northern China and established the Yüan dynasty. He managed to subjugate Korea in 1273, after years of fighting, when the Korean ruler married Kublai Khan's daughter and proclaimed Korea a vassal state. In 1279, Kublai Khan finally succeeded in defeating the Sung dynasty of south China, uniting all of China under one rule for the first time since the T'ang dynasty fell in 907 CE. The khan, however, was not satisfied with just ruling all of China and Mongolia. He believed that to make China the center of the universe, all other nations must become subjects or vassal states. Those that refused, he would conquer. There was one more realm worth conquering after Korea and China. Kublai Khan decided to add the island nation of Japan, with all its riches, to his empire.

In 1281 Kublai Khan made his second attempt to conquer the

stubborn islands. He had tried to take Japan in 1274, but before his forces could gain a serious beachhead, a huge storm blew in and destroyed most of the fleet. Despite the fact that the loss may have been partially due to his generals' inexperience with a sea campaign—after all, the Mongols were horsemen of the steppes, not sailors—Kublai Khan decided he could win if he just had a larger fleet and invading army. Now that he controlled the resources of Korea and the shipbuilding yards of south China, he decided he could build that fleet. It would be not just a larger fleet, but the largest fleet in history. It was far larger than the Spanish Armada and would be unmatched until modern times.

He ordered the Chinese and Korean shipwrights to begin construction of over four thousand ships. In contrast, the Spanish Armada was made up of fewer than three hundred vessels. A task of that magnitude would be daunting to any nation even when spread over many years, but the khan went further, demanding the fleet be ready within the year. The newly subjugated southern Chinese shipwrights already resented their Mongolian masters. The brutal pace demanded by an impossible timetable made this worse.

At this time the Sung ships, especially oceangoing vessels, were considered the finest in the world. The Chinese had pioneered the use of watertight compartments, rudders, and metal-reinforced fittings, yet many of the ships they built for their khan lacked even well-crafted mast steps. They were thrown together—and possibly sabotaged—in the rush to meet the deadline. The Korean shipbuilders were not as resentful, but they knew how to build only one type of ship: flat-bottomed boats suitable for Korea's narrow tributaries. They had no experience with building large, oceangoing vessels. However, even the efforts of all available Chinese and Korean shipbuilders were not enough, and after a year far fewer than the four thousand demanded were completed. Rather than increase his deadline, the impatient Khan decided to conscript existing boats to make up his fleet.

Unfortunately, most of the existing ocean-ready ships had already been pressed into the Mongols' service. The only other available boats were riverboats. While the khan had proved himself a willing student in most cases, he did not bother to learn the difference between riverboats and ocean vessels. That or he simply did not care. Oceangoing vessels have a deeply V-shaped keel to give them stability in the wind and waves. In contrast, riverboats have flat bottoms to allow them passage over shallow riverbeds and against the current. But this shallow configuration means that they are unstable in any turbulence. Regardless of the differences, thousands of riverboats were collected and added to the growing fleet. Perhaps it was thought that their flat bottoms would make them suitable as landing craft. By the time the Mongol fleet was ready to sail, it included 4,400 ships carrying approximately 140,000 soldiers and 60,000 sailors. The khan put General Atahai in command of the combined fleet, despite the fact that the latter had never commanded even a single ship. This was the same mistake that doomed the Spanish Armada three centuries later.

The first part of the new fleet sailed for Japan in May 1281. The rest of the ships suffered delays gathering and did not meet up with the first part of the fleet until July, leaving them to suffer the elements and harassing attacks by the Japanese ships for weeks. The combined fleet then advanced on Takeshima Island in Imari Bay. Everything seemed to be going the Mongols' way. The khan's forces had the technological edge, using long-range weapons as cover fire against the samurai from their ships. Their arsenal included the world's first-known exploding projectile, a shell with a fuse filled with shrapnel and gunpowder. But the Japanese had spent the time between invasions preparing for the khan's return by building walls to reinforce their shoreline. Once the Chinese soldiers landed, they faced fortifications and the disciplined fury of the samurai. On the first landing, despite heavy losses, the samurai succeeded in driving the invaders back to their boats before they could establish a beachhead.

The Mongol general refused to accept defeat. He kept his fleet at anchor and made plans to renew the attack. Before he could, however, a massive typhoon blew into the bay. The Mongol ships were anchored offshore and unprotected from the weather. It was a mistake a seaman would not make, but a general did. On August 12, four thousand ships of the greatest fleet ever gathered disappeared. All the flat-bottom riverboats and landing craft were quickly overturned, swamped, or destroyed by the first great waves of the storm. The boats thrown together in haste with faulty construction broke up in the violent storm. The only ships known to survive were a few hundred deep-keeled ocean vessels. By the end of the storm, four thousand ships had been shattered or sunk and more than seventy thousand men had drowned. This remains the greatest single loss of life at sea in history.

The Japanese called the storm *kamikaze* or "divine wind." The loss broke the back of Mongolian expansion. It also triggered a Japanese cultural belief of racial superiority that lasted until World War II.

Kublai Khan never completely recovered from the loss, though he never stopped trying to enlarge his empire. The myth of Mongol invincibility had been shattered. His determination to take Japan without learning from his first failure proved devastating. He had lost his first fleet to a similar storm, so there was no excuse for it happening again just a few years later. Yet he sent an invasion fleet across the sea during typhoon season. His demands for more and more ships also resulted in the deforestation of Korean lands. His impatience led to a hastily gathered fleet of inferior ships never designed to handle the open sea. His choice of a commander with no knowledge of the sea compounded his other mistakes, resulting in the loss of a fleet larger than the D-Day invasion force of World War II.

The divine wind may have destroyed the fleet, but only because the Great Khan's mistakes doomed it.

16

NEARLY THE
ULTIMATE EGO TRIP

An Accidental
Reformation

nless your head is on the chopping block, there are few
better gigs than being king. In sixteenth-century Europe,
monarchs were thought to be divinely appointed by God.
This meant that kings tended to get what they wanted. There is
perhaps no better example of this than Henry VIII, a lascivious
English king who is most famous for establishing the Anglican
Church when the pope refused to grant him a divorce. By refusing
to annul Henry's marriage, Pope Clement VII permanently undermined the Catholic presence in Britain and lost the church
vast amounts of wealth stored in English churches. The ramifications of the pope's decision persist to this day. Even now, there
is an ever-raging battle between Irish Catholics and English Protestants, a legacy of Clement's ill-fated refusal to accommodate
Henry.

Henry VIII was never supposed to be the king. His older
brother, Arthur, died in 1502 before ever taking the throne. Their
father, Henry VII, had orchestrated a marriage between Arthur
and Catherine of Aragon. It was a purely political union, typical

for that era. Catherine was the daughter of King Ferdinand and Queen Isabella of Spain, and their marriage was meant to cement an alliance between the two countries. Arthur's death created obvious challenges to such an agreement. It was resolved that young Henry should marry his brother's wife but such a union was considered forbidden by the Bible. Nevertheless, Henry VII was able to secure a dispensation from Pope Julius II to allow the marriage of his second son. To enable this Catherine swore that her marriage with Arthur had never been consummated, that they had never had sexual relations. Both Spain and England pressured Julius to waive the biblical prohibition and he did so in 1503. The future king of England was only twelve years old. Due to Henry's youth, the marriage was delayed until Henry had succeeded his father in 1509.

Their marriage was not to be a happy one, though. Catherine bore Henry three sons and three daughters, but all of the children except one (Mary) died very young. The British law of primogeniture meant that the oldest living male in the royal family would someday inherit the throne. If there was no direct male heir, there would be a question as to who was entitled to be king. Such questions had torn England apart more than once. In part due to these concerns for the nation's stability and in part due to his colossal ego, Henry felt that he needed a son of royal blood. As Catherine aged, it became ever more apparent that she was not going to bear him a male heir. She was no longer of ideal childbearing age, and every prior attempt had been fruitless. Moreover, Henry VIII had taken a fancy to a lady of the court, Anne Boleyn. It was common for kings to have mistresses, but a bastard son would not solve the question of needing an heir.

Henry decided that he must end his marriage to Catherine so that he could marry Anne. He attributed Catherine's inability to bear a son as evidence that his marriage to Catherine was not sacred. As proof of this, he cited a passage from the Bible, Leviticus 20:21—"And if a man shall take his brother's wife, it is an unclean thing . . . they shall be childless." It bothered Henry little that this clearly contradicted the dispensation granted his father by Julius years earlier. That dispensation initially permitted his marriage to Catherine. Henry dispatched Cardinal Thomas Wolsey to seek an annulment from the new pope, Clement VII.

Getting that annulment proved not to be so simple. As before, politics influenced the pope's decision. This time, however, politics worked against Henry. Between 1523 and 1527, Clement's loyalty had oscillated among France, Spain, Charles V, and various Italian princes. This prompted troops from the Holy Roman Empire to invade Rome. But the emperor, Charles, had not ordered such an attack and was embarrassed by his troops. Even so he capitalized on his newfound leverage over the Catholic Church and its pope. Unfortunately for Henry VIII, Charles happened to be Catherine's nephew. Charles had little interest in removing his relative from a position of power. He preferred to maintain a line of British succession through Catherine, as that would mean England would one day be ruled by his cousin. Spain also pressured Clement to deny Henry's request. Spain also was far more generous in its donations to the church than England was, and thus Clement refused to grant an annulment. It was the first concern of any Catholic pope to preserve the church and its influence. In the still highly religious sixteenth century, Clement had to be as political as he was spiritual to accomplish this.

Henry was unfazed. He maneuvered to replace the late archbishop of Canterbury William Warham with Thomas Cranmer, the Boleyn family's chaplain. Warham annulled Henry's marriage and remarried him to Anne. Clement responded by excommunicating Henry. This bothered the king little. Henry proceeded to establish a church independent of the Vatican that would be managed by none other than himself. Catholics in England thus became a threat, as Henry construed their adherence to Catholicism as a tacit challenge to his authority. Catholics were thus persecuted for political rather than theological reasons, as Catholic dogma differed little from the tenets of Anglicanism. One of the first victims of this sectarian violence was the venerable Thomas

More, a cardinal who was executed for refusing to attend Anne's coronation. This was but the beginning of a cycle of violence that would persist in England for years.

Henry VIII ended up having six wives and three true heirs (Edward by Jane Seymour, Mary by Catherine, and Elizabeth by Anne). After Henry's death, Edward took the throne but died of illness shortly into his reign. Mary restored Catholicism as the official religion and earned the nickname "Bloody Mary" for the violence that ensued. Elizabeth took the throne and reestablished the Church of England. The Virgin Queen proved to be one of England's greatest monarchs; in the end, Henry's fear of not having a male heir proved groundless.

Clement, beholden to the leaders of Spain and the Holy Roman Empire, was forced to make a difficult choice. Yet he should have anticipated Henry's reaction. Henry was an egomaniac who would stop at nothing to get what he wanted. England was the most independent of the kingdoms. The pope also misjudged the mood of his time. In 1517 Martin Luther posted his ninety-five theses on the cathedral door. Clement could have appeased Henry and retained a powerful ally. While his decision would have undoubtedly angered Spain and the Holy Roman Empire, it is unlikely that either would have abandoned Catholicism in the way that Henry did.

Clement's decision ultimately paved the way for centuries of sectarian violence in England and created a schism within the church. Even the religious tradition of the United States has its roots in Clement's decision. The Puritans who first came from England were a viscerally anti-Catholic sect of Anglicanism. Those Puritans would never have existed without the Church of England. There was a Church of England because the pope misjudged his own influence and Henry VIII's independence. Clement's mistake thus had far-reaching implications for the political and religious landscapes of England, Europe, and indeed, the world.

17

||||||||||||||||||||||||||||||||||||||||||||||||||||||||||||||||||||||||||||||||||||||

KNOW WHO YOUR
ENEMY IS

Montezuma Welcomes
the Conquistadors

1519, MEXICO

||||||||||||||||||||||||||||||||||||||||||||||||||||||||||||||||||||||||||||||||||||||

magine the following situation: You are the leader of a vast empire. A small force of foreigners, the likes of which you have never seen, have come to your land with advanced weaponry, strange beasts, and debilitating diseases. Within days of arriving, they ally with your empire's biggest rival. They then raze large parts of your empire's second most important city, killing thousands of your subjects in the process. The leader of the opponent is a warmongering megalomaniac bent on plundering your nation's treasures and subjugating your people to his crown and his god. The survival of your empire and customs depends on resisting this aggressor with your overwhelming numbers and knowledge of the terrain. Would you welcome the strangers into your capital?

In 1519, Aztec emperor Montezuma II faced such a situation. Spanish conquistadors under Hernán Cortés had forged an alliance with the Aztec's primary rivals, the Tlaxcala. They had freshly attacked Cholula, the religious hub of the empire, and massacred up to thirty thousand of its citizens. Cortés then marched on Tenochtitlán, the capital of the empire. He sent a threatening message to Montezuma: Resist and Tenochtitlán will end up like Cholula.

This must have been difficult for Montezuma. Despite the Aztecs outnumbering the conquistadors, victory over the well-armed Spaniards was no sure thing. Even if he were victorious, the battle would no doubt incur serious casualties and potentially leave the empire vulnerable to attacks by rivals like the Tlaxcala. Montezuma chose instead to try to placate the Spanish with gifts and hospitality. He welcomed them into Tenochtitlán as honored guests for several months. The risk-averse emperor deemed the costs of resisting the conquistadors to be too great. All this was complicated by the very different, bearded, and powerful conquistadors seeming to fulfill a sacred Aztec myth about one of their gods returning.

Montezuma's decision was not entirely impractical. After all, the Spanish's mass of native allies, superior firepower, metal weapons, and armor made the prospects of victory grim or at least costly. Costlier than he could afford since the Aztecs' subject tribes had been roused and were likely to continue to be a problem. Consider also that the Aztecs had never before encountered Spaniards. Their pale skin and strange language were frightening enough to the Aztecs, not to mention the warhorses, guns, and steel armor. The invaders had also brought smallpox with them; as the disease ravaged the native peoples, it no doubt seemed that the Spaniards were endowed with some supernatural powers. It is not altogether surprising that Montezuma capitulated to the conquistadors. Not surprising, but disastrous.

Montezuma made a grievous error, however. It was not long before he was a prisoner within his own home: a puppet controlled by Cortés. Montezuma yielded to Cortés's demands of replacing Aztec idols with shrines of Christian saints. He showered Cortés with gifts of treasure and pledged his loyalty to the Spanish Crown. Despite his compliance, Cortés held Montezuma hostage as protection against a potential revolt by the Aztec people.

When conquistador Pánfilo de Narváez arrived near Tenochtitlán to arrest Cortés (Cortés had initially been ordered to establish trading partnerships with the natives, not conquer them), Cortés had to temporarily leave the city. He left a small force at Tenochtitlán and engaged in a daring attack on Narváez's troops during the night. He then rushed back to the capital to stymie unrest. In his absence, his troops had slaughtered many of the Aztec nobility during a religious celebration. Scholars dispute the motivation for the massacre; Spanish sources maintain that the massacre was to prevent a human sacrifice or to preempt a planned attack by the Aztecs. Aztec sources state that the Spaniards were enticed by the jewelry and treasures on display during the ritual. Either way, Cortés returned to Tenochtitlán to face an angry Aztec population that turned against Montezuma for appeasing the Spaniard. The Aztecs elected a new leader and laid siege to Montezuma's palace with the Spanish trapped inside it.

Cortés's conquistadors were between a rock and a hard place. At first, they sought to use their puppet king to convince the Aztecs to let them escape to the coast in peace. Montezuma addressed the Aztec people from the palace's balcony. Once again, sources differ on the events that followed. Spanish witnesses stated that Montezuma was jeered and pelted with rocks, causing the injuries that eventually lead to his death. Aztec accounts maintain that Montezuma was killed by Cortés when he had outlived his usefulness. Cortés then led his troops outside of Tenochtitlán. Some of the forces escaped on a hastily crafted bridge, whereas others cut their way through Aztec resistance. The Spanish were harried by Aztec pursuers and were almost defeated before finding refuge in the home of their local ally, the Tlaxcala. With their ally's armies, they seized control of Tenochtitlán and eventually defeated the Aztecs. They were helped by a devastating smallpox epidemic that struck the city. Aztec survivors were banished from the region, and the city was razed. It would form the foundation for what would become Mexico City.

Montezuma's weak-willed response to Spanish aggression

doomed his empire. If Montezuma had been bolder, he might have staved off the conquistadors and let his empire survive another day. It is possible that such a defeat would have changed the complexion of Spanish exploration in the region. After all, Cortés's success inspired countless other ventures into the Americas; had he instead been slaughtered by local "savages," it is doubtful that enterprising young men would have found the New World so enticing.

Montezuma's biggest failing, though, was not his lack of boldness. It was instead his failure to understand his enemy. Cortés was driven by his desire to bring God to the heathens, to bring glory to himself and to Spain, and to collect hefty amounts of gold in the process. There was no reason to let the Aztecs or their culture live. Had Montezuma understood Cortés the man, he would have realized that the Spaniard never intended to spare the Aztecs. He would not have first allied himself with their enemies had he planned to be a friend. The Aztecs were merely another civilization to be conquered for the glory of Spain while their treasures were shipped overseas to fill Spain's coffers. There was never anything temporary about Cortés's stay in Tenochtitlán. The conquistadors were invaders, not guests, and Montezuma failed to realize the distinction until it was too late. His entire nation paid for the mistake.

‖‖

18

UNDERESTIMATED THE OPPOSITION

Short Temper and a Long Parliament

1627–1629, ENGLAND

‖‖

There's an old saying that goes: "Don't bite the hand that feeds you." It's simple, sound advice. When you are dependent on another, it's a good idea to ingratiate, not alienate, that person. If you cannot abide such dependence, you'd best wean yourself from it. The English King Charles I, the king of England from 1625 to 1649, seemed to have trouble with this basic notion. Charles repeatedly undermined Parliament, the institution on which he relied for revenue collection during his reign. Charles embarked on a number of fruitless wars that drained his coffers. By biting the hand that fed him, while simultaneously begging to be fed, Charles set the stage for a dramatic political transformation that would forever change England.

At the beginning of the seventeenth century, Parliament had a vague, impermanent role in governing England. Parliament was, in essence, a glorified tax-collection agency. It was summoned by the king when he needed revenue and dissolved at his discretion. Parliament had no real authority over the king; its only leverage was that it could refuse to collect taxes for him. In such an event, the English king lacked a practical means to compel Parliament to cooperate. An uncooperative Parliament could totally frustrate royal policy.

The members of Charles's first Parliament in 1625 were tired of their indeterminate role in governing and sought to expand their influence. Much of the king's regular income came from his ability to collect customs duties. Traditionally, Parliament granted the monarch the right to collect such duties throughout his reign. This Parliament chose to grant this right for only one year; its members believed that doing so would force Charles to keep Parliament in session.

Parliament was too bold. King Charles was a petty, authoritarian man with little tolerance for Parliament's antics. Charles was, at the time, engaged in a costly conflict on the European mainland called the Thirty Years' War. Charles's backing of the continental Protestants was supported by Parliament and eased their concerns about his marriage to Catholic Princess Henrietta Maria of France. Yet his first Parliament was less enthusiastic about George Villiers, Charles's choice as commander of the English expedition.

Villiers was a family friend (indeed, perhaps he was more than a friend; it is speculated that he had a sexual relationship with James, Charles's father) and the Duke of Buckingham. He had earned the derision of Parliament in just about every way a British gentleman could. He was crass, had shown military ineptitude, and had clandestine affairs in Ireland, which reflected his apparent support of Catholicism over the Church of England. Parliament moved to impeach Villiers but was thwarted by Charles, who dissolved the body to protect his friend. When Villiers was assassinated a year later, the public celebrations that ensued deepened the rift between the king and the members of Parliament.

Charles provoked further unrest by financing the war with a "forced loan," a tax levied without Parliament's consent. Though the Five Knights' Case in 1627 affirmed the king's right to imprison those who refused to implement these taxes, Charles was still short on funds and reconvened Parliament. Incensed by the forced loan, Parliament conditioned their authorizing new funds on Charles's approval of a new constitutional document, the Petition of Right. The Petition of Right ruled there should be no taxation without the consent of Parliament. It said that there should be no imprisonment without cause shown. It forbade the billeting of soldiers or sailors on householders against their will and stated that there should be no martial law to punish ordinary offenses by sailors or soldiers.

The law effectively limited the king's power to act without Parliament's approval. The king accepted the new law. This second Parliament was prorogued in 1628 and recalled for a second session in 1629 when a crisis arose. Charles had violated the Petition of Right by confiscating the property of MP John Rolle for his refusal to pay tonnage and poundage, two customs duties on imported and exported merchandise. The king still had the right to dissolve Parliament. They scrambled to pass a number of provocative resolutions condemning both Catholicism and the collection of customs duties before being forced to adjourn. A final resolution garnered support but did not pass before Parliament was dismissed. It stated that any individuals who were complicit in the illegal collection of customs duties would "be reputed a betrayer of the liberties of England." The members were solidly on the high ground, and Charles looked little more than a despot when he went on to imprison eight members of Parliament for criticizing him.

Charles was tired of dealing with Parliament. He made peace with France and Spain, eliminating a sizable drain on the kingdom's resources. In an unprecedented display of absolutism, Charles would rule the next eleven years without calling Parliament. It became the era referred to as the Eleven-Year Tyranny. Without Parliament's assistance, Charles had to get creative when it came to revenue collection. He resurrected a 1229 law called the distraint of knighthood, which required all men of a certain income to attend the king's coronation to be knighted; Charles then fined anyone who had been absent from his coronation in 1626. He also collected "ship money." Ship money was a tax applied to coastal towns during times of war to offset the costs of their defense. Charles chose to levy the tax despite the fact that England was not at war. While royal courts validated the collection of ship money, Parliament and its supporters viewed this as a gross abuse of power. These efforts, supplemented by the illegal granting of monopolies and by revoking royal gifts to Scottish nobility, enabled Charles to scrape by.

Charles was able to maintain this tenuous financial position only because England was not involved in any costly wars. Unfortunately for Charles, this was about to change. Charles, who was by birthright also the king of Scotland, sought to establish a unified church in his kingdoms. Without consulting Scottish political and religious leaders, he ordered that Scotland use a new prayer book that mirrored England's Book of Common Prayer. Scotland was heavily Presbyterian and believed the book was an attempt to convert the Scots to Anglicanism. The Scots responded in 1638 by replacing their Episcopalian government (rule by bishops) with a Presbyterian one. In what was to be called the first Bishops' War, Charles accompanied his troops to suppress the rebellion and disband this new Scottish government. The campaign was inconclusive and the costs great. Finally a truce was declared, mostly because Charles needed to secure more funds. However, both parties knew the truce was temporary. Charles was forced to call Parliament in 1640. In exchange for forfeiting the right to ship money, Parliament granted him a large sum that eventually would prove inadequate by the war's end. He disbanded Parliament after only a month; this session was later called the Short Parliament.

His treasury rejuvenated, Charles resumed the conflict in 1640. The second Bishops' War did not end well for Charles. English forces were handily defeated in a number of battles; the Scots went on to occupy the northern regions of Northumberland and Durham. Charles was forced to sign the humiliating Treaty of

Ripon. The treaty required Charles to pay an indemnity that he couldn't afford. Scottish forces would continue to occupy English territory until Charles called Parliament and secured the payment; until he did, he was forced to pay the Scots the then large sum of £850 daily. As strange as it might sound, Charles was forced to *pay* the Scots to occupy English land.

Charles's costly mistakes had finally caught up to him. When Charles called Parliament again, it had the leverage to demand a number of reforms. To get needed money, Charles abdicated the right to disband Parliament at will. He also consented to bans on ship money and fines in distraint of knighthood. The royal courts that had rubber-stamped Charles's policies were eliminated. This Parliament would become known as the Long Parliament because it would remain in session for twenty years. The men of Parliament were also English patriots. Charles could have pursued an amicable relationship with them had he chosen to. This would have equipped him with the means to pursue his domestic and foreign priorities. There was never a serious disagreement with the king's goals. The problem was one of style. Charles's treatment of the members of his Parliament as enemies and his resentment, attempts at intimidation, arrests, and intentional illegal actions set the stage for the English Civil War and his eventual execution. It was the first ever of an English monarch by his own people.

19

UNFORESEEN CONSEQUENCES

Charles I Deals with the Scots

1640, ENGLAND

||||||||||||||||||||||||||||||||||||||||||||||||||||||||||||||||||||||||

Charles I is well-known for his feuds with Parliament over his arbitrary use of power and the English Parliament's resulting unwillingness to fund his policies. If Charles had wanted to make money, he probably should have just written a book. The title could have been *Getting Executed for Dummies*. Charles's pigheadedness brought about the English Civil War, a conflict that he lost. Despite his actions, Charles retained the throne and, more significant, his head. Charles should have been content with his life, but he was a victim of his colossal ego. He was unwilling to endure the inevitable restrictions on royal power that Parliament imposed. Charles also attempted to negotiate an under-the-table deal with the Scots to wrest control from Parliament. He was defeated yet again, and his scheme eradicated any sympathy harbored by Parliament and the English public. Charles was executed, and England entered a period of Parliamentary rule called the interregnum.

In 1640, Parliament was called by Charles so that he could pay debts incurred during the Bishops' Wars. Parliament used the opportunity to impose a number of restrictions on the Crown. Parliament denied Charles the right to dissolve its sessions at will; it also imposed constraints on a number of dubious measures Charles had used to acquire funds during the Eleven Year Tyranny. The first fifteen years of Charles's reign, a comedy of errors on the king's part, are described in mistake 18.

Charles was none too happy with Parliament's newfound powers. In an early act of defiance, Parliament had impeached his friend and adviser Thomas Wentworth, the Earl of Strafford. Strafford was viewed as a symbol of absolute monarchy that needed to be eliminated. For the execution to proceed, Charles had to sign the death warrant. Charles was still incensed about how Parliament had treated his old friend the Duke of Buckingham; he was loath to see another friend and ally die. Wentworth sensed Charles's dismay and convinced him to go through with the execution. For all of Wentworth's flaws, he was loyal. He did not want to give ammunition to anti-Royalists, at this crucial juncture, by forcing the king to spend goodwill in his defense. Charles signed the warrant and Wentworth went to the gallows in May 1641.

Wentworth's sacrifice proved inadequate. As lord deputy, the earl had been vilified for his suppression of Catholicism. Shortly after Wentworth's death, Ireland revolted. The rebels were emboldened by Charles's apparent weakness and the political turmoil that by then gripped England. The Irish were also worried by England's behavior during the Bishops' Wars; they feared that the Long Parliament would take measures to squash Catholicism if they did not act first. The Irish sided with the Old English, a group of Catholic Englishmen who had lived in Ireland for generations, against the Protestant New English settlers. The Irish regarded the New English as aligned with Parliament. Thus the Catholic coalition professed loyalty to Charles even as it rebelled against English settlers. Though Charles had played no role in fomenting the rebellion, many in England believed the king was involved in a papal conspiracy to undermine Anglicanism. When Charles called for funds to quell the rebellion, those in Parliament doubted his motives. They believed that Charles would use the troops against Parliament after the rebellion was taken care of. Parliament denied him the requested funds and attempted unsuccessfully to pass an ordinance wresting control of the military from the king. This, coupled with rumors that Parliament intended to impeach the king's Catholic wife, Henrietta, was the last straw for Charles.

In January 1642, Charles made perhaps the greatest mistake of his underwhelming career. Charles accurately suspected that some members of Parliament had colluded with the Scots during the Bishops' Wars. Accompanied by four hundred soldiers, Charles entered the House seeking to arrest five members of Parliament on charges of treason. It was the first and last time such a thing happened. The members in question had been tipped off and escaped before he arrived. When Charles demanded that Speaker William Lenthal hand over the renegade MPs, Lenthal responded, "May it please your Majesty, I have neither eyes to see nor tongue to speak in this place but as the House is pleased to direct me, whose servant I am here." It was a statement of disrespect; Lenthal was functionally declaring loyalty to Parliament, not the Crown. It was a decisive moment in the court of public opinion. Royalists had argued that a strong king was crucial to stability, but this episode merely illustrated Charles's impotence. Fearing for his life, Charles fled north with his family, intending to raise an army to fight Parliament.

The country was divided. Parliament found support primarily in coastal towns and in the navy, whereas the landlocked inner regions remained loyal to Charles. Charles raised the Royal Standard at Nottingham and set up court at Oxford. The beginning of the war was inconclusive, though the Royalists were victorious in a number of early skirmishes. Each side pulled out all the stops to gain an advantage: Charles negotiated a ceasefire in Ireland to free up Royal troops there, whereas Parliament solicited Scottish assistance by offering them a number of concessions. The tide began to turn in 1643 with a series of Parliamentary victories. In 1645, determined to end the war, Parliament raised the New Model Army. The English military was previously divided into an array of militias tied to a single garrison. In contrast, the New Model Army was a band of professionals that could be deployed anywhere in the country. Under the leadership of Sir Thomas Fairfax and Oliver Cromwell, the New Model Army defeated Royalist forces and pushed Charles into Scotland. The Scots handed Charles over to Parliament. Charles attempted to escape before eventually being interred in Carisbrooke Castle.

Charles was, all things considered, lucky. Though many in Parliament favored reforms to balance against royal excess, even the most radical members preferred that Charles remain on the throne. Yet Charles subscribed to the belief that he was the king by divine right. He would not stand for a weakened Crown. In an effort to regain his power, Charles made a deal that an Irish army be raised and even invited the French to send soldiers to help him crush the New Model Army and the Parliament. Cromwell found those letters and made them public, alienating many of the king's supporters. Charles finally made his worst, and last, mistake. He negotiated a secret deal with the Scots called The Engagement, which stipulated that Scotland would invade England and restore Charles to the throne in exchange for the establishment of Presbyterianism for three years.

As promised, Scottish forces invaded England. Royalist uprisings were quickly suppressed, with the exception of a few protracted sieges. A Parliamentary victory at the Battle of Preston effectively ended the war. Charles, realizing that he could not win, submitted a proposal to reform the government to Parliament's advantage. The measure passed. Yet some, like Cromwell, believed that Charles was too dangerous to let live. Cromwell used his New Model Army to arrest members of Parliament who had voted in favor of restoring Charles to the throne. For his betrayal, Charles was put on trial for treason. Because he had earlier made deals with the Irish and even the French, everyone knew Charles had sold England out again to the Scots. Despised by his countrymen for his betrayal, Charles was sent to the executioner's block. Oliver Cromwell would rule England, Ireland, and Scotland as its Lord Protector during the interregnum. Only his death in 1658 allowed Charles's son, Charles II, to reclaim the throne.

Charles I was a despot and a fool. He squandered countless opportunities to make peace with Parliament. His refusal to share power was paid for with blood, eventually his own. He was willing to sell out any belief to retain or regain power. Charles thought that no one in Parliament had the stomach to call for his execution, but he was wrong. The reforms passed in response to Charles's intransigence were instrumental to England's political development. The irony is that Parliament would never have had the leverage to enact such reforms had Charles simply cooperated from the beginning.

‖‖

20

MISJUDGED THE ENEMY

A Fortunate Shot

1687, PARTHENON, GREECE

‖‖

The Parthenon, built by Pericles, was the crown jewel of ancient Athens. The elegant, columned building was created to honor Athena and serve as a treasury for the riches of the Dorian League. It stood atop the Acropolis as the embodiment of Greek classical art and culture. For over two thousand years its marble columns and sculptured eaves survived largely intact, despite the ravages wrought by the Romans, the Christian Byzantines, the Roman Catholics, the Franks, and the Ottoman Turks. In 1670 the building retained enough classic beauty that Turkish writer Evliya Celebi called it "a work less of human hands than of Heaven itself" that "should remain standing for all time." However, the Parthenon could not survive the conflict between a determined Venetian general and a desperate Turkish aga.

Since 1667, the Christians had attempted to drive the Ottoman Turks out of Europe. The Turks were determined to hold their ground, including within their territory the city of Athens. In 1684, Venice sent Francesco Morosini and their entire republic fleet to face them. He conquered Preveza and Lefkada. The

Turks responded by escalating their military preparations. The Venetians knew they could not possibly match the Turks' increased forces, but according to historian Dimitrios Kambouroglou, "The Venetians had discovered the secret for conquering the world. They didn't trouble themselves to have their own armies and generals. They rented them."

By 1685, Venice had managed to hire a massive volunteer mercenary army. Francesco Morosini was appointed commander in chief of all military operations against the Turks, and Count Otto von Königsmark was hired to run the mercenary army. Together they succeeded in driving the Turks out of the entire Peloponnese, establishing the new kingdom of Morea for Venice. The Turks began gathering their forces in the rest of Greece, while Morosini and the other leaders of his multinational force determined how to counter them. It was decided to make Athens their next prime target for liberation.

The problem was that the Athenians didn't really want to be liberated. The city was doing well, and its merchants were prosperous. They sent a delegation to Venice to request that the army stay away. Venice agreed, but only if the Athenians paid a fee to stop the invasion. The Athenian delegation agreed to a price, and Morosini promised they would not be disturbed. He saw no real tactical value in taking Athens from the Turks anyway, especially if the Athenians did not want it done. Militarily Athens was of no value because its capture would do little to hinder the Turks' advance. Any troops stationed there could be provisioned only from the sea. If the Turks attacked, the city would have to be abandoned and, of course, would be destroyed.

However, political pressure for Morosini to take Athens continued to mount. Morosini might have been able to hold his ground if another delegation of Athenians had not arrived during a critical war council meeting, insisting that the Turks holding Athens were all but broken. They promised that the dignitaries inside of Athens would add their own assistance to any attack and ensure its success. The other leaders pressed Morosini to take advantage of this obvious opportunity. Morosini decided he had no choice but to attack. He was determined, however, to do it on his terms, hoping for no Athenian casualties.

The Turks expected Morosini to attack Athens. To them, their hold on the fortified temples of the Acropolis prevented an invasion of mainland Greece. Since the Acropolis was the only defensible position in the city, the Turks focused their energies on fortifying it against the already legendary power of the Venetian guns. As the Turks got word of Morosini's preparations, they strengthened the west wall, tore down the Temple of Athena Nike—using its parts to build a rampart for cannons—and built a support tower. Then, in what would turn out to be a fateful decision, they placed most of their stores of munitions and gunpowder inside the Parthenon. To the aga Ali, this choice was obvious. The Parthenon was the largest and most substantial building on the hill. Any other location would leave the stores more vulnerable to weather and potential enemy fire.

Knowing he was up against a formidable enemy, Morosini feinted, sending a portion of his fleet to Evvia. As the ships sailed off, the Turks assumed the threat was over and relaxed. Reinforcements were moved to face this new threat. The next morning they awoke to find the entire combined might of the Venetian fleet anchored at nearby Piraeus, prepared for a lengthy siege. The panicked Turks, now badly outnumbered, all headed for the heights of the Acropolis, where they sent the women, children, and noncombatants into the Parthenon for safety. Ali not only felt it was the strongest and safest building on the rock, he also felt certain that the Venetians would never dare damage such an important temple and landmark.

The Athenian Greeks, now caught between a Turkish-held rock and a Venetian army, quickly chose the likely winner and met Morosini's forces at the dock. They offered valuable intelligence in exchange for protection for themselves and their city. (Pillaging conquered cities was still not unheard of.) Morosini sent a small force to occupy the city and protect the Greeks from the Turks. The Athenians then returned home and hid their valuables.

Morosini, still trying to avoid a fight, offered to allow the Turks safe passage if they surrendered. Ali refused. He had ammunition and men, and he knew that the serasker, the supreme commander of the Ottoman army, was on his way with a relief army.

Morosini sent his main force, under the command of Königsmark, around the city to set up positions for an offensive on the Acropolis. Under fire from the Turks, Königsmark's gunners placed their cannons and began firing on the hill. Shortly after the bombardment began, an escaping Turk informed the Venetians that Ali had moved all the ammunition and nonmilitary personnel into the Parthenon. Morosini ordered Königsmark to target the Parthenon.

Over four hundred shells struck the celebrated temple before one, either lucky or well aimed, sailed through a hole in the roof and struck the stored ammunition. The Parthenon exploded, knocking out the ceiling, most of the walls and damaging or destroying most of the priceless sculptures. At least three hundred Turks, mostly women and children, were killed, either in the explosion or from flying chunks of marble. The entire Acropolis burned for three days. Königsmark was dismayed and heartbroken by the destruction. Morosini, however, reported it as a "fortunate shot."

The Turks still refused to surrender, waiting for the serasker's army to save them. However, when the serasker arrived, Königsmark's army was ready and waiting. Seeing the Venetian force arrayed against him, the serasker retreated without firing a shot. With no hope remaining, the surviving Turks surrendered. The Parthenon had been destroyed for nothing.

Though Morosini's destruction of the Parthenon is viewed by most as a horrendous error in judgment, to him it was simply the price of victory. The Parthenon was an enemy fortress, an objective to take as cheaply as possible. The fact that the enemy filled it with munitions simply made his job that much easier. Apparently, most Venetians agreed. Upon returning from his campaign, he was made doge of Venice. Yet his victory had no lasting impact on the war. A year after Morosini's victory, Athens was retaken by the Ottoman Turks. An Athens no longer crowned with the full glory of the Parthenon.

21

||||||||||||||||||||||||||||||||||||||||||||||||||||||||||||||||

PENNY-WISE AND COLONY-FOOLISH

How Raising Taxes Cost
the British America

1770–1773, COLONIAL AMERICA

||||||||||||||||||||||||||||||||||||||||||||||||||||||||||||||||

In the current political climate, it is career suicide to support
higher taxes. Taxes are seen as growth-killers and drains on the
pocketbook. Most voters prefer the candidate who will lower
taxes and not those who create new ones. If you think the political
rhetoric surrounding taxes is incendiary today, you should take a
peek in an American history textbook. The contemporary political group the Tea Party might be considered a fringe movement
by some, but their views are mild and mainstream when compared to the beliefs and actions of the original Tea Partiers from
the American Revolution. The recalcitrance of British leaders—
namely, King George and the leading members of Parliament—in
dealing with the American colonies eventually contributed to the
Revolution. Had they been more accommodating toward the colonists, had they simply been able to see and treat them in the same
way as they did Englishmen in England, the soon-to-be states
would have likely remained loyal to the Crown for some time.

Boston in 1770 was a volatile city. Beginning in 1767, the British Parliament passed a series of acts called the Townshend Acts.

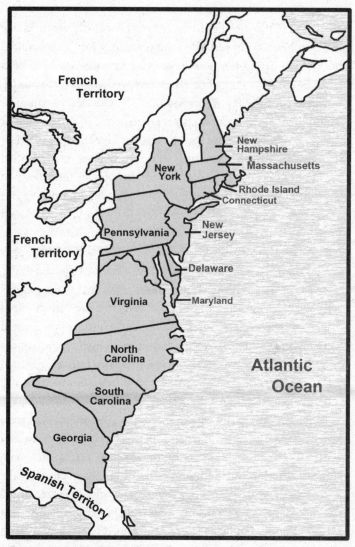

The American Colonies

Britain was in dire need of revenue to pay for costly ventures like the Seven Years' War. It needed money to pay for the continued stationing of troops that were protecting the colonies from both French and Indian aggression. They also needed money to pay for the salaries of British government officials stationed in America. Beyond these aims, the new tax acts were political. Britain sought to establish a precedent for future taxation. Like the Spanish, they saw the wealth of the Americas as a way to finance the British government's needs. The taxes would also punish the colony of New York for its failure to comply with the 1765 Quartering Act (which mandated that colonists provide British soldiers stationed in America with housing and supplies).

The Townshend Acts had been preceded by the 1764 Sugar Act and the 1765 Stamp Act, both of which were opposed under the mantra "No Taxation without Representation." Colonists opposed the taxes for economic reasons and cited the British Bill of Rights to support their claims. Parliament refuted this argument by stating that colonists were de facto represented by Parliament via "virtual representation." In other words, they were represented by the members as a whole despite there being no members of Parliament elected from the colonies.

When the Stamp Act was repealed, the Townshend Acts were enacted. These included duties on paper, paint, lead, glass, and tea. There was no income tax or value-added tax, so the main source of taxation was duties on goods that moved through the ports. The acts were passed in conjunction with other acts aimed at clamping down on smuggling. These included broader powers to search houses and businesses for smuggled goods as well as an increase in the number of vice admiralty courts aiming at prosecuting smugglers.

The reaction to these acts was intense and vehement. Some responses were intellectual, such as John Dickinson's series of essays titled *Letters from a Farmer in Pennsylvania*, which challenged the constitutionality of the measures. These letters were addressed to the Massachusetts House of Representatives, which sent a petition to King George III asking for the repeal of the acts. These letters in effect challenged the right of Parliament to tax the colony. When the House refused to rescind the letter, Provence of Massachusetts Governor Francis Bernard dissolved the legislature. This action was met with retaliatory boycotts aimed at forcing repeal. Opposition to the acts became so stiff that Colonial Secretary Lord Hillsborough felt the need for a substantial troop presence in Boston. Several incidents continued to inflame colonial anti-British sentiment. First, a merchant ship owned by John Hancock was seized on allegations of smuggling. The case was highly publicized as an example of injustice wrought by British customs officials, though the charges were eventually dropped. Several minor clashes occurred between British soldiers and colonists. When Christopher Seider, an eleven-year-old boy, was killed by a customs official, the situation became even tenser. Sometimes referred to as the first casualty of the American Revolution, he became a heart-wrenching example of the dangers of the escalating tensions.

Again and again, Britain alienated its American subjects. Many today don't realize that the Tea Act actually lowered the price of tea in America. The historical irony was that America's Founding Fathers were smugglers of tea who stood to lose money owing to increased competition. They also would be paying more taxes for the new goods included, losing both ways. Thus they engineered a campaign against the act. As the colonies become more rebellious, the British responded with harsher, more authoritarian laws and actions. When Parliament decided to place Boston under de facto martial law, the result was a general, public resentment. The king's authorities reacted by stationing large numbers of soldiers in the city. The troops were vilified, harassed, and distrusted by the Bostonians.

On March 5, the tensions in Boston manifested in one of the most pivotal events leading up to the revolution. Private Hugh White, a British sentry, was stationed near a customhouse. A young apprentice began harassing a British captain by the name of John Goldfinch; White responded by striking the boy with the butt of his musket. A heated argument between White and the boy's companions drew a larger crowd. As the crowd began to become a massive and threatening mob, White retreated up the customhouse's steps. Captain Thomas Preston was observing the situation and dispatched a regiment of troops to relieve White and control the crowd. The crowd of several hundred Bostonians formed a semicircle around the troops and began shouting insults and throwing snowballs and rocks at them. Private Hugh Montgomery was knocked to the ground by a club-wielding tavern keeper; he then fired into the crowd and shouted for his companions to do the same. Despite receiving no such order from Preston several fired their muskets. Their shots killed three members of the crowd instantly, fatally wounded two others, and injured eleven more people.

The incident presents an interesting case of the circumstances that can create a dangerous and volatile situation. The situation would have never escalated without the tax policies because it was this system of taxation that created the hefty antagonism toward the British soldiers who supported the officials who collected the taxes. It is no doubt true that the soldiers on the square in Boston were fearful for their lives; nonetheless, the murders were rightly viewed as a flagrant breach of justice. This mistake made by the Parliament was made immeasurably worse that day by a few brash British soldiers. The incident became known as the Boston Massacre.

The soldiers were tried in a Suffolk County court. In an effort to make the trial as fair as possible and to avoid alienation of moderates and retaliation by other soldiers, the jury was made up of men living outside of Massachusetts. Few lawyers wanted to defend the soldiers. Their case was eventually taken up by the prominent lawyer and future firebrand of a patriot John Adams. In a separate trial, Preston was acquitted when it was found that there was no evidence he had ordered his troops to fire. Adams persuasively argued that the situation called for self-defense, and that the soldiers' actions were thus justified. Six of the soldiers were acquitted on these grounds; two more were found guilty of murder because there was overwhelming evidence to suggest they had fired directly into the crowd. Adams finagled the judgment down to a manslaughter conviction for these two soldiers. The punishment for manslaughter at the time was to be branded on the thumb. Adams was too successful for the good of the Crown. The consequence of the light punishment was a pervasive feeling of injustice that spread throughout the colonies. They saw the sentences as a sign that British soldiers could shoot American colonists with impunity.

The reason this incident was such a significant blunder is that it became a rallying point for future calls-to-arms against the British. Before, the colonists' grievances had been mostly fueled by pocketbook concerns. The massacre lent an element of justice and personal threat to their cause that had been lacking before. While the Revolution might very well have occurred absent an event such as the Boston Massacre, the incident created substantial anti-British sentiment in colonies outside of Massachusetts. It demonstrated that the British troops and officials were a threat to everyone in the colonies, even those not directly affected by the new taxes.

After the fact, many attributed King George's insensitive attitude regarding his American subjects to his mental illness. However, by this time Britain had a constitutional monarchy, and the king was more of a figurehead than a ruler. The collective error was made by Parliament, a group of men without the competence to win the hearts and minds of the colonists and ultimately keep the colonies under British control.

The Boston Massacre highlights the significance of macropolitical action as well as the importance of normal individuals in guiding history. Mistakes were made by King George III and Parliament that precipitated conditions that resulted in the mob and the shootings. Though its error was obvious, the British Crown failed to learn from the massacre. It maintained its system of taxation, and in response to the Boston Tea Party of 1773, it implemented what colonists would dub the "Intolerable Acts," a series of punitive acts meant to make an example of Boston. Rather than find mutual ground, both sides escalated the conflict. Three years later more shots were fired at Lexington and Concord and the American Revolution had begun.

22

|||||||||||||||||||||||||||||||||||||||||||||||||||||||||||||||||||||||||||||||

PRIDE

Ingratitude and Ambition

1776–1780, THE AMERICAN REVOLUTION

|||||||||||||||||||||||||||||||||||||||||||||||||||||||||||||||||||||||||||||||

You should remember the name of Horatio Gates as being one of the revered Founding Fathers of the United States. That you don't have that recollection is his own fault. The painful fact is that one of the men who helped win the American Revolution also almost lost it, twice. The reason was simply that he would not accept his own limits. This man who did much, but also sullied his name, was commander at one of the young America's greatest victories and helped organize the Continental Army. Yet you probably do not know his name because of what else he did, and tried to do.

Brigadier General Horatio Gates was, as many American colonists then were, born in England. His parents were in service (hired help on a Scottish estate). As a young man this may have helped him obtain the influence to be given a commission in the British army in 1745. As a lieutenant, Gates served first in Germany. There he showed his skill at organization and became his regiment's adjutant (aide, chief clerk, and quartermaster). Gates was good at organizing and keeping records. He was good at keeping the men fed and armed. It is a talent that every army needs. He was soon transferred to Canada as an aide-de-camp to General Charles Cornwallis.

Not being of noble blood or from a wealthy family limited Horatio Gates's chances of promotion. The higher ranks in the British army were actually bought and sold, not given out for merit. The purchase of commissions was a way to ensure only the right people would be officers. When a captain stationed in the distant colony of Maryland became ill and had to sell his commission, Gates had a chance to purchase the rank at a good price. Encouraged by General Cornwallis, young Gates was able to borrow enough money to buy the captaincy. Moving to Maryland, he took command of his new infantry company and promptly found himself leading the men during General Edward Braddock's ill-fated wilderness expedition against the French and Indians. Among others on the trek through the wilderness were George Washington, Charles Lee, and Daniel Morgan.

Horatio Gates did not last long once the shooting started. Hit in the chest early in the fighting, he was carried from the battlefield by a private from his company. Likely this saved his life as the battle was a disaster and the wounded English soldiers left behind were scalped then killed. The young captain almost died from his wound anyhow. In future battles throughout his career Gates seems to have shown a reluctance to place himself where he might again be shot. But this did not interfere with his noted ability to turn organizational chaos into order.

Once Gates recovered, he was placed in a staff position on an expedition to the West Indies commanded by an old friend, Brigadier General Robert Mockton. Again Gates's administrative skills served him well. When the venture ended in success, he was chosen by Mockton to deliver the good news to London. As was traditional in such cases, Horatio Gates was promoted to major. He was also granted the large sum of a thousand sterling-silver coins that helped him purchase a lieutenant colonelcy. But the promotion at first did not work out as Gates had hoped because there were no active-duty openings for the rank, and he was put on half pay. Half pay meant literally that. The officer was on standby with nothing to do and was paid half the normal amount for his rank. The smaller salary was a disaster for someone without family money who still had to support his household and act and dress like an officer. When in 1762 an opening for a lieutenant colonel appeared in the crown colony of New York, Gates accepted the position and returned to North America and a full paycheck.

It was at about this time that Gates's friend General Mockton thought he had a great opportunity for both of them. The general hoped to get a high-ranking command position with the British East India Company. In the eighteenth century, the East India Company maintained what was a private army in India, often tapping regular officers to lead it. The position almost always guaranteed wealth. East India Company officers received a portion of any loot taken from the often incredibly rich local rajas and cities they conquered. The catch was that to be free to take the job you had to resign and sell your commission. Both Gates and Mockton did this and then the East India Company position Mockton sought went to someone else, meaning Gates, who had quit, hoping to become Mockton's number two, was also out of a job. Understandably, not long after this Gates and Mockton had a falling-out. But this split meant most doors in England were now closed to the civilian Horatio Gates. He did have some money from selling his commission so he bought 659 acres in Virginia. He moved his family there, purchased slaves, and set up a plantation. It is no surprise, considering his skill at organization, that the plantation thrived. Over the next few years he became a respected member of the community and was elected first a local justice and then a lieutenant colonel in the Virginia militia.

In 1775, Horatio was an ambitious, common man who had clawed his way up in a military system that favored the wellborn and wealthy. As an officer, Gates knew he was an extremely capable administrator, but he was sensitive to the fact that he had not commanded troops in battle since the time he was so badly wounded with Braddock early in his career.

After hearing about Lexington and Concord, Horatio Gates knew what would follow. He went to his fellow Virginian George Washington and offered his services. When the Continental Congress appointed Washington commander in chief, he had both Gates and Charles Lee appointed generals. General Gates was also the adjutant general (chief clerk and administrator) for the new army. In this he excelled, creating procedures and practices that were used throughout the Revolution and beyond. He then spent some time as second in command of the Canadian Department; the name described that army's target.

When things went badly on the Canadian border, Gates was recalled to again assist Washington. Bringing Pennsylvania and New Jersey Continental Army regiments with him, Horatio Gates had a chance to be part of one of the most decisive victories of the entire war. He joined up with Washington on December 20 at Valley Forge.

The revolutionary army was at a low point. Many already felt the war had failed and that what remained would be crushed in the spring. Washington proposed a bold attack on the Hessians in Trenton, New Jersey, on Christmas Day. Brigadier General Gates disagreed and felt that the colonial army should use the rest of the winter to move farther away from the British positions. Washington prevailed, and his attack on Trenton changed the tide of the war. Gates was not there. He had voluntarily left on sick leave a few days before the attack.

A short time later, General Gates was to be sent back to the Northern Department, comprised mostly of the New York colony, intending to serve as second in command to the abrasive General Philip John Schuyler. Instead of reporting to his post, Gates went to meet with members of the Continental Congress, asking them to lobby for him, not Schuyler, to be the top northern commander.

Washington and his supporters in the Congress disagreed. Gates was given the choice of accepting his orders as second in the northern district or returning to his old job as adjutant general for Washington. He chose to go back north. Almost immediately on his return, Gates, General Schuyler, and three thousand continentals found themselves under siege in Fort Ticonderoga by a large British army under General John Burgoyne. When the British managed to place artillery in a position that made the fort untenable, the two generals cooperated and were able to escape with the entire garrison. It was a well-organized and successful escape that visibly frustrated Burgoyne. The empty fort fell, but no American soldiers were lost or captured. This may have been Gates's best combat action ever, something he would mention to the members of the Congress.

At this point the already contrary General Schuyler became so negative that he was relieved of command, and Gates was finally put in charge of the northern district (minus the fort). He did an excellent job of raising the countryside and organizing the recruits even as Burgoyne marched south down the Hudson. Generals who saw that their men were well fed and taken care of were popular, and with their homes threatened, the local frontiersmen flocked to join the army Gates was commanding near Saratoga, New York. But once Burgoyne was close and the battle imminent, the conservative Gates clashed with the more aggressive officers under him, including Daniel Morgan and Benedict Arnold. When on September 17, 1777, Morgan led his riflemen in a harassing attack, several other units spontaneously joined in. The impromptu battle was an American victory, forcing the British to retreat into their defended camp. Even though it was a victory, Gates was upset that such a risk had been taken without his approval. Relations between him and the courageous and popular Benedict Arnold soon got so bad that Gates removed Arnold from command.

Even with Burgoyne on the defensive and his own army outnumbering the British three to one, Gates chose to simply hold a fortified position on the Beamis Heights. So it wasn't until October 7 that another battle began. Even then it was the British who moved, not the cautious Gates. Burgoyne's supplies were running low and this led him to attempt to try to flank the American position. The flanking forces were discovered long before reaching the American line and were themselves attacked and driven back. Benedict Arnold was the commander of the left flank, and at a minimum, he had planned the battle. Other sources have him leaving his tent and commanding personally. The British not only were driven back but lost part of their outer defense line. General Gates commanded not from the front lines, but from his headquarters.

Benedict Arnold was a political ally of the now-departed General Schuyler and was out of favor with Gates, who took sole credit for the victory as the commanding general. It was the beginning of a bitterness that would end in the formerly devoted revolutionary becoming a . . . Benedict Arnold, a traitor.

The next day Burgoyne retreated to the town of Saratoga over frozen roads in a frigid downpour. Gates's army followed and again surrounded the British. Low on supplies, trapped, badly outnumbered, and discovering the relief army he had been promised under General Henry Clinton would not be coming, the British general surrendered. It was the largest American victory of the war, and Gates took full credit for it.

General Gates's supporters in the Continental Congress began to point out how he had won a great victory while George Washington had little success. Horatio Gates had successfully taken over the northern district and so then he wanted to do the same with the entire war. He began actively working through his allies in the Continental Congress for him to replace George Washington. The Congress created a Board of War and made Gates the president of it. Ignoring the conflict of interests, Horatio Gates returned to also command the Northern Department. But Gates did little to take advantage of his victory or the weakened British presence in Canada. Washington was able to win the political battle. In 1880, George Washington gave General Gates the option of actively leading a column of soldiers in attacking the British-allied Indians or moving south and taking over the Eastern Department. After a short time Gates was then shifted to the Southern Department, where his skills in army building and commanding a battle were needed.

As soon as Horatio Gates arrived in the southern district, he prepared to move against the British. Unfortunately Gates ignored the local commanders and chose the worst route possible to get to the battle. It passed through a swamp with little available food. Because of this mistake, when his army finally was facing Cornwallis, his men were exhausted and half starved. Gates still had a chance to move away, but he chose to fight Cornwallis then and there, despite his soldiers' condition. The battle near the town of Camden, South Carolina, was a disaster from the beginning. The numbers were about even, but half of the American force was militia. Gates had never really commanded militia in a set-piece battle. He greatly overestimated its ability. Placed in front of the best British infantry, the colonial militia broke almost immediately. This left the continentals, the trained soldiers, to fight alone against the entire British force. They held for a while, but when nearly surrounded and attacked in the rear by cavalry, the regulars too broke. Over a thousand valuable regular soldiers and all the army's cannons and baggage were captured. General Gates led the retreat and was off the battlefield before his regulars were forced to make a fighting withdrawal. He traveled a short way with the militia that had fled first. Then he rode on another 60 miles to Charlotte and then yet another 120 miles to Hillsborough, North Carolina, leaving what remained of his army without a leader. The man who wanted to replace George Washington proved incapable as a courageous commander.

Gates was soon back where he belonged, handling details at Washington's headquarters. Placing the best administrator in the position of field commander almost cost the Americans the Carolinas and extended the war. This was a case of personal ambition over common sense and politics over merit. Gates was a great round peg, but he wanted to be in a square hole, which led to a costly defeat. His failure we see repeated throughout the history of the American democracy. Even though his skills helped make the Continental Army possible and he was the commander at Saratoga, history has never forgiven Horatio Gates for using politics to undermine George Washington.

23

OUT OF TOUCH

Too Little

Sometimes the greatest mistake a leader can make is to do nothing at all. This is especially true of King Louis XVI of France, who ate while his people starved. His failure to understand his people's needs brought about the bloodiest revolution the world has ever seen. And it cost Louis his greatest possession . . . his head.

Louis lacked assertiveness and personality as a child. His parents ignored him in favor of his elder brother, another Louis, Duke of Bourgogne and the dauphin (heir), whom all hopes fell on as the future king. Our Louis, Louis-August, occupied himself by taking up locksmithing, his favorite hobby. But when his brother, the elder Louis, died suddenly, he became the dauphin at the age of nine. So Louis's hobby had to take a backseat as he brushed up on his king-making skills. A few years later, his father, yet another Louis, and the dauphin of France, also died and Louis-August became the next in line for the French throne.

His grandfather, the king named—you guessed it—Louis XV, spent time preparing the boy. The king felt that young Louis's greatest duty was to marry and have sons. So, at the tender age of fifteen, Louis married the Austrian princess Marie Antonia, known in America as Marie Antoinette. The French people bitterly opposed the marriage. They believed that their alliance with Austria had forced them into the Seven Years' War with Britain, which nearly bankrupted the country. The average Frenchman and -woman despised the foreign princess and viewed her as an outsider. Public opinion worsened when the couple failed to produce an heir. Louis's inability to perform was taken as a direct reflection on his people. Rumors of Louis's impotency ran rampant. Though Louis's grandfather, the king, had fallen out of favor years ago, he was at least virile and guaranteed a peaceful transition. When the old king died in 1774, Louis still had no heir.

The reaction to Louis as king was almost entirely negative. Times were hard, the economy stuttering, and food shortages in Paris threatened. Pornographic circulations depicting the childless royals littered the countryside. They showed Marie as a prostitute and poked fun at Louis's ineptness as a locksmith and his inability to "place the key." Finally on December 19, 1778, Marie gave birth to Marie Thérèse Charlotte. Though a male child would have been held in higher regard, the birth did put a stop to some of the ridicule. It did not make Louis a sudden hit in the public forum, however.

Word reached Paris about lavish parties being held at Versailles and the amount of food consumed at these events. Other indulgences included dresses, jewels, and elaborate hairstyles for Marie. She rose, maybe not as a beloved queen of France, but as the reigning queen of fashion. She sought favor by creating fantastic hideaways for herself and her friends. At Petit Trianon, a sort of petting zoo for grown-ups, patrons could try their hand at country living, pretending to be milkmaids and shepherdesses. And while real country folk died from starvation and disease, Marie and her friends dined on tea and cakes while discussing the joys of simple life. It was her way to escape the humdrum life of being a monarch and showed just how out of touch the monarchy had become.

The people became all too aware of this disconnect. They felt the monarchy had alienated them years before Louis's reign when it moved the capital from Paris to Versailles. However isolated, Louis could not fail to notice the effects of the devastation caused by the winter of 1788. France had not seen a winter as harsh as this for over ninety years. Bread became scarce and crops failed. Louis tried his hand at finance in order to raise money. He had already drained the national coffers by helping finance the revolution in America and turning a blind eye to his wife's spending. So he decided the best way to raise money was to raise taxes. His king-making skills obviously didn't include basic economics. He overtaxed the people, bringing the price of bread up to the equivalent of one month's wages. Louis's attempts to stabilize the economy failed dismally. At least he finally came to the conclusion that he needed a qualified minister of finance.

Louis hired Jacques Necker for the job. Necker hit the ground running. He raised interest rates and divided the taxes more equally. He stated that the government's duty was to ensure all of its citizens had grain. This made him hugely popular with the people. He excelled in people pleasing and knew what it would take to quell the masses. He decided to publish a royal spending report. However, he knew that if the truth about royal expenditures were put on public display, it would cause an uprising. So he did what so many politicians throughout history have done. He lied. He fiddled with numbers and used new techniques in mathematics to prove that the country did not have a deficit but actually had a financial surplus. Hooray! All that starving and dying had been for nothing. The people could bask in the wealth of their nation. Not so fast!

Necker knew his tactics would not be able to fool the masses for long. The government was in real trouble. He advised the king to call in the Estates-General. The Estates-General ran like a parliament or congress with three houses rather than two. The first two houses, or estates, represented the clergy and the nobles. The Third Estate represented the people. Most of the French masses felt they were being grossly underrepresented because 97 percent of the population was represented in this one estate and any decision made there could be outvoted by the other two. To add a more powerful voice to the Third Estate, a man by the name of Maximilien de Robespierre stepped in as a deputy.

Robespierre quickly pleased the representatives of the poor and middle-class French when he demanded that the clergy and nobles pay taxes. His demand was met with ridicule by the first two estates. Then the Third Estate was locked out of its meeting room. This didn't stop them. They met in a nearby tennis court and agreed to continue meeting until they had written a constitution. All 577 members of what would now be called the National Assembly signed the agreement. It was the creation of the Tennis Court Oath, as the agreement would come to be known, that sparked the next events.

Riots broke out in the streets of Paris and mobs raided the armories. Fully armed, they stormed the Bastille. The Declaration of the Rights of Man was drafted stating that "all men are created equal." Sound familiar? Then, on October 5, 1789, a mob consisting mostly of women working in the fish markets of Paris marched on Versailles to protest the shortage of bread. The stinky fish ladies armed with knives killed the king's guards and demanded that the king return to Paris. The National Assembly forced the king to sign documents limiting his power. For a short time, France was a constitutional monarchy. The king thought if he could escape to Austria he would be assisted by his wife's family. So he packed up the wife and kids and made a break for it. He almost made it. They were captured just miles away from the Austrian border. But now the men who had taken over running France believed that Austria would retaliate for their treatment of the royal family. Fearing Austria would attack, they needed to rally the masses. So they declared war first.

But now the Directorate had to decide what to do with Louis. If Austria won the new war, they would most likely reinstate the king. So alive, Louis was a liability and threat. As for Marie, well . . . she was just plain disliked. She was accused of giving away troop movements and disclosing national secrets. This "proved" her loyalty was to Austria. The time had come. After the September Massacres, in which sixteen hundred noble and clergy prisoners were killed, the people already had a taste for royal blood. On January 21, 1793, the people of France guillotined their own king.

The death of Louis was not the end of the revolution. The Reign of Terror lasted another year and claimed the lives of tens of thousands of people, including Louis's wife, Marie, and Robespierre himself. However, the revolution also brought about great change locally as well as globally. It saw the end of the Catholic Church as a power in France, the demise of the class system, and the end of slavery in the French West Indies. Eventually, it brought democracy to its people. It was also the beginning of the end of feudalism as people everywhere began to see themselves as equal. Not at all what Louis or his predecessors had in mind.

24

DISMISSED OUT
OF HAND

No Steam

1802, PARIS

||||||||||||||||||||||||||||||||||||||||||||||||||||||||||||||||||||||

The American inventor Robert Fulton sat waiting for an audience with Napoleon that never came. He had met the emperor a few years earlier and tried to interest him in his manpowered submarine. Napoleon had not been impressed. It would be another seventy-five years before submarines became a viable weapons system. Perhaps it was because of this that Fulton never got his meeting. That was Napoleon's loss.

Encouraged by the American consul (ambassador) to France, Fulton had already created a full-size version of what he had crossed the Atlantic to offer to Napoleon. His steam-driven paddlewheel boat was sailing on the Seine River at speeds of over three miles per hour. He never got to show Bonaparte the boat that could sail without wind, and he could not interest anyone else in the emperor's government. Eventually Robert Fulton returned to America, where he continued to develop his steam engine and ships powered by it.

In 1805, England and France were once more at war. On the shore of the English Channel, over a hundred thousand French soldiers waited to invade Britain. With them were enough flat-bottomed boats to carry most of the army, its horses, and its cannons. At the time, there were fewer than thirty thousand troops, mostly of poor quality, on all of the British Isles. If the French could reach the English shores, they would be able to sweep across England; London would fall within days. But the Royal Navy blocked the way. To conquer Britain, Napoleon had to get his army safely across the Channel. The British blockaded his ports, and an attempt to clear the way for the invasion failed when the combined French and Spanish fleets were crushed by Admiral Horatio Nelson at Trafalgar. The French army marched east and England did not face another invasion for over a century.

The English Channel can be rough, and its winds, unpredictable. Even the highly skilled British sailors were sometimes driven back to their ports by easterly winds. Occasionally the Channel's winds dropped, leaving sail-driven ships stalled. By this time back in the United States, Fulton's steam-driven ships were moving up and down canals and rivers at five to six miles per hour. Had Napoleon held that meeting and supported Fulton's efforts he would have been able to move his army across the Channel any time it was calm. The trip would have taken just a few hours. That ability alone would have forced the English fleet to stand watch permanently off every one of the French ports just to prevent that from happening. The moment they sailed away, the invasion could have been launched.

With Fulton's steam-driven ships instead of barges, Napoleon just might have conquered England. Without English money to finance their wars against Napoleon, Prussia, Austria, and Russia would have been unable to resist the French demands. Without Wellington leading a British army in Spain, a quarter million

Frenchmen would not have been lost or tied up in a sideshow. Then there would have been no one left to resist the French emperor and no one in Europe who could have afforded the fifteen years of war that finally defeated the French. If Bonaparte had supported Fulton's steamships, there still might be a French throne and a Bonaparte on it even today.

25

A FATAL GESTURE

Burr-Hamilton Duel

1804, NEW JERSEY

Today, we are used to what we see as hard-edged politics. When President Barack Obama went on a road trip to promote his American Jobs Act, former opponent John McCain angrily tweeted about the "ugly, Canadian built tax-payer funded bus" that Obama was riding in. It just goes to show how silly political rivalries have become. Once upon a time, such rivalries were life-or-death affairs and, by George, they were interesting. You'd need a dictionary to follow the highfalutin language of men like Alexander Hamilton or Aaron Burr as they traded insults. Hamilton once referred to the latter as "profligate, a voluptuary in the extreme." Theirs was the most famous political rivalry in American history, and it ended with Hamilton the loser of a deadly duel. As entertaining as the story is, it's clear that Hamilton, so brilliant in so many ways, was a fool to accept Burr's challenge. Hamilton chose not to fire at Burr, and in return received a musket ball to the stomach. This left his party without a leader and his family without a father, all because he was too proud to decline the duel and too pure to actively participate in one.

Their feud began in 1791, when Burr won a Senate seat that had been held by Philip Schuyler, who happened to be Hamilton's father-in-law. Hamilton was the secretary of the treasury and a leading member of the Federalist Party, whereas Burr was a Democratic-Republican. As a Federalist, Hamilton supported greater centralization of power, the creation of a national bank, a system of tariffs, and strong trade relations with Great Britain. Hamilton counted on having a Federalist majority in the Senate to pursue these policies, and Burr's defeat of Schuyler threw a wrench in his plans. Leading up to the 1800 election, Hamilton circulated a letter among his party harshly criticizing President John Adams, also a Federalist. The letter was leaked to the press. This put Hamilton publicly at odds with a president from his own party and many rumored that Burr was behind its release.

The letter divided Federalists, undermined Adams's reelection campaign, and embarrassed Hamilton. Back then, the vice president was determined by who got the second most electoral votes, not by a shared ticket. In 1800, the election was between Federalists John Adams and Charles Pinckney versus Democratic-Republicans Thomas Jefferson and Aaron Burr.

At the time the Electoral College was not constrained by state laws as to how to vote. When the election occurred, more states were won by the Democratic-Republicans. Republican electors were each supposed to cast a ballot for Jefferson and a ballot for Burr, except for one elector who would not vote for Burr. This would have the effect of giving Jefferson the presidency and Burr the vice presidency. Yet they failed to execute the plan, and Burr and Jefferson ended up with equal electoral votes. By rule, the decision was left to Congress. The Federalists, who controlled the House of Representatives, soon planned to use their votes to give Aaron Burr the election.

Hamilton believed that Burr was a dangerous, immoral man. He used his influence to sway the Federalist vote and ensure that Jefferson became president. He later expressed his dismay that the Federalists even considered supporting Burr, describing such a move as "signing their own death warrant." Burr was dropped from Jefferson's ticket in the 1804 election and ran as an independent for governor of New York. Hamilton again sabotaged Burr, campaigning vigorously for Republican opponent Morgan Lewis. At a political dinner, Hamilton so criticized Burr that one onlooker described him as having a "despicable opinion" of the vice president. This description infuriated Burr, but Hamilton refused to apologize for the way his words were perceived. Burr believed that Hamilton's attacks were a dishonorable violation of decorum, and challenged Hamilton to a duel. Though the cause was flimsy at best, Hamilton accepted.

Dueling was a crime aggressively prosecuted in the state of New York, so Burr and Hamilton met on July 11, 1804, at a popular dueling site in New Jersey. Each man arrived with a second, William Van Ness for Burr and Judge Nathaniel Pendleton for Hamilton. A doctor was also present. Hamilton shot first, and his bullet was high and to the right, far from hitting Burr. Burr returned with a shot that fractured Hamilton's ribs, tore through his organs, and lodged in his spine. Pendleton later said that Burr moved toward Hamilton as if showing regret before departing with Van Ness. Hamilton's family physician, David Hosack, arrived just after the duel and tended to Hamilton, who gasped, "This is a mortal wound, doctor," before falling unconscious.

Hosack took Hamilton back across the Hudson River and briefly revived him. Hamilton conveyed that "Pendleton knows that I did not intend to fire at him." This was confirmed by Pendleton and also by a letter written by Hamilton the night before the duel. In it, Hamilton said that he was "strongly opposed to the practice of dueling" and that he was resolved to "throw away my first fire." Perhaps Hamilton hoped that Burr would return the favor. Yet if so, Hamilton should have more obviously conveyed his intent. Standard practice was to fire into the ground, whereas Hamilton fired in Burr's general direction. While his shot was six feet high and four feet wide of Burr, it is possible that Burr believed Hamilton intended to hit him. Some historians yet believe that Hamilton intended such a thing and merely misfired. They use as evidence the presence of a deadly hair trigger on the pistol. Whatever happened, Alexander Hamilton's mistake cost him his life and the United States one of it greatest leaders.

Yet Hamilton, a former general, would have been aware of such a device. His mistake was either not shooting Burr or at least not making his pacifist gesture more obvious. Burr himself was quoted as saying that he would have hit Hamilton in the heart were it not for the mist. This violent bravado caused utilitarian philosopher Jeremy Bentham to refer to Burr as "little better than a murderer." Whatever the case, Burr's political career was over. He escaped prosecution for the duel and was later arrested but acquitted on charges of treason. Before his death, he publicly lamented that he should have realized "the world was wide enough for Hamilton and me."

Alexander Hamilton died the day after the duel. With Adams retiring, John Marshall ascending to the apolitical Supreme Court, and Hamilton's death, the Federalist Party was left without a leader. It gradually dwindled until it no longer existed, ushering in the Era of Good Feelings, the United States' only period of true single-party domination. The duel itself remains a recurring subject in popular culture, appearing in "Got Milk" ads and *Saturday Night Live* skits. While modern politicians should not kill each other, one cannot help but wonder if the campaign rhetoric might be a bit more polite if that option remained.

26

PUNISHING YOUR FRIENDS

Jefferson's Embargo

1807, UNITED STATES

During Thomas Jefferson's inaugural address in 1801, he described his vision of how the fledgling United States should conduct its foreign policy: "peace, commerce, and honest friendship with all nations, entangling alliances with none." Jefferson's devotion to this principle would be tested throughout his presidency. The Napoleonic Wars, which pitted Britain and France against each other in a life-or-death struggle, challenged America's ability to stay neutral. Each nation frustrated American trade with the other, and in response Jefferson declared an economically ruinous embargo. Jefferson tried too hard to avoid an entangling alliance at the expense of commerce. By violating this principle, Jefferson undermined the American economy and set his country on the path to war.

The trouble began when Britain began attacking American ships and impressing her sailors. *Impressing*, in this case, did not mean flirtatious bravado; rather, the British would kidnap American sailors and force them to serve in the British navy. To avoid fighting the French, British sailors often deserted and enlisted on

American merchant ships. British press gangs would assail these ships and reclaim the soldiers, but they would often impress Americans in the process. In the successor to the 1794 Jay Treaty, which established trade and settled territorial issues between the two nations a decade earlier, American diplomats James Monroe and William Pinkney sought to negotiate the end of impressment. American signing of any treaty was contingent on the British ending impressment. Yet Britain believed that acquiring soldiers for the war effort outweighed the risk of alienating the United States, and thus the treaty collapsed.

Before the treaty negotiations began, Jefferson encouraged Congress to pass the Non-Importation Act of 1806. This act established a list of goods that could be manufactured in the United States and blocked their importation from Britain. Implementation of the act was delayed in hopes of reconciliation, but it was enacted after the treaty failed. In February 1807, the British asked for the United States to return three deserters who had joined the crew of the U.S.S. *Chesapeake*. The request was denied, as the sailors in question were American-born and had served in the British navy only because they had been illegally impressed. In June, the *Chesapeake* crossed paths with the H.M.S. *Leopard*. The *Chesapeake*'s commanding officer, Captain James Barron, refused to hand over the men. The *Leopard* fired on the *Chesapeake*, killing three and injuring eighteen more. Barron was forced to surrender. The British seized the three men in addition to taking a legitimate deserter.

The *Chesapeake-Leopard* Affair was a gross violation of American sovereignty, a national humiliation, and a public outrage. Jefferson began to consider enacting an embargo against Britain. Secretary of the Treasury Albert Gallatin tried in vain to dissuade Jefferson, arguing that economically and politically, "I prefer war to a permanent embargo." He correctly predicted that an embargo would be inefficacious and difficult to implement. Gallatin argued that "government prohibitions do always more mischief than had been calculated" and that he had doubts it would "induce England to treat us better." Yet Jefferson, though long sympathetic to free commerce, was unmoved. On December 21, at Jefferson's urging, Congress passed the Embargo Act of 1807. The act closed American ports to exports and restricted British imports. A few supplementary acts were also passed to clarify enforcement mechanisms and eliminate loopholes, though they proved ineffectual.

The embargo was an economic and political disaster. The southern states relied on selling their crops to international markets, and the northern states relied on shipping. While American manufacturing, particularly the textile industry, got a small boost from decreased competition, the overall effect was depression and unemployment. The British adapted to the embargo by expanding trade with South America. Britain also benefited from irate American shippers, who continued to purchase British exports and deliver American goods. The United States had revolted over unfair taxes and now its own government was doing something far worse for the young economy. This smuggling was extremely common and supported by the public, who viewed the embargo with disgust. Protests rippled along the eastern coast and the embargo was openly flouted. Some pockets of the country bordered on rebellion.

With the public so discontented, Jefferson was forced to back off the embargo. Just days before leaving office, Jefferson signed the Non-Intercourse Act of 1809, which replaced the Embargo Act. The act lifted all embargoes on American shipping except those bound for British or French ports. Like its predecessor, it was largely ineffective and was destructive to the economy. It was very difficult to prevent American ships from trading with the belligerents after they had already left American ports. Yet such was Madison's problem, as Jefferson was no longer president. With a floundering economy and a diplomatic crisis, Jefferson had left Madison in an unenviable position.

Jefferson's chief objective was to avoid war, and in that aim he was successful. Yet war eventually came, in part due to Madison's own failings but also because of Jefferson's ineptitude. Jefferson deviated from the small government, laissez-faire principles that make him so revered to this day. The economy is a fickle thing that surges and withers in an often inexplicable way. The Embargo Act was a rare case in which depression inexorably and unequivocally resulted from a single government intervention. Even men like the brilliant Thomas Jefferson have lapses of judgment, and this was such a case. He should have listened to his adviser Gallatin, a man with a keen economic instinct. Instead, Jefferson dangerously weakened his country with war on the horizon.

27 and 28

UNPREPARED FOR THE UNEXPECTED

Napoleon Attacks Russia

1812, RUSSIA

The terrible irony of Napoleon Bonaparte's near total defeat in Russia was that he should not have attacked there in the first place. There were many reasons not to attack Russia, and his strategy was based on a false assumption. The result was the loss of his Grande Armée and a collapse of prestige that the French emperor never recovered from.

Why did Napoleon attack the massive and fairly backward Russian Empire? While it had once been an ally, relations had become strained. The young czar no longer trusted the French, and with good cause. But a look at the numbers showed that Russia posed little threat. Russia was a large nation, but not a rich one. It could maintain an army of only three hundred thousand as compared to the almost million Frenchmen at arms. The Russians might have caused problems for Poland, a French ally, but little else, both because of the strength with which the French would react and their own army's limitations. Napoleon was able to amass six hundred thousand soldiers on its border when he decided to invade Russia. That was double the size of the Russian army.

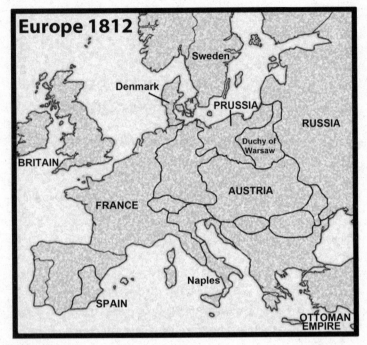

Europe in 1812

The stated reason for attacking Russia was to punish them for failing to enforce the Continental System. Beyond all other nations, England had been the emperor's nemesis. But with the Royal Navy always in control of the English Channel, there was nothing directly that Napoleon could do. The British not only had an army causing havoc in Spain but were also the paymaster for any nation that was willing to oppose the French. English gold and silver had and would finance the Prussians, Austrians, and Russians when they moved against France. And the source of the vast wealth the British spent was the duties and taxes on their massive merchant fleet. That fleet made its money carrying trade for all nations and transporting English goods all over the world. Bonaparte knew this and that was where he struck back.

By banning the British ships from entering any port in Europe, he could cut off the income that was financing his enemies. The Continental System was hardly popular, even in France, much less in other nations, for good reasons. British goods and those from the Americas were often cheaper or better. Also there was a market, at now inflated prices, for French wine and all sorts of other European goods in Britain and the Americas. So when the French tried to enforce the ban on trade in those countries they controlled, smuggling became big business. In nations that were dubious allies, particularly Russia, the system was ignored entirely, and British goods poured onto the Continent through St. Petersburg and other Russian ports. Because it was legal to trade with Russia, the British goods could then be easily shipped all over Europe. To break the British, Napoleon felt he had to force Russia to obey his restrictions. The invasion of Russia was to be a limited war. From the beginning, the French plan was to force the czar to accept a treaty that closed Russia and then they would withdraw.

Beyond an economic incentive, Napoleon liked the idea of invading Russia. He had conquered the rest of Europe. He could just march his armies into Russia with no English Channel to cross.

HARD TO ENFORCE

The British attempts at enforcing the embargo were futile. Within months, the smugglers of Cornwall and other coastal areas were bringing in large quantities of just about everything and getting rich in the process. There was never a shortage of French wine or perfume in London. What their embargo did do was prevent the ships from the newly independent United States from profiting from the lucrative European trade. This and other measures England felt justified in using caused the War of 1812.

Russia was the last major continental nation not cowed or occupied by the French. It was the only European nation he had never conquered. And before the war even began, it seemed a sure win.

But there were several problems with any invasion of Russia, ones that the Teutonic Knights and Charles of Sweden had already encountered. Napoleon either felt he had dealt with each one or ignored them. The first was the nature of the countryside. Compared to anywhere in the rest of Europe, Russia was thinly populated and the peasants were poor. The normal practice for the day was for an army to live off the land. Basically foragers spread out from the army and took anything edible. But that was not possible in Russia. There were not enough farmers, and there was too little food to support so many soldiers.

Napoleon was aware of this and prepared depots in Poland. The Grande Armée had hundreds of wagons carrying food and fodder to accompany the invasion. The problem with this came when the system broke down. Food is no good in storehouses if it cannot reach the troops. Nor had he planned to march as far into Russia as he did. In the fall of 1812, between the weather, the roads, and the Cossacks, the stored food could not get to Moscow or even later to the retreating army. It had to wait for them to march back to it.

WAR: MOTHER OF INNOVATION

Bonaparte held a contest and gave a prize to anyone who could create a better way to preserve food so it could be carried in wagons or stored for months in depots. We benefit today from the winning solution: canning. Yes, we have canned corn today because Napoleon wanted to feed his army better while it invaded Russia.

Distance was a giant factor. In a time when an army walked everywhere, the long, empty spaces of Russia put a further strain on every aspect of the invasion. All of the rest of western Europe could fit inside Russia with room to spare. This allowed the Russian army to trade space for time. Russian troops simply retreated ahead of the French into a countryside so vast they could not be pursued. Napoleon and his staff knew the distances, but they had no experience that would prepare them for what that meant. The simple fact was that Russia was so big that there weren't even accurate maps such as the French were used to planning with.

Roads were also a factor. Armies marched on roads, and the supply wagons that carried the food, fodder, and ammunition for the Grande Armée needed good roads to keep up with an advancing army. There were plenty of roads on the map of Russia. The problem was that there were roads and there were routes that had been marked as roads. Most of the Russian roads were not like those of Europe, solid and dry all year around. In Russia, what looked like a main road on the map was often a winding dirt pathway with no improvements. In snow or mud, such roads slowed the march and stopped dead anything with wheels. Most Russian roads also were not well marked and would disappear in a heavy snow. As always Napoleon and his staff carefully prepared the routes and timing in advance, but they were unprepared for the primitive conditions of Russia's roadways. Nor were they ready to pursue a Russian army that was moving into unmapped territory.

The first plan failed. That was to meet and defeat the main Russian army early, force a peace, and return to Poland for the winter. That did not happen. The new plan was to take Moscow, and this would force a treaty. What the French did not understand was that Moscow was not Paris. In this less-advanced nation, Moscow was an important city, but not so vital to trade, travel, or even to the Russian government that its loss would cripple their nation. There was another entire capital, used in the summers, at St. Petersburg.

Finally there was the cold weather. The Russian winter was infamous. Once it set in, you could lose an army trying to retreat back through those long, empty distances in the cold and snow . . . and Napoleon did.

The invasion of Russia was a gamble that was not necessary. Was it decided by a determination to isolate England at all costs, was it prompted by the need to have all of Europe under French control, or was it the result of overconfidence and hubris? There were problems and unknowns. Napoleon knew the concerns and not only went ahead anyhow but kept following the Russian army, in hopes of forcing a treaty, all the way to Borodino and then to Moscow. Invading Russia cost Napoleon his Grande Armée and a quarter of a million soldiers, and eventually he lost his throne too. All in a war he did not have to fight.

29

||||||||||||||||||||||||||||||||||||||||||||||||||||||||||||||||||||||||||||

HE HESITATED
AND LOST

Too Late and Too Little

DECEMBER 1812, MOSCOW

||||||||||||||||||||||||||||||||||||||||||||||||||||||||||||||||||||||||||||

One of the other disastrous decisions that Napoleon made on this campaign was to remain in Moscow too long. Napoleon had arrived in the Russian capital on September 14, 1812, and found the city almost empty with little food left behind. The city itself had been partially burned at the order of the retreating Mikhail Golenishchev-Kutuzov. But Bonaparte did not take the hint. He seemed unable to accept that the Russians were not being forced to sue for peace and kept waiting for their offer.

The decision to depart was not made until the weather had begun to change and food was running short. His reluctance is shown by the fact that, although Napoleon decided to withdraw back to Vilnus, Poland, for supplies, he did not leave for another two weeks. That delay was decisive in the destruction of the Grande Armée by its bitterest opponent, the Russian winter.

A lack of supplies was what forced the withdrawal. When the Russian campaign had begun, it was Bonaparte's stated intention to force the Russian army into battle as soon as possible, defeat them, and dictate a peace. The Russians did not cooperate, withdrawing constantly deeper into Russia and stripping the land behind them of food. (Yes this was incredibly hard on the local peasants, but that was, or is, the Russian way of making war.) What this meant was that while Napoleon had established depots to support his army, he soon had to move too far to the east for the supplies to be accessible. There had been no plan to march as far as Moscow or feed an army that far from the Polish depots.

The French army had to once again live off the land, and the Russian countryside offered very little. This is why even in Moscow Napoleon rationed food. When they finally retreated back toward Poland, the French soldiers were burdened with much loot, but little food. Quickly a pound of gold might be a pound of meat, if any could be found to buy. Most of the Frenchmen's loot was discarded along the march, much to the joy of the hovering Cossacks and local peasants.

To complicate matters, the Russians managed to maneuver their position in a way that forced Napoleon to return by the same route he had taken into the country. But that area had already been stripped twice of food. French foraging parties often returned with little or nothing. Whenever a forager or anyone else fell behind or was separated from the army, he would be attacked by the ever-present Cossack light horsemen. If they did not forage, the army could not eat, and when the French foraged, they often were ambushed. The lack of food and clean water led to disease. Weakened men are subject to typhus, cholera, and fatal diarrhea. Even suicide became a problem as men were tested past their limits.

Then came the winter. It was one of the earliest and coldest in Russian history. Yet the French had to march through and not stop or they would starve. Temperatures dropped to minus 20°F, and men literally froze to death in their sleep or even in the saddle. So common was it for a soldier to simply give up and collapse into the snow that it had a nickname: "doing a bear." Each day's march meant a thousand or more Frenchmen lost from the ranks. The Grande Armée left Moscow with nearly a hundred thousand soldiers in its ranks. Less than thirty thousand crossed the Nei-man River to safety.

The sole and entire fault for this disaster has to be laid at Napoleon Bonaparte's feet. The Russians implemented their plans well, but the delay and winter was what allowed them to turn defeat into victory. Had Napoleon simply left Moscow in October, then history would have been very different. But he chose to stay and lost an entire army.

30

||||||||||||||||||||||||||||||||||||||||||||||||||||||||||||||||||

EGO OVER REALITY

Best Offer

||||||||||||||||||||||||||||||||||||||||||||||||||||||||||||||||||

One failure by Napoleon Bonaparte set up the situation that led to the worst diplomatic decision of his career. It began in Moscow, one of the two capitals of czarist Russia. Already about two weeks too late, on October 3, 1812, Napoleon ordered the Grande Armée to prepare to depart Moscow. It was another two weeks before the hundred thousand soldiers actually began marching west toward Poland. Things went wrong almost from the beginning. The weather turned early, and it became the coldest winter in a century. Slowly, and then not so slowly, Bonaparte's army disintegrated. He had started the campaign against Russia with over two hundred thousand soldiers and that many again of reluctant allied and garrison troops on his flanks. By the time the Grande Armée's survivors approached the Nieman River and safety, there were less than thirty thousand men at the colors. The army that had conquered almost all of Europe was no more.

On December 5, 1812, Napoleon called together those marshals who were left. He announced that he was leaving the army in their hands, with his brother-in-law Marshal Joachim Murat in charge. Napoleon would be hurrying back to Paris to ensure that the loss of over two hundred thousand Frenchmen, virtually his entire field army, did not cost him the control of France. It shows just how things stood that while traveling back across the nations he had formerly dictated demands to, Napoleon was in disguise as the secretary to the diplomat Armand Augustin Louis de Caulaincourt. The entire convoy consisted of just three wagons and a small escort of Neapolitan (Italian) troopers. The emperor felt he had no choice. In his own words to Caulaincourt, "In the existing state of affairs I can only maintain my grip on Europe from the Tuileries." The reality was much darker. The following weeks would show that most of Europe would take advantage of Napoleon's weakness and declare their independence. Back in Paris, Napoleon performed miracles. He called up the next classes (annual groups) of recruits and trained a new army. By the next spring, he led a new army ready to march. It was short on horses, guns, and experienced officers, but Napoleon was also full of regained confidence.

Austria, Prussia, and Russia formed the Grand Alliance. Soon other nations, even Sweden, joined in opposing France. Only Italy and the German states (Germany was fifty years from being unified as a country) that were close to France stayed loyal to the French emperor. The armies of allied nations had not suffered in Russia, and they were ready to ensure Napoleonic France would never again be a threat. Prussia, Austria, Sweden, and Russia soon formed a coalition that was supported and financed by Britain. Together they could field 800,000 soldiers. In the summer of 1814, columns of allied troops began moving against the rebuilt French corps in Germany and France herself. Napoleon could field an amazing 350,000 men to oppose them. Of these, about 190,000 were in the army led by the emperor. Several battles followed in which the allies defeated the French when Napoleon was not with them, but the emperor was on the winning side when present, such as at Dresden. The result of all this was that Napoleon still felt he had a chance to emerge victorious and reassert his control of all Europe; meanwhile the allies were even more determined to defeat him once and for all. Both sides had lost heavily, but the French could not afford the losses.

The final battle of this campaign took place around the city of Leipzig in mid-October of 1814. It has since been known as the Battle of Nations for obvious reasons. Napoleon concentrated virtually his entire army of about 190,000 men and 750 cannons around the German city. The allies attacked Napoleon with over 300,000 soldiers and 1,335 guns, with more approaching. The French did well the first day, and the second was indecisive. But on the third day everything fell apart for Napoleon. His army was driven back into the city, the entire Saxon corps of 30,000 men changed sides, and parts of Napoleon's defensive positions were overrun. On October 18, Napoleon ordered a general retreat. The problem was that his remaining 120,000 soldiers had to all use the same bridge. Chaos reigned, and by nightfall the bridge was so congested no one could escape. With the French army trying to flee, the allied forces were able to push into the city. Most of the Italian and German soldiers in the French army deserted. Several important French generals were captured, and eventually someone panicked and blew up the only bridge, leaving almost 30,000 French soldiers on the wrong side. The disaster cost Bonaparte most of his army. Those who were still at the colors were disorganized and demoralized. Over the next weeks many felt the war was lost, and they deserted.

The battle for Leipzig had been also expensive for the allies, and their agreed-on commander, Austrian Prince Karl von Schwarzenberg, retained an almost psychotic fear of Bonaparte. They had seen the French emperor recover from the loss of his entire army less than a year earlier, so even though Napoleon had shattered his army again at Leipzig, the allies were not confident he was or could be beaten. Also, even the generous British subsidies they all received could not balance out the cost of maintaining their large armies.

Austrian Prince Klemens von Metternich was one of the creators of the concept of realpolitik: doing what is practical and possible and worrying about the moral concerns later. Just a month after the allied victory at Leipzig, in November 1813, he convinced the gathered kings, princes, and emperors at the Congress of Vienna to offer Napoleon Bonaparte peace terms. The terms were generous. They included the provision that Napoleon would remain emperor of France and that his son by Marie Louise would be his heir. This made Austria happy as Marie Louise was the Austrian emperor's daughter. France would retain control of Belgium and the Rhineland. Its northern border would remain the Rhine River, long a French goal. Both areas were rich in resources and industry. There would be no reparations, and Napoleon's France would be an equal member of the nations of Europe. These were called the Frankfurt Proposals. So if he accepted, Napoleon Bonaparte would remain the leader of an enriched France, in spite of having a recently crushed army. The allies would get to declare a victory and bring their armies home.

Napoleon arrived near Paris with an army of thirty thousand. He called up more recruits, but few appeared. Who wants to fight in a war most see as already lost? Lord Wellington's British army was pressing to invade France from the south. The rapid advance of the allied armies also meant most of the reinforcements Bonaparte might call in from the distant French fortresses were trapped behind the allied lines, and most were in the process of surrendering. With little hope of raising an army large enough to even defend France and with his support wavering at home, the French emperor went with pride and ego instead of common sense.

Napoleon Bonaparte said no. He refused the terms or to negotiate further. Five months later, on April 11, 1814, with Paris occupied and his army gone, the former emperor of France was forced to sign the Treaty of Fontainebleau. Instead of ruling all of France, he became the "emperor" of the small Mediterranean island of Elba with a staff of thirty-five and an army of eleven hundred soldiers. In 1815, his bid to return to power ended with his defeat at Waterloo. Napoleon died in May 1821, a prisoner on the distant and rather bleak South Atlantic island of St. Helena.

‖‖‖

31

TERRIBLE TIMING

A Useless Little War

1812, WASHINGTON, D.C.

‖‖‖

There were few cases in history of timing worse than the United States' declaration of war with Britain in 1812. The reasons for starting the war were many and even valid. The Americans had cause to be angry. The year 1812 was only twenty-nine years after the end of the American Revolution. There was still a good deal of resentment on both sides. Nor had the Americans forgotten that it was France who came to their aid and ensured the victory at Yorktown. However, the reasons for not starting a war were practical and apparent, or at least they should have been.

In Europe, the Napoleonic Wars were raging. Britain was paying subsidies that covered much of the cost of maintaining the army of anyone who would challenge the French. To punish the British, the French emperor had been enforcing, since 1806, the Continental System. It excluded British merchants and goods from every nation on the Continent. Because Napoleon controlled most of Europe at the beginning of 1812, this affected just about every European nation's port except Russia's . . . and he was invading Russia. The British had responded by declaring a blockade on France and her allies. Caught in the middle were the American merchants. They were suddenly blocked by the Royal Navy from trading with most of their European markets or importing goods from them. Also, the French seized any American merchant ship that had also traded with Britain or had any British goods on it. So the merchants were not happy with either side, but they were angrier at the British. The French confiscated almost five hundred ships from 1806 to 1812. During that same period, the British boarded and kept over a thousand ships. Understandably, the American merchants who owned those ships were upset. But since the Royal Navy controlled the seas, it was the navy that was the subject of American wrath.

The British were always short trained sailors. To begin with, the conditions of the ordinary English seaman were difficult. Seamen lived in crowded quarters, ate poor food, and were subjected to severe discipline. Many sailors had been "pressed" into service, kidnapped on land by gangs of sailors or professional pressers and forced to join the crews. Also, the pay was so low that it barely covered the expenses the navy charged them. This meant that when they could, many seamen jumped ship.

In the days before computers and photos it was a simple matter to change your name. John Paul Jones did it. His real name was John Paul Duff, and he had been born in Scotland. There was also a need for trained seamen to man the American merchant ships. The food was good, and the pay was several times that of a seaman in the Royal Navy. Furthermore, if the officers didn't approve of something a seaman did, he got fired, not flogged. So many of the British sailors that "ran," simply changed their names and bought easily obtained forged papers that said they were Americans. Then they could sail on American hulls.

The problem of British sailors running to join American ships became so great that the Royal Navy began a practice of stopping all American ships and inspecting their crews. If you sounded English, or Welsh, or Scottish, that was enough for them to grab you. If they occasionally impressed a few Americans in the process, no one in the admiralty was concerned. It was illegal, under international law, to stop another nation's ships at sea and impress members of its crew. But that didn't deter the British. International law works only if there is someone to enforce it, and the oceans of the world were controlled by the Royal Navy.

When in 1807 the American brig the *Chesapeake* refused to stop and be inspected by the Royal Navy's *Leopard*, that ship fired on the *Chesapeake*. Three American sailors were killed and eighteen injured. The entire encounter took place just three miles off Norfolk, Virginia, clearly in American waters and seen by the whole city. In reaction to this and other incidents, President Thomas Jefferson issued the Embargo Act, banning American ships from trading with the British. Because they already could not trade with the rest of Europe, this was an economic disaster for New England.

Hundreds of miles to the west, in what is now Indiana, British representatives from Canada were arming the local tribes and encouraging them to attack American settlers. This culminated in the Battle of Tippecanoe, where future President Henry Harrison defeated them. Because of this as well, anger at the British rose to a high pitch. Both in the ports and on the frontier, everyone wanted another war with the English.

In the election of 1810 most of those elected were war hawks who demanded the United States go to war with England. The fact that France was still considered a friend and was also fighting Britain was an added encouragement. So on June 18, 1812, the U.S. Congress issued a declaration of war against Britain. It also was without good sense. In 1812, the new United States was totally unprepared to fight a war against one of the most powerful nations with the most powerful navy in the world. It had a navy so small as to not really matter. The U.S. Navy consisted of a handful of excellent seamen, but they were badly outnumbered by the dozens of frigates in the Royal Navy. The Americans had no ships of the line. A frigate had between thirty-six and forty-four small cannons; the more than one hundred British ships of the line each had between sixty-four to a hundred cannons that were two to three times larger. At sea the United States was outnumbered and outgunned. The individual American frigates were better than their British counterparts, but the country never even tried to build a ship of the line. The Americans were also taking on a navy that had been constantly fighting and winning sea battles for fifteen years.

The American army was also pitifully small. Because they believed that it was the militia that had won the Revolution, the new nation put its faith in citizen soldiers who could be called to arms when needed. In all but the last encounter of the war, this proved disastrous. Furthermore, once they were at war with England, the ships of the American merchant fleet were fair game for the hundreds of British vessels. Rather than helping the ship-owning merchants, who had been wronged before the war, the declaration of war made things even worse for business.

So why did Congress feel they could declare war on Britain? The answer is what was happening in June 1812 in Europe. Napoleon was at the peak of his power. He was master of Europe from Spain to Poland. The Grande Armée was just beginning to invade the last of his mainland opponents, Russia. Everyone but the Russians expected he would defeat them just as he had every opponent except Britain. The French navy was in the midst of a building program, and it looked as if the British would have its hands very full and few resources to spare for the Americans.

Five months later, Napoleon had lost his entire army. By the spring of 1814, all of Europe had united against France and defeated Napoleon. The irony here is that because the Continental System was gone, the American merchants could have traded freely, except that now because of the war, the Royal Navy seized or sunk anything flying an American flag.

The United States started a war because they felt the British were distracted. But within months Napoleon was on the defensive, and within two years he was defeated. American attempts to grab Canada failed, and U.S. foreign exports sat in warehouses. When Napoleon was exiled in 1814, the United States found itself alone fighting a war against Britain. It did not go that well. The White House was first painted white to hide the scorch marks caused when an English army set it on fire.

The War of 1812 was simply unnecessary. Every cause for the war was gone before the war itself ended. With France defeated, trade was opened up everywhere. The British had no need to impress sailors because they soon had mothballed much of the fleet. The battles in the Midwest did settle the border with Canada, but no new territory was gained by the Americans. The United States was lucky. It could have found itself pitted against the best army in Europe and the full might of a navy ten times the size of its own. Tired of war, the British agreed to the Treaty of Ghent in December 1814. This basically reset everything to where it had been before the war, started. The United States gained nothing. America had started what became a meaningless but dangerous war at the exact wrong time and was lucky not to have paid a higher price.

32

OUT OF TOUCH

Sou-Wise and Franc-Foolish

1814, FRANCE

fter Napoleon was banished to Elba in 1814, Louis XVIII returned to the throne of France. Supported by the allies, the Bourbon had little trouble establishing himself as the king of France. The one problem he did have was that perpetual one plaguing rulers everywhere. There was never enough money to do that he wanted or needed to do. France was recovering from two decades of near constant warfare, and its economy was still stuttering. Things were further complicated by the return of the nobles who had fled from the terror of Napoleon. They wanted to reclaim the lands and homes they had left, but these had also been bought in good faith by the Frenchmen now living in them. Further, if Louis allowed the nobles to reclaim their now-broken-up estates, this would drive tens of thousands of peasant farmers from their land. No one wanted another wave of mobs of displaced and angry peasants roiling Paris and blaming the government. That had not worked out so well for the last French king in 1789.

Louis XVIII had another thing that may have kept him awake nights. This was the continuing popularity of Napoleon. While Louis made hard decisions and raised taxes, the days of the emperor began to look better. And although people had not forgotten the pain and cost of Napoleon's wars, they also remembered the glory and successes. And Bonaparte himself was still yet another financial burden. The Treaty of Fountainebleau, in which Napoleon agreed to be banished to Elba, included a clause that said the French government would provide the funds needed for the former emperor to support his household, personal troops, and the island.

It was likely that from the day he arrived on Elba, Bonaparte was thinking about his return to France. The irony was that Louis XVIII made the decision for him. He did the one thing that ensured the dreaded return would happen. His treasury stretched to the limit, Louis decided to economize by not sending Napoleon the money he was promised and needed to survive. Perhaps he thought Napoleon would be unable to react. Elba had no real resources and no one would lend the former emperor money. After all, as king of France, Louis had been pledged the support of all the other nations in Europe and their armies. What could Napoleon, eleven hundred infantry, and four light cannons do? By facing Bonaparte with the very real prospect of poverty and disgrace, the French king gave the former emperor no choice. Staying on Elba without his stipend was no longer tenable. In effect, the French king forced his proud former enemy to return to France. He created a Napoleon with nothing to lose.

On March 1, 1815, Napoleon and his soldiers sneaked off Elba on three ships and landed in France. The emperor marched to Paris, and every military unit sent to stop or arrest him instead joined him. When Michel Ney, still a marshal of France for Louis XVIII, announced that he too would be siding with Napoleon, it meant that the last of the French army had become the emperor's again. Louis fled Paris in disguise while the city celebrated

Bonaparte's approach. It was an approach Napoleon was forced to make because Louis had effectively cut off his allowance. It took two battles, Ligny (against the Prussians) and Waterloo (against the Anglo-Dutch), and tens of thousands of deaths for the other nations of Europe to return Louis XVIII to the French throne.

33

A COMPROMISE
THAT WASN'T

Kansas and Nebraska

1854, UNITED STATES

F or all the partisanship in American politics today, there is no issue that can polarize like slavery could. For the first half of the twentieth century, slavery dominated the public conversation. The union was held together by a series of compromises from about 1820 to 1850. Around 1850, the compromises began to unravel, creating substantial rifts between and within the two major political parties. Two important politicians—Senate Democrat Stephen A. Douglas and President Franklin Pierce—made an egregious error by supporting the Kansas-Nebraska Act, which repealed the Missouri Compromise. The act had far-reaching implications. Beyond intensifying the split over slavery, the act energized the antislavery movement and compelled the creation of the Republican Party. The Whigs ceased as a political entity. American politics has been dominated by Republicans and Democrats ever since.

The Missouri Compromise was orchestrated in 1820 by Henry Clay, a three-time presidential aspirant and one of the most important senators in history. Along with his colleagues Daniel Webster and John C. Calhoun, he preserved a tenuous peace in the decades leading up to the Civil War. He was called "The Great Compromiser" for a reason. Whenever the country was at odds over slavery, Henry Clay managed to secure a solution that placated each side.

The Missouri Compromise delayed rather than solved the explosion. For decades, there was an even balance between the number of slave states and free states in the Senate. Both sides wanted to secure a majority in the U.S. Senate so that they could advance legislation favorable to their position. Men like Clay preferred to maintain the balance and preserve the status quo; each concession promulgated by him and his congressional allies was meant to defuse tension over the slavery issue. The Missouri Compromise, for instance, sought to settle the question of slavery in territories gleaned from the Louisiana Purchase. The bill prohibited slavery in territories north of Missouri. It also welcomed Missouri as a slave state and Maine as a free state. While some major figures criticized the bill—the elderly Thomas Jefferson warned that the compromise was but a reprieve from mounting tensions, and many Southerners felt the bill disadvantaged them—it did help stabilize the union . . . for a time.

The slavery issue would not go away, however. In 1836 and 1837, Arkansas and Michigan were added as a slave and a free state, respectively. The addition of slave states Florida and Texas in the 1840s was matched by Iowa and Wisconsin. An important question centered on what to do about territories gained during the war with Mexico. Clay, by this point an old man, had one more compromise up his sleeve. The Compromise of 1850 was passed. It allowed the residents of the Utah and New Mexico territories to decide the slavery question for themselves upon gaining statehood. It also admitted California as a free state and implemented the Fugitive Slave Act, a measure that banned slavery in Washington, D.C., and obligated Northern states to help recapture fleeing slaves. Clay, Calhoun, and Webster all died within a few years of

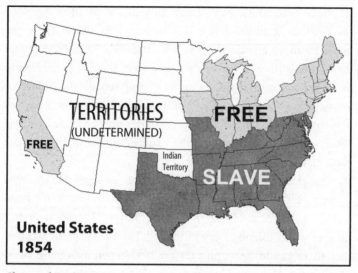

Slave and Free States

that compromise's passage. With them died the hope of stalling the conflict between the slave and free states.

Without Clay's guiding hand, tensions escalated. Stephen A. Douglas, the Democrats' leading senator, put forth the Kansas-Nebraska Act in 1854. The act was a de facto repeal of the Missouri Compromise in that it treated these territories in the same way Utah and New Mexico were treated. It granted all fledgling states the right to decide whether slavery should be permitted, rather than stipulating that any future state north of Missouri must be free. The bill incensed Northerners who felt the measure would jeopardize the abolitionist movement. It caused an influx of agitators into the new territories as each side vied for control. The result was a miniature civil war in what was referred to as "Bleeding Kansas," in which men like abolitionist John Brown organized brutal raids on the homes of proslavery Kansans who then organized reprisals.

Senator Douglas believed that popular sovereignty—that is, ceding the right to decide the slavery issue to the population of the territory itself—would help preserve the union and was the most democratic way of handling the issue. Bleeding Kansas was an example of that democracy gone awry. There the battle to attain a majority vote left numerous casualties. Douglas was unwilling to take a real stance on slavery, preferring to avoid the controversy that came with being strictly abolitionist or proslavery. He was a man of political expedience, not a man of principle. The debate over popular sovereignty versus absolute abolition would not end, and the issue would frame his political career later in the decade.

Douglas was not alone in his mistake, however. He was able to secure his compromise's passage in the Senate, but the act faced a stiff battle in the House of Representatives. President Franklin Pierce was initially leery of the bill. He was correctly worried that there would be significant political repercussions to overturning the Missouri Compromise. Douglas convinced him by arguing that the Compromise of 1850 had already invalidated the Missouri Compromise by granting popular sovereignty to Utah and New Mexico. The argument was not technically true because the Missouri Compromise affected only the territory from the Louisiana Purchase, and the territories of New Mexico and Utah were gained in the war with Mexico. Nonetheless, Pierce was convinced and threw his support behind the compromise's repeal. With the president's backing, the Kansas-Nebraska Act was able to pass in the House of Representatives.

The change infuriated the abolitionist movement. Before the Kansas-Nebraska Act was passed, the antislavery forces were a disorganized hodgepodge of Whigs, Free-Soilers, and Northern Democrats. Opposition to the act forced these groups to crystallize their antislavery sentiments under one banner: the Republican Party. Members of the new party varied in their levels of devotion to the cause (even Lincoln wasn't in favor of immediate abolition), but the Kansas-Nebraska Act united them in a coherent political movement. It wasn't long before the Republican Party was fielding major candidates in elections across the United States.

One of the most high-profile elections occurred in 1858. Abraham Lincoln, who had earned recognition with his harsh criticism of the Kansas-Nebraska Act upon its passage, was running for the Senate in Illinois against none other than Stephen Douglas. The famed Lincoln-Douglas debates brought national attention to the popular sovereignty debate. While Douglas squeaked out a victory, Lincoln became the figurehead of the Republican Party. In 1860, Lincoln defeated a fractured Democratic Party for the presidency when it fielded two candidates, the proslavery Southerner John C. Breckinridge and Stephen Douglas.

Never before had the nation been as polarized. The benefits of the past compromises were lost until no alternatives remained. By adding this uncertainty to the process, the Kansas-Nebraska Act vastly increased the insecurity of both sides. This attempt by the Democratic majority in Congress at adding democracy into an unstable situation aggravated tensions, ultimately bringing about the American Civil War. Nor did the party of the compromisers benefit. In the post–Civil War era, Republicans would control Congress and the presidency, with few interruptions, until the economic upheaval of the Great Depression. In the interests of their careers, their party, and their country, Douglas and Pierce failed. When wisdom was needed, they instead proposed a compromise that was not one.

34

||||||||||||||||||||||||||||||||||||||||||||||||||||||||||||||||||||||||||

DOING NOTHING IS DOING SOMETHING

James Buchanan's Inaction

1856, WASHINGTON, D.C.

||||||||||||||||||||||||||||||||||||||||||||||||||||||||||||||||||||||||||

James Buchanan was the right man at the wrong time. He was intelligent, hardworking, and savvy. He aspired to be his era's George Washington. Ever cautious of the temptations of power, Buchanan became one of only a few presidents in history who chose not to run for a second term. He was a "doughface": a Northern Democrat with Southern sympathies who, if he had possessed more ability, could have ameliorated some of America's pre–Civil War rifts. Buchanan's legacy will always be tarnished, however, because of his inability to stop the bloodiest war in American history. Buchanan's failings become even more apparent when stacked up against the legacy of his successor, Abraham Lincoln. Many regard Buchanan as history's worst president, and justifiably so. If he'd had the stomach to nip the Civil War in the bud, America's history would have been very different.

Buchanan inherited a difficult situation. The North and South were split over the issues of slavery and states' rights. The partisanship of today's Congress scarcely compares to the rancor of the

1850s, in which Congressmen would wallop one another with canes or draw pistols on each other. In regions like Kansas, miniature civil wars popped up as radical abolitionists and proslavers raided each other's homes and towns. The South felt its rights were under siege. Democrats were very suspicious of the upstart Republican Party. Abolitionists felt deeply that the United States was the last Western nation in the world to allow slavery.

Buchanan's predecessors had done little to ease the tension: Zachary Taylor had been against expansion of slavery in western territories and had little sympathy for secessionists, but he died early in office. Millard Fillmore's principal act was to sign the Compromise of 1850 and the infamous Fugitive Slave Law that incensed the North. Franklin Pierce was just plain ineffectual, foolishly pushing for the Kansas-Nebraska Act.

Buchanan's presidency was unspectacular. He was selected as the candidate in large part due to his lack of controversial opinions. With the rancor so strong, everyone who held a major office had made too many enemies. Buchanan had been the ambassador to Great Britain during the voting for controversial bills like the Kansas-Nebraska Act. Because he was overseas, he was never forced to take a stand and so eluded much of the criticism that could be leveled at other candidates.

That is not to say that he was not politically active. Earlier, during the infamous *Dred Scott* case, the Supreme Court decided that blacks in America had no constitutional protection. Buchanan pressured Justice Robert Cooper Grier to side with the majority, giving the court leeway to broadly declare the Missouri Compromise of 1820 unconstitutional as well. The implication was that popular sovereignty, not national policy, should determine the status of slavery in territories and fledgling states. His support for popular sovereignty, often called "states' rights," was a product of his Southern sympathies. Buchanan wanted desperately to avoid disrupting the slave state–free state balance of representation in the Senate. But neither balance nor cooperation was common during his presidency. Due to fissures within the Democrats, as well as an economic panic in 1857, Republicans gained a plurality in Congress in 1858. Relations between Republicans and Buchanan soured as party members frustrated his agenda, and he responded by vetoing numerous significant pieces of legislation. Republicans even made an attempt to impeach Buchanan on corruption grounds, though they never succeeded.

Such inefficacy is to be expected of any government in gridlock, when the presidency and Congress are controlled by different parties. Buchanan's biggest failing was not his ineptitude in dealing with an uncooperative Congress. His true error lay in his dealings with the South as they seceded. Buchanan, as promised, did not run for president in 1860. The Democrats fielded two candidates, John Breckinridge and Stephen Douglas. With two Democrats splitting votes, it was a foregone conclusion that Republican Abraham Lincoln was going to win the presidency. Southerners were extremely worried that Lincoln would attempt to abolish slavery, though in fact Lincoln merely wanted to limit the emergence of new slave states. The risk of secession was palpable. General Winfield Scott even requested that Buchanan supplement federal bases in the South with troops, as he suspected Southern states were on the cusp of seceding. Southern-leaning Buchanan ignored Scott's advice and did not reinforce the forts.

In Buchanan's final address to Congress, he did what he did best: straddled the fence. He issued a feeble condemnation of the South's impending secession while simultaneously chastising the North for its "unconstitutional and obnoxious enactments." He stated that secession by the South was illegal, but that he believed revolution by the Southern "injured States" was justified due to the North's gross violations. He went on to explain that the South's decision did not warrant a military response by the North and that any forceful attempt to stop the South seceding would be illegal. As president he virtually gave the Southern states permission to at least peacefully secede. He suggested Congress issue an explanatory constitutional amendment, giving the states popular sovereignty on the question of slavery, though neither side felt inclined to listen to him. He was roundly criticized for his luke-warm response.

On December 20, 1860, South Carolina declared its secession. Six other states shortly followed suit. The states seized federal as-sets and formed the Confederate States of America. As president, Buchanan was forced to defend the Union. Eventually Buchanan cleaned house, replacing Southern sympathizers in his cabinet with hard-line Northern Democrats. The new cabinet attempted to secure emergency executive powers to marshal a response, but their efforts fell flat with an uncooperative Congress. The North retained one fort: Fort Sumter, off the coast of Charleston, South Carolina. Buchanan chose not to reinforce the garrison in ex-change for promises of noninterference. Someone may have for-gotten to mention his plan to the Confederate commanding officer in Charleston, Major Robert Anderson. Then again, the major may have just ignored it. Anderson seized Sumter, further exacerbating relations between the North and South. Buchanan attempted to reinforce the besieged fort with a civilian ship, but it was attacked by Confederate artillery. Buchanan failed to respond to the aggression. Instead, he lay paralyzed: He made no further attempts at reconciliation, nor did he make preparations for war that would have enabled Lincoln to better handle the rebellion. When Lincoln became president, the nation was split, and noth-ing had been done to deal with it.

Buchanan left Washington a weary man. He had done nothing and the result was a shattered nation. He had not possessed the fortitude required to stand and weather the storm. The conse-quences of his being a weak president in difficult times were tens of thousands of deaths, a civil war, and the devastation of the Southern states. It is fortunate that a man of Abraham Lincoln's caliber succeeded him, for had Buchanan's successor resembled him in his lack of tenacity or inept leadership, the United States might never have been restored. Buchanan lacked the decisiveness that a good president requires. His ineptitude paved the way for America's greatest tragedy, the Civil War. Had he had some moxie or a shred of courage, history might have remembered him as a great man and not for a war that pitted brother against brother.

35 and 36

DESIGN FLAW

The Confederacy

1861–1865, RICHMOND, VIRGINIA

When they began their rebellion, the leaders of the Confederate States of America made two mistakes that were never rectified. One was inherent in the structure and political basis for the new nation. The other mistake they made was choosing and retaining a president who was chosen because of his devotion to that philosophy. These two leadership failures both crippled and eventually doomed the Confederate states in a way that even the brilliance of Robert E. Lee and the unquestioned courage of his soldiers could not overcome.

When seven Deep South, cotton-growing states seceded from the union in response to Abraham Lincoln's election, there was a vaguely rudderless feel to the rebellion. The new nation was made up of strong-willed state governments as opposed to a powerful central government. No central figure rose to unite the new nation. Rather that nation was founded because the states wanted more independence. The new Confederate States of America was just what the name says. A confederation is formed when most of the real power remains in the hands of the members and not the whole. It is a good way to guarantee states' rights but not the way to run a war.

The constitution of the Confederate States of America was much like that of the United States, though it ceded greater rights to the states and stipulated legal protections for slave owners. The Civil War tested the vitality of the Confederacy, and it failed. President Jefferson Davis did not realize the folly of establishing a country that lacked central authority when it was on the cusp of debilitating warfare. The only hope the South had of defeating the North was if they were organized and unified. Even the Romans and Athenians knew central control was vital in times of war. But the states were rebelling against the increased power of a central government. Jefferson Davis was not an incompetent leader, but he never lost his commitment to the superiority of the states to the federal government he headed. He could not move beyond that original concept, even as the new nation fell apart around him. Soon the Confederate president was overwhelmed by the onerous task of organizing and then running a new government with very limited authority to raise taxes or soldiers and hampered by the recalcitrance of uncooperative governors. It was a blueprint for defeat. As historian Frank Owsley put it, the Confederacy "died of states' rights."

In 1860, Abraham Lincoln was elected president of the United States. Worried that Lincoln would aggressively curtail slavery, seven states broke off from the country. Their stated reason was that the federal government had usurped the powers that were given in the Constitution to the individual states. The issues that this related to were slavery and taxes. Several states specifically addressed the issue of slavery as being the impetus for secession; Confederate Vice President Alexander Stephens would later describe the "cornerstone" of the new government to be the "great truth that the negro is not equal to the white man, that slavery—subordination to the superior race—is his natural and normal condition." It was a tenuous principle to build a country on. Indeed, the Confederacy's constitution mirrored that of the United

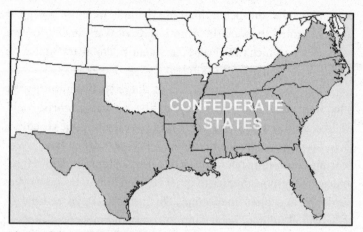

The Confederate States of America

States, except it had provisions protecting slave owners and ceding greater authority to the states. Though most Southerners did not even own slaves, they believed that the federal government should not interfere with states on the question of slavery. The new country was thus born in response to what was viewed as federal meddling. To prevent this from ever happening again, they ensured that the states held most of the power and the Confederate government had to act through them.

Under normal circumstances, a nation might survive on such principles. These were not normal circumstances. The Confederacy was at war from its inception. Confederate leaders had to grapple with the difficulties of establishing a new nation while simultaneously facing the Northern military threat. The North had many advantages: an industrial economy, greater population, more railroads, a superior navy with the eventual ability to blockade Southern ports, and international legitimacy. The South's hope was that the Northern public would be unable to stomach going to war with their Southern brethren. After the battle of Fort Sumter turned the secession into a shooting war, each side was convinced that it would be victorious within weeks. The Confederacy depended on such a thing; they simply were not equipped to win a protracted war. The American Civil War went on for five years, during which time Davis consistently demonstrated that he was the wrong man for the job.

When the Confederate president did exert his authority, he often went about it in the wrong way. The one area where he could wield a good deal of influence was in coordinating the rebellion. Here his personal faults interfered. Jefferson Davis was an overbearing, controlling man. He tried to do it all himself. This refusal to delegate responsibilities to others caused him to become overburdened and often ineffectual. For instance, Davis refused to cede overall military leadership to commanding general Robert E. Lee until very late in the war. Lee controlled only the Army of Virginia and was unable to use his genius to coordinate a national defense. Davis also failed to coordinate his generals, which sometimes resulted in incoherent or nonsupporting strategies. The South sought to win a defensive war, fending off Union troops until the Northern public tired of conflict. This was not a bad strategy, but it meant that the emphasis had to be on punishing the Union and not protecting the states. But each governor and Confederate senator insisted that his state was equally vital. Since the Confederate government depended on the states for taxes and soldiers, Davis insisted on defending all Southern territories with equal effort. This made the Confederates vulnerable in the vital Western theater and then just about everywhere. The old and proven maxim of "He who defends everything defends nothing" was forgotten. Finally, Davis appointed friends like Braxton Bragg as generals but failed to relieve them even if they proved to be inept.

Davis's micromanaging of the army was not his only failing, however. He feuded often with members of his own cabinet as well as with state governors. The result was that the governors withheld troops from national service—for instance, Texas argued that it required soldiers to defend against Native American raids and thus could not fully commit to the war effort. Davis had been hoisted by his own petard. Whenever he made demands on the states, they countered with claims of national infringement on states' rights. When Davis authorized conscription in an effort to secure more troops, he was viewed by some as a tyrant overstepping his bounds.

Davis was not completely insensitive to these views. For this reason he was loath to levy taxes to finance the war effort, correctly anticipating that higher taxes would anger the people. Instead, he authorized the printing of money to pay for the war. The result was crippling inflation that hampered the Confederate economy. Their economy also suffered from a devastating blockade imposed by the Union's navy. Davis had pinned his hopes on European intervention. The Southern states produced the majority of the world's cotton, and thus Davis believed the British factories would be unable to handle a disruption of that supply. The British cloth industry in 1860 was almost entirely dependent on Southern cotton. All of the Confederate leaders were sure that rather than lose production in a good part of their factories, the British would order the Royal Navy to open the ports. The U.S. Navy in 1860 would have been unable to challenge even a small part of the British. Davis expected Britain to side with the Confederacy. This was not to be. Britain had stockpiled cotton before the war; moreover, the British public was against slavery, and thus British officials would have had difficulty making a case for intervening on behalf of the slave states. By 1862, Egyptian and Indian cotton filled the void. Davis had overestimated the economic significance of his new country and underestimated his potential ally's repugnance at slavery, even though Britain was a world leader in repressing its practice elsewhere.

Ultimately, Davis lacked the ability to unite the Confederate states and truly mobilize them to the war effort. He failed to foster connections with the Confederate citizenry. A resident of Virginia thought of himself as a Virginian, not as a Confederate. Jefferson Davis did nothing to change this and cloistered himself within Richmond, rarely directing his energies to rally public support for the war effort. His obvious favoritism toward the rich and power-ful gradually wore on the nerves of common folks. Because Davis was so unpopular and committed to states' rights, governors were not criticized within their state when they refused to cooperate with him. Davis made rash economic and military decisions and alienated the people he depended on most. Because the Confederacy did not believe in a two-party system, opposition to Davis never crystallized into a coherent political entity. The result was that politicians had difficulty creating effective alternatives to the policies of the Davis administration. Instead, political thought in the South was stagnant, driven primarily by the whims of an incompetent control freak. Had Davis possessed the ability of his counterpart, Lincoln, the South might have won. History should then be thankful for Davis, if only because his failings brought about the end of slavery in America.

The structure and philosophy of the Confederate States of America guaranteed that it could not efficiently fight a war. The leadership, in particular Jefferson Davis, made the problem worse and the central government less effective. There is no knowing how history might have changed if this had been different. Though without states' rights and slavery, there would have been no American Civil War to begin with. So perhaps the seeds of the Southern states' failures were in the states' cause itself. Just as failure was guaranteed by their choice of the man who was their first and only president.

III

THE RELUCTANT GENERAL

Opportunity Lost

1862, VIRGINIA

IIIIIIIIIIIIIIIIIIIIIIIIIIIIIIIIIIIIIIIIIIIIIIIIIIIIIIIIIIIIIIIIIIIIIIIIII

The Union had an excellent chance of winning the American Civil War in the spring of 1862. Had the opportunity not been bungled there would have been six hundred thousand fewer dead Americans and a lot less bitterness. This lost opportunity is today known as the Peninsular Campaign.

The most accepted way to win a war in the nineteenth century was to demonstrate you had won by capturing the other side's capital city. Napoleon thought he had done this with Moscow in 1812, forgetting the Russians had two capitals. It was always the goal of the Germans when invading France to capture Paris. They actually did so in 1871, and it sealed their victory. One of the most important strategic geographic considerations of the American Civil War was that Washington, D.C., sits just over a one-hundred-mile march from the Confederate capital of Richmond, Virginia. The capture of Richmond was the main objective of the Army of the Potomac when it was formed. It was also the objective of that army's first campaign of 1862. By all rights and measures, the

Union Army should have captured Richmond that April rather than after a costly siege in 1865.

When the Southern states seceded, many of the coastal forts held by the U.S. Army were lost. The first and most famous of these was Fort Sumter. But a number of coastal fortifications remained in Union hands. One of these was Fort Monroe, which controlled the eastern tip of the Virginia Peninsula. Because they held this fort, it was possible for Union commander General George McClellan to disembark the entire Army of the Potomac, all 118,000 soldiers and all their cannons, horses, and equipment, uncontested. This meant he was in place and organized by the end of March, and by April 4 he was ready to move on Richmond.

The landings had caught the Confederacy by surprise. Most of its army was away, and only seventeen thousand Confederate soldiers were available to defend their capital. The city was in a panic, many sure it would fall soon. Provisions were discussed regarding the transfer of the Confederate government to another state. Morale would have been low for the outnumbered defenders. If Richmond fell so soon into the war, then some states might even have lost heart and sought to rejoin the victorious Union. A negotiated peace on Union terms would have been likely.

Fortunately for the Southern cause, despite the fact that the Union had six times as many soldiers, it also had George McClellan as its commander. There was no finer trainer or organizer, or more popular commander, than McClellan. His men loved him, and he had turned them into a potent military machine. The problem was McClellan must have been reluctant to see his creation harmed. The seventeen thousand Confederate defenders hastily constructed a thin line of defensive positions that stretched from Yorktown, Virginia, to the Warwick River. Their commander, General John B. Magruder, hoped to just slow down the Union advance long enough for reinforcements to reach Richmond and hold the city itself. The rest of eastern Virginia was written off by necessity.

McClellan took a look at the Confederate positions and decided they were too tough for his hundred-thousand-plus soldiers to attack. He greatly overestimated the number of men he was facing. Sure any strong attack would be repulsed easily by so many dug-in defenders, he settled down with his entire army and began a monthlong artillery bombardment. By the time McClellan finally stirred and attacked Confederate General Joseph E. Johnston, he had force-marched his entire army there to back up the defenders. This still left the Southerners outnumbered almost two to one, and so the day before McClellan finally ordered the assault, the Confederates withdrew. After a month of preparation, the entire army was ready to fight its way in and the defenses were empty.

The Union troops pursued, and Johnston's rear guard was engaged the next day near Williamsburg. They suffered badly, but Johnston was able to break contact and move his army to the suburbs of Richmond. Cautiously moving toward Richmond, McClellan sent forces out to occupy the eastern portions of Virginia. They met little resistance in most places. When Norfolk fell, the Confederates were forced to scuttle their first ironclad ship, the *Virginia* (*Merrimac*).

Before McClellan's divisions could reach Richmond, a series of heavy rains caused the rivers to peak and split the Union forces. There was a chance for Confederates to hit two of the Union corps that were isolated near Seven Pines, Virginia. This time it was Magruder who did not press the attack when the Southerners finally went in, so nothing significant resulted. The Confederate commander Joseph Johnston was wounded in that attack. So Jefferson Davis relieved Magruder and appointed the next highest ranking general in Richmond to handle the city's defense, Robert E. Lee.

Lee inspired the men, and he had strong defenses built all around Richmond. He then ordered the dashing cavalry commander J. E. B. (Jeb) Stuart to ride completely around McClellan's slowly approaching Union Army. In doing so, Stuart was able to disrupt the Union advance and confirm that the right flank of the

Union Army was weak and badly placed. Lee now had 72,000 men facing McClellan's 110,000-plus. Still, Lee took the offensive, leaving only 25,000 soldiers to face McClellan's still slowly advancing army. He took the other 47,000 men and attacked its flank. On June 26, Lee's forces broke through the Union line near Gaines's Mill, Virginia. McClellan was now sure he must be badly outnumbered and began to withdraw. The retreat did not stop until the Army of the Potomac had reached the relative safety of Harrison's Landing. More fighting followed, known as the Seven Days' Battles, but it resulted in severe casualties for both sides and little else. Eventually, the bulk of the Union forces were ferried back to their bases in Maryland.

McClellan had the opportunity to capture a weakly defended Richmond and possibly end the Civil War. All he had to do was move with the urgency the opportunity called for. His caution and hesitancy lost him the advantage of surprise and then he overestimated the opposition's size. As he neared Richmond, McClellan allowed himself to be chased away by an inferior force. There was never another opportunity for a single, decisive, and war-ending victory, and McClellan's timidity wasted this one. In April of 1865, the war ended only when Richmond fell after months of bloody trench warfare.

38

KNOW YOUR SUBORDINATES

A Bad Beginning

1863, GETTYSBURG

||||||||||||||||||||||||||||||||||||||||||||||||||||||||||||||||||||

The Battle of Gettysburg was Robert E. Lee's one great defeat. More than that, it was his battle to win or lose, and he made several uncharacteristic mistakes that unquestionably lost it. There are literally entire sections of some libraries that contain nothing but remembrances by those who were there and speculation as to why the Confederacy lost this battle. Often overlooked in any discussion of the strategy and tactics used over those fateful three days are the mistakes that Lee made before the first shot was even fired.

The first of these was Lee's choice of corps commanders. Until just before Gettysburg, the Army of Northern Virginia was divided into two corps. They had been commanded by James Longstreet and Stonewall Jackson. But Jackson was killed by his own picket at the Battle of Chancellorsville. Until this time, each corps had served its own role in General Lee's victories. Jackson had been the master at moving his men quickly and striking the Union's flank or rear. His infantry was sometimes referred to as "foot cavalry" because of their ability to march so rapidly and still fight. Longstreet was the anvil to Jackson's hammer. Longstreet tended to react slowly, even to urgent orders, but he did not panic when pressed. He was well organized and dependable. Lee decided to keep the cautious but competent Longstreet, but he needed to balance that choice with a commander or commanders that would be as aggressive and daring as Stonewall Jackson had been. In an attempt to make his army more flexible, General Lee also reorganized into three corps from two.

The choice of an officer who hesitated to obey orders during a battle has often been questioned. But James Longstreet was far superior to the other two corps commanders Lee appointed just before the Battle of Gettysburg. Each of the two men he selected were so badly flawed that the choices affected the battle and the defeat. Those men were Ambrose Powell Hill and Richard "Dick" Ewell.

A. P. Hill had been famous for his aggressive leadership. When he expected a battle, he put on a red calico hunting shirt. This made it easy for his men to see him and made him a target for enemy snipers. His men would spread the word when they saw Hill was wearing his "battle shirt," and they would get ready to fight. His infantry command, until promoted, was known as the Light Division. Hill had earned the command of a division with the skill and decisiveness he had shown during the Peninsula Campaign. The Light Division was not organized any differently from other infantry divisions, but it marched more quickly than most other units. This made it invaluable to the corps commander, Stonewall Jackson, in several battles. Under Hill, the Light Division had played an important role in the battles of Second Bull Run, Fredericksburg, Chancellorsville, and Antietam. At Antietam Hill, he had forced-marched his entire division at double speed for over ten miles and then thrown them directly into the attack. It had turned the battle.

Hill seemed the ideal candidate to replace Stonewall Jackson and command Lee's III Corps. There was one tragic problem that changed all this. The problem was one that was not even mentioned in most histories written after the war. That was because those histories were largely written by Hill's fellow "gentlemen" officers. During the Mexican War, Ambrose Hill had gotten very familiar with some of the local women. As a result he was infected with syphilis. The disease had progressed slowly, but was now in its later stages. The effects of third-stage syphilis include mood swings, irrational reactions, physical weakness, and difficulty concentrating. During the Battle of Gettysburg, the commander of one third of the Confederate Army was often physically weak and hesitant. The disease destroyed his effectiveness just when Hill's aggression and leadership were needed the most.

Ambrose Hill had a problem that was just not spoken of; in contrast, Dick Ewell's was readily apparent. He had lost a leg and nearly died after the Battle of Second Bull Run (Second Manassas). Before this loss, he had been one of Jackson's favorite division commanders. Ewell returned the favor by idolizing Jackson. The problem was if you were not Jackson, Dick Ewell was often short with you and impatient. But that was Ewell before he lost his leg and spent months recovering from the wound. The recovery seemed to have taken something out of him. He had lost that edge that made him so effective. You can call it his fighting spirit, but whatever he needed to push his men around an army and then lead them against its rear was gone. His unwillingness to press his tired men in an attack when ordered was often said to be a major factor in the Southern loss.

It is the job of the top commander to know his subordinates. In this, Lee failed. Just before the Battle of Gettysburg, Robert E. Lee appointed three men to command the three corps of his reorganized army. He retained James Longstreet, who was given to "the slows" but was reliable. Lee then gave the two other corps, two-thirds of the entire Army of Northern Virginia, to a man broken in both will and body and to one who was going insane from a venereal disease.

‖‖‖

39

GLORY OVER FUNCTION

Without His Eyes

1863, GETTYSBURG

‖‖‖

There should not have been a Battle of Gettysburg. The battle was not fought where or in the way Robert E. Lee had originally planned. Much of the fault for this has to be laid on the absence of cavalry and the lack of any intelligence regarding the Army of the Potomac's location. With the exception of mostly unreliable spies, the source of all intelligence on enemy movements during the Civil War was the cavalry. They both scouted the enemy and screened their army from the other side's cavalry. Or at least they normally did, but not before the Battle of Gettysburg. The day before the battle, Lee still thought that the Army of the Potomac was near Washington, D.C., not forty miles away.

The Army of Northern Virginia was operating far into Pennsylvania, which was hostile territory. There were no friendly locals to pass on anything. Lee knew they would be traveling through unfriendly territory and would likely draw out the Army of the Potomac. Yet when his army was just crossing out of Virginia, he ordered J. E. B. (Jeb) Stuart to split off and go on a sweeping raid through Union territory.

Since the start of the Civil War, the Confederate cavalry had dominated their Union counterparts. They had consistently outrode, outfought, and outthought the Union horsemen. Their most newsworthy feats were great raids that had swept behind or around the Army of the Potomac. Jeb Stuart was the master of these rides. His maneuver behind McClellan during the Peninsular Campaign had helped force the superior Union Army to withdraw, ultimately saving Richmond. He had repeated these raids several times, always disrupting the Union plans and drawing after him large formations. So it made some sense that Lee would agree to send Stuart and the majority of the army's horsemen off on another such attack. If the Union Army reacted as it had before, by sending a few infantry divisions to block Stuart and even more cavalry to chase him, the Confederate horsemen could tie up substantial Union forces. The disruption might also delay the Army of the Potomac's departure from Washington because there would be an urge to stay close to and defend their capital.

Unfortunately, for Stuart's raid to be effective, the Union forces had to react in the way that Lee expected and wanted. It also meant that the Army of Northern Virginia would be traveling with barely enough cavalry to screen its own movements and would have none to scout with. That turned out to be too high a price.

The raid did accomplish one benefit. The bulk of the cavalry attached to the Union Army rode off after Stuart. Both Robert E. Lee and General George Gordon Meade, who was commanding the Army of the Potomac, were operating blind. Stuart certainly sowed confusion and fear. With several thousand horsemen, he cut a swath of destruction, defeated a few garrisons, and even captured a massive supply train full of ammunition, food, and blankets—everything an army can use. In fact, he was too successful. The four hundred captured wagons slowed down his entire column and delayed his return to Lee. It was not until the end of the second day at Gettysburg that Stuart rode in. The cold reception he received when he entered Robert E. Lee's tent was deserved. Lee never planned to fight at Gettysburg, and had he known Meade and his army were close, he could have pulled back to the nearby position he had already selected. But without their "eyes," the two armies literally blundered into each other.

Stuart was slow to return and distracted by the captured wagons. Lee had agreed to and ordered Stuart's raid. Both Lee and Stuart have to share the blame for what proved to be the Southern horsemen's disastrous absence in the days before the Battle of Gettysburg.

40

||||||||||||||||||||||||||||||||||||||||||||||||||||||||||||||||||||||||||||

THE PRICE OF
OVERCONFIDENCE

Pickett's Charge

||||||||||||||||||||||||||||||||||||||||||||||||||||||||||||||||||||||||||||

Most of the chapter titles in this book are wordplays meant to introduce the mistake covered. They use irony, or even puns, to offset the pathos and the pain caused by the leadership mistakes and failures. But when you are talking about courage . . . and futility, there are few choices of title better than simply saying Pickett's Charge. It sits among a pantheon of just a few other valiant and doomed efforts that demonstrate so clearly both the glory and the cost of war. It was the last great effort of the Army of North Virginia and the Confederacy.

The Battle of Gettysburg happened by mistake. Both armies blundered into each other and were drawn in piecemeal. Robert E. Lee's stated intention, if he met the Army of the Potomac, was to fight a defensive battle. He had selected a position he planned to pull his army into and then make the new Union commander, George Gordon Meade, attack him. But on defense or not, fight he would because the Confederacy desperately needed a victory. It needed a major victory in the east because the west was lost. Ulysses S. Grant was besieging Vicksburg, and when that city fell, the entire Mississippi River was in Union hands. The Union naval blockade had closed all the Southern ports, and with no trade and the strains of war, the Confederate economy was collapsing. The Union states had seven times the population of the Southern ones. Since the start of the war, the Army of North Virginia had sustained almost a hundred thousand casualties. Considering that the army only had seventy-two thousand soldiers in it at Gettysburg, its casualties had been about 138 percent. Some men had been wounded and returned, the rest had to be replaced, and in doing so, the limited manpower of the Southern states had been expended. There were no more recruits to replace any further Confederate losses. The Union could easily replace their losses, but they were also recruiting immigrants just off their ships in droves.

The Confederacy was not without hope, but it needed a victory or something as spectacular. There was one chance that their goal of a negotiated separation could be achieved. The elections of 1864 were approaching, and former general George McClellan (of Peninsular Campaign timidity) was the Democratic candidate challenging Abraham Lincoln. McClellan was the peace candidate and had pledged to end the fighting and seek a negotiated treaty with the South. His promise had appeal to many war-weary Northern voters. But to be sure of defeating Lincoln that November, McClellan needed to show the war was far from won, and a big Confederate victory would almost guarantee him the presidency. The Army of Northern Virginia was in Pennsylvania to create such a situation. A victory, a city such as Baltimore or Washington, D.C., threatened, or even just an extended period of the Army of North Virginia rampaging up the Shenandoah Valley could put McClellan in office. Lee needed that big win and had overwhelming confidence in his soldiers. A win meant that McClellan would get elected and make peace. An added benefit was that such a victory might even encourage the European nations to demand the Union blockade of all the Confederate ports, which was strangling their cotton export–based economy, be lifted.

There was a chance that England or France might even offer military support, as France had to the American colonists only eighty years earlier.

So once the armies met, Lee had to win. A draw, or withdrawal, would not be enough to ensure McClellan's election or to show Europe that the Confederacy could effectively bring the war north. While by the third day of the battle the Confederates had pushed back and punished the Union corps facing them, there was no victory. Much of Lee's army was spent, but then so were many of the Union's brigades. Lee had been fighting the battle as an aggressor but still felt he was winning. He believed that just one more push was needed to break the Army of the Potomac and save the Confederacy. Lee was wrong. Meade's army was firmly in place and determined to not give way. They had held their own and punished the Confederates. Just as important, they were now on Union soil and defending their homes. Where in the past when the Union soldiers had broken after two days of hard fighting, this battle was different. Diaries and accounts remarked on their determination. It was new and a factor Robert E. Lee did not consider.

The men of the Army of Northern Virginia had never failed. They believed in General Lee, and he knew they would do anything he asked of them. What he asked on that day was one final charge that would break the Union center. For this he turned to his last intact corps, that of Lieutenant General James Longstreet. It was composed of three divisions, one of which was led by General George Pickett, for whom the attack was named. Longstreet argued against the charge. He was notably conservative, and Lee was confident his soldiers could cross the thirteen hundred yards under fire and push through.

The charge was not to go in without all the support Lee could provide. It would be preceded by the heaviest artillery bombardment of the war. The Southern artillerists would literally fire off nearly all of the ammunition they had. Pressure was to be put on other parts of the Union line by the other two corps, to prevent

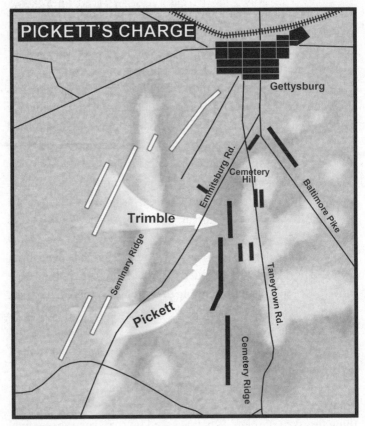

Pickett's Charge

the center from being reinforced. J. E. B. (Stuart) had orders to lead his cavalry around the entire position and then charge in behind where Pickett's men were to attack. Pressed from both sides, the center of the Army of the Potomac would break. Split in two, Meade would have to order a withdrawal. Lee would have his victory. He might even be able to get between Meade and Washington, D.C. That threat alone might force negotiations.

The plan fell apart before Pickett's charge even started, though there was no way for Lee to know this. Stuart's still-tired horsemen were seen as they rode toward the Union rear. The first unit that saw them was a brigade of the Michigan cavalry led by the youngest general in the Union Army, George Armstrong Custer. The general saw the long column behind Stuart and knew he was badly outnumbered, but he ordered his Wolverines to charge. That charge doomed Pickett's men. The Southern horsemen had to stand and fight. More Union horsemen joined in, and eventually Stuart was forced to retreat. There would be no attack on the rear of the Union center.

The Southern artillery barrage was intense, but failed to soften the Union infantry. Firing uphill they could not see where most of their shots landed. As a result, most of the cannonballs landed behind the infantry. It was spectacular, but ineffective.

So when the Confederates charged across the three quarters of a mile between them and the Union soldiers, they were facing an enemy that was expecting them, was determined to hold, and was undamaged. The Union Army had brought up artillery overnight and reinforced their center. When the Confederates charged, they were met with a storm of shot and canister on both flanks. Longstreet's three divisions melted under the intense fire. Still the Confederates closed ranks and advanced. Of the fifteen brigade commanders in Pickett's division, eleven were killed or wounded. The men showed raw courage and amazing devotion. A scant few brave Confederate soldiers reached the Union line, but they were pushed back. Units were shattered. Losses in some were as high as 60 percent. These were losses the Confederacy could not replace. When Lee ordered Pickett to form his brigade and prepare to defend against a counterattack, Pickett replied, "General Lee, I have no division."

There was no counterattack. The Union Army was too battered to mount one. They barely pursued what remained of Lee's army back to Virginia. Lee needed a victory, and he convinced himself that the men of his army could give him one. To get that victory, he chose to fight in a place not of his choosing, without his cavalry for half of the battle, and ended the battle by throwing away seven thousand lives in an attack that had little chance of succeeding. While he attempted to rally the survivors, General Robert E. Lee was heard to tell General Cadmus M. Wilcox and his men that the disaster was "all my fault." It was.

‖‖‖

41

CHOOSING POLITICS OVER THE MAN

The Compromise Selection of Andrew Johnson

1865, UNITED STATES

‖‖‖

The vice presidency of the United States is a peculiar institution. Because the vice president has so few day-to-day responsibilities, candidates are often selected based on their appeal to voters not accessed by the presidential candidate. For instance, Republican moderate John McCain chose far-right Governor Sarah Palin to be his running mate in 2008 to energize hardcore conservatives. In the nineteenth century, such ticket-balancing was often regional rather than ideological. For this reason, Abraham Lincoln replaced fellow Republican Hannibal Hamlin with Southern Democrat Andrew Johnson during his reelection campaign of 1864. Andrew Johnson was known to favor the Southern view of states' rights while not supporting secession. His role was to make the ticket more acceptable to the voters in the border states, such as his own state of Tennessee.

Lincoln was obviously not expecting to be assassinated, but during such a volatile time he should have prepared for such a contingency. After Lincoln was shot, Johnson pursued policies that must have made his predecessor turn in his freshly dug grave.

The obstinate Johnson frustrated the fledgling civil rights movement, failed to rein in a vindictive Republican Congress, and foiled Northern Reconstruction efforts. The agony of Reconstruction did not have to happen. Lincoln should have selected a more capable successor; enticed by the politically expedient option, Lincoln unwittingly set the stage for Johnson to jeopardize everything Lincoln fought for.

Andrew Johnson was born into poverty, but later he earned considerable wealth via his tailoring business. He served in both houses of the Tennessee State legislature before being elected to five consecutive terms in the House of Representatives. During this time he fanatically advanced the Homestead Act, which provided American citizens land in an effort to settle "unpopulated"—by white men—territories. He served as Tennessee's governor from 1853 to 1857 before becoming a senator. When talk of secession began to boil, Johnson pledged loyalty to the Union while reaffirming his belief in the legitimacy of slavery. As other Southern congressmen resigned their seats upon formation of the Confederacy, Johnson chose to retain his position even as Tennessee voted to secede. He criticized secession as unconstitutional and aggressively campaigned against it in his home state, to no avail. His devotion to the Union earned him considerable respect among Northerners.

After ingratiating himself with Lincoln and other Republicans, he was a natural choice to serve as military governor to Tennessee upon Northern occupation of the state. During this time, he ostensibly moderated his views on slavery. Where he had once described black Americans as "inferior" in matters of intellect and asserted slavery be protected by the Constitution, he began to describe slavery as a "cancer on our society." Johnson's true feelings were reflected in other statements, though. It was not that Johnson supported abolition so much as he preferred it to disunion. On the matter, he is quoted as saying, "If you persist in forcing the issue of slavery against the government, I say in the face of heaven: Give me my government and let the negroes go." Johnson was truly devoted to national unity, and it was for this reason Lincoln selected him as his vice presidential candidate.

During his first term, Lincoln's vice president was Hannibal Hamlin, a Republican from Maine. Lincoln faced former general George McClellan when he ran for reelection. The principal issue was of course the Civil War. The Democratic Party in the Union was divided between "Copperheads," who supported reconciliation with the South, and "War Democrats," who supported Republican war efforts. McClellan was very ambitious and smarting from his failures when commanding the Army of the Potomac. He ran as the Democrat candidate, despite disagreeing with that party's antiwar platform. The Republicans combined with the War Democrats to form the National Union Party, which fielded a Lincoln-Johnson ticket. Lincoln selected Johnson, despite the men's stark differences in opinion on slavery, because he calculated that Johnson would buoy him to victory. Lincoln won the election handily and probably could have done so without Johnson. Though there was no way of knowing the repercussions of his choice at the time, his running mate cost the nation greatly.

Lincoln was assassinated on April 14, 1865, shortly after Union General Ulysses S. Grant had finally forced Confederate Commander Robert E. Lee to surrender. With Lee's help, the rest of the Southern forces surrendered. Johnson was also targeted for death, but his would-be assassin lost his nerve. In the immediate aftermath of Lincoln's death, Johnson vowed to continue Lincoln's policies. He decisively dealt with the conspirators involved in Lincoln's assassination and swiftly established a working relationship with the former president's cabinet. Lincoln had already begun putting Reconstruction policies in place before the war ended, and he also had selected Johnson in part for his experience as Tennessee's wartime military governor. Lincoln intended to fully embrace the South rather than punish it. His belief was that harsh sanctions would only exacerbate tensions and prevent wounds from healing. His intent to rebuild rather than punish the South highlights the irony of his assassination. Confederate sympathizer

John Wilkes Booth thought slaying Lincoln would benefit the South, but his actions served only to enrage the North and radicalize Republicans in Congress. They nixed Lincoln's accommodating plans for Reconstruction in favor of a more punitive program. Johnson did little to calm their tempers, and it was not long before he felt forced to sabotage the new Republican agenda.

Republicans in Congress were not incredibly desirous of reintegrating the Southern states. Beyond lingering resentment toward the South over the Civil War, Republicans feared that restoring former Confederate states to their previous status would enable the Democratic Party to wrest control of Congress. Freeing the slaves had the effect of increasing the South's number of members in the House of Representatives. Before the Civil War each slave had only counted as three fifths of a person when determining representation. Now they each counted as a full citizen. Thus Republicans preferred to be able to continue to enact legislation without having to deal with an influx of former Confederate legislators. To prevent this, the Republicans placed many constraints on readmission to Congress.

Johnson's Southern white supremacist roots began to re-emerge during his presidency. His actions now were the opposite of what Lincoln had desired. Johnson criticized Republicans for protracting Reconstruction and refused to heed their concerns about the black codes. These were laws enacted in the former Confederate states that prevented Negroes from voting. He vetoed Republican legislation to renew the Freedman's Bureau, a Lincoln-era program that sold land confiscated during the war; instead, Johnson attempted to restore this property to the aristocrats who had originally owned it. Congress later passed a watered-down version of the bill that garnered enough support to override Johnson's veto, but the altered version of the bill was less equipped to assist former slaves. Johnson also vetoed the 1866 civil rights bill, which sought to eliminate black codes and give former slaves all the rights accorded to other citizens. Johnson's justification for his veto was that eleven out of the thirty-six states were not represented due to Republican refusal to readmit Southern congressmen. The Republicans overrode his veto.

To truly guarantee protections for freedmen, Congress proposed a Constitutional amendment to enumerate rights for all citizens regardless of race. The Fourteenth Amendment guaranteed voting and civil rights for freedmen. Because the Southern states had been economically devastated by the war, the amendment also promised that the Confederate debt need not be repaid. This was meant to be a conciliatory, moderate gesture, but it fell on deaf ears. Johnson rallied against the amendment, using his influence to block ratification. It would not be ratified until 1868.

Republicans made considerable gains in Congress in 1866 and were able to override his vetoes. This rendered President Andrew Johnson impotent. They continued their campaign of punishing the South while attempting to secure rights for freedmen. Johnson had such strained relations with Congress that he could do little on the South's behalf. He continued to encourage Southern leaders to refuse to ratify the Fourteenth Amendment and to generally drag their feet in accommodating Republican efforts. Republicans were so incensed at Johnson that they passed the Tenure of Office Act, which required Johnson to consult the Senate before removing executive officers from their positions. When he suspended Secretary of War Edwin Stanton without the permission of Congress, the House of Representatives impeached him. It was a nakedly partisan attempt to punish Johnson for frustrating Reconstruction policies. Johnson narrowly avoided being impeached by the Senate, as a few courageous senators refused to succumb to petty politics.

Johnson was never supposed to be president. He was a compromise candidate who shared little ideological commonality with either Lincoln or the Republicans. In the wake of the Civil War, the country needed a strong president who could engineer a coherent plan for Reconstruction. Johnson was not that man. Distrusted by the former Confederates for remaining with the Union and by the Republicans for favoring Southern views, he was a president without any political allies. He was a Democrat in a Republican-dominated government. His main agenda was to thwart Republicans; such an uncooperative attitude did nothing to mend the scars of the war. In reaction the Republicans continued to punish the South. Lincoln should have selected a man who would carry out his mission should he prove unable. Johnson, because of his petulance, his stubbornness, and his Southern bias, could not carry out Lincoln's plans.

|||||||||||||||||||||||||||||||||||||||||||||||||||||||||||||||||||||||||||||

42

PROMOTING OUT DOES NOT ALWAYS WORK

And One Became Vice President

1900, NEW YORK

|||||||||||||||||||||||||||||||||||||||||||||||||||||||||||||||||||||||||||||

n 1881, New York political power resided with the Republican machine, controlled largely by Senator Thomas Platt, and the Democratic machine, controlled by the now-notorious politicians of Tammany Hall. The two rivals had little else in common until a charismatic upstart named Theodore "Teddy" Roosevelt decided he wanted to be part of the governing class. With reform-minded ideas and the energy to see them through, Teddy Roosevelt represented a serious threat to the status quo of politics of New York State for both parties. In an effort to get rid of him, they got more than they bargained for.

Thomas Platt spent years working his way up the ladder of the Republican political machine in upstate New York, eventually modeling his own political methods on the infamous Democratic machine based in Tammany Hall. Unlike the Democrats of Tammany, Platt's organization did not seek personal wealth, just political power. Known as "the Easy Boss" because he ruled with a soft touch, Platt built important friendships with major business owners while helping to ease government regulations. After moving to Manhattan, Platt became the primary political boss of New York's G.O.P. He met with local and state politicians almost every Sunday at what became known as the "Amen Corner" because his subordinates always agreed with him, but that was before he met Teddy Roosevelt.

At the age of twenty-three, Theodore Roosevelt became the youngest state representative in New York's history. Though elected by the Republican Party, he quickly proved he would not be bound by its constraints. He began leading a group of young reformers known as the "Roosevelt Republicans." They focused on reform and corruption issues while opposing the political machinery of both the Republicans and the Tammany Hall Democrats. Roosevelt soon exposed a Tammany Hall–backed judicial corruption scandal involving New York Supreme Court Justice T. R. Westbrook and railroad magnate Jay Gould. He became the youngest minority leader of the assembly, and he collaborated with the Democratic governor Grover Cleveland to pass reform legislation. He left only because of the trauma caused by the death of both his wife and his mother on the same day. He moved west to have a new beginning.

However, the Republicans still had a use for him. In 1886, they needed someone to run in a three-way race for mayor. An independent candidate actually had a chance to win. The party machine knew that the chance of any Republican winning was next to impossible, but they nominated Roosevelt to keep their party on the ballot. Most of the Republican regulars, in fear of a third-party victory, abandoned Roosevelt to vote for the Democratic nominee, leaving him to finish in third place.

Roosevelt left New York politics after the election and did not return until 1895, when he received an appointment to the Board of Police Commissioners. As police commissioner, he attempted to clean up the massive corruption, bribery, and rot that permeated the New York Police Department, often heading out in the middle of the night with journalist friend Jacob Riis to hunt for derelict police officers. Unfortunately, they had little trouble finding them. He also went after the police chief and the inspector.

Some of Roosevelt's actions, especially his determination to uphold the laws forbidding alcohol sales on Sundays, stepped on some toes. Politicians in both political parties had interests in many drink establishments. Republican boss Senator Platt, who needed to appease certain business interests, tried to get Roosevelt to drop the fight to enforce the Sunday laws, but Roosevelt refused. Platt then warned that, if pressed, he would use his power in the legislature to end the police commission entirely.

Fortunately, another choice appeared when William McKinley won the presidency. McKinley was willing to give Roosevelt the position of assistant secretary of the Navy, but only if Platt, as the senior senator from his state, gave his approval. Platt, despite his reservations about Roosevelt, did so, realizing this was an opportunity to get Roosevelt out of New York. It seemed an ideal solution.

A year later, after leading his Rough Riders in the Spanish American War, Roosevelt returned to the city as a war hero. Platt had spent the time solidifying his position as the unquestioned leader of the New York Republican Party, but the Republicans were in trouble. They were desperate to hold on to the governor's mansion, but there had been so many scandals and problems within the party that to the voters there was little to separate the Republicans from the corrupt Tammany Democrats. Fearing a heavy loss, Platt reluctantly realized that Theodore Roosevelt represented the party's best chance for a victory. Roosevelt promised to work with Platt, so Platt backed him. Roosevelt won a close election, turning the tide by proclaiming that a vote for him was a vote against Tammany Hall.

Once Roosevelt was in office, Platt discovered that Teddy's idea of "working with him" meant something far different from what Platt intended. Rather than carry the party line and make the expected appointments as payback, Roosevelt made the most lucrative appointments based on merit. Roosevelt allowed Platt to pick appointees, but only from a list that he supplied. He refused to be Platt's puppet, while trying not to alienate him totally. Roosevelt's continued crackdown on corruption and his determination to pass civil legislation that benefited the workers, angered Platt's business supporters. It came to a head when Roosevelt pushed through a tax on public franchises, an attack at the very heart of Platt's financial supporters. They screamed for him to rein in his governor. Platt then found he had no way to do it. The senator watched as his hold on the party faded because he could not control Roosevelt. He had to get rid of the governor before Platt's political machine was completely destroyed, but he couldn't just throw the elected war hero out.

The death of vice president Garret Augustus Hobart gave Platt an idea. He consulted with Mark Hanna, the top Republican political boss in the nation, and suggested Roosevelt be nominated as vice presidential candidate for 1900. Roosevelt would then be prevented from running for a second term as governor. He would be out of Platt's hair, at least for a while. Hanna thought it a very bad idea, but Platt insisted. President McKinley remained stubbornly neutral.

It took some effort, but Platt finally managed to convince Teddy Roosevelt to consider the job, making it clear that reelection as governor would be very difficult, if not impossible, without Platt's support. But Senator Platt promised he would support him for vice president. For his part, Roosevelt knew the job to be little better than a four-year vacation. He wrote "it is not a stepping stone to anything except oblivion." However, convinced it was better than no job at all, he agreed to consider it.

Platt's machine worked so well no one could stop Roosevelt's nomination. Only Hanna withheld his support. When someone queried him, he retorted, "Why, everybody's going headlong for Roosevelt for Vice President. Don't any of you realize that there's only one life between that madman and the presidency?" Hanna however, finally relented and made the nomination unanimous. Roosevelt accepted, determined to make the best of things.

With war hero Roosevelt campaigning for him, McKinley won with a large margin. Platt celebrated and attended the inauguration primarily "to see Theodore Roosevelt take the veil." He had managed to send his difficult governor into political seclusion for the next four years—or so he thought.

On September 5, 1901, Leon Czolgosz shot President McKinley. A week later McKinley died, and Theodore Roosevelt became the twenty-sixth president of the United States. Instead of sending his wild maverick into political obscurity, Thomas Platt's machinations ended up putting him into the highest office in the land. As president, Teddy Roosevelt's reform efforts were much more effective.

A man had two sons, one went to sea and the other became
vice president, neither was heard from again.
—OLD POLITICAL ADAGE

43

||||||||||||||||||||||||||||||||||||||||||||||||||||||||||||||||||||||||||

A WHOLE LIST OF
FAILURES

Titanic

||||||||||||||||||||||||||||||||||||||||||||||||||||||||||||||||||||||||||

You cannot do a book on leadership failures without a section on the sinking of the *Titanic*. While the result was positive—improved safety standards—the event was unquestionably one of the most traumatic in naval history. It was hoped that the lessons learned in the sinking of the *Titanic* and the loss of so many lives would prevent any repeats of the same errors. It seems that was not the case. When the *Costa Concordia* capsized off Italy's west coast in January 2012, it didn't take long for people to compare the incident to the *Titanic*. The temptation was understandable. Each liner was a luxurious mammoth that sunk due to gross negligence on the part of the captain. The captain of the *Titanic* ignored warnings of icebergs in an attempt to cross the Atlantic in record time. The captain of the *Concordia* took his ship too close to the shore as a favor to the head waiter, who wanted to wave to his family. The similarities end there: The *Concordia* incident, though tragic, had casualties measured in the dozens, whereas over fifteen hundred of the *Titanic*'s passengers were claimed by the sea. The *Titanic* was not the deadliest maritime disaster in history (that would be the 1987 sinking of the MV *Doña Paz*, in which more than four thousand people died when the ferry crashed into an oil tanker), but it is by far the most famous. The story of the *Titanic* is so compelling for its senseless loss of life, the distasteful classism that governed the allocation of lifeboats, and the hubris of the ship's captain, Edward Smith. The combined failings of Smith, who ignored iceberg warnings, and the leadership of the White Star Line, which neglected to equip the ship with sufficient lifeboats, left an indelible mark on the Western imagination. If the experts had the sense to see through the unsinkability myth, the tragedy, and its subsequent effects on maritime safety regulations, would never have occurred.

When the *Titanic* was completed in 1912, she surpassed her sister, the *Olympic*, as the largest passenger steamship in the world. It was a triumph of engineering ingenuity, measuring 882 feet in length and possessing a massive steel hull and a pair of powerful steam engines. The ship was more than gargantuan. Its opulence was unrivaled: The ship featured a telephone system, a barbershop, a lending library, fine cuisine, and expensive furnishings. The amenities for first-class passengers included a gym, a pool, and a squash court. Acquiring a first-class ticket was quite pricey, and thus the passenger list included a number of wealthy individuals ranging from renowned businessmen to famous actors.

Yet one thing the ship lacked was lifeboats. The ship was equipped to hold sixty-four lifeboats, a fleet that would have accommodated more than four thousand people. The White Star Line decided that the *Titanic* should carry only twenty lifeboats. While this number exceeded the minimum dictated by the Board of Trade, the boats could hold only about a third of the ship's carrying capacity. The board's regulations had not been adjusted to accommodate the growing size of ships, as extra sailors would be required on board for the sole responsibility of managing the lifeboats in an emergency. White Star managing director J. Bruce

Ismay presumably desired to cut costs by not equipping the ship to full capacity. Doing so, he signed the death warrant of fifteen hundred passengers.

The *Titanic* departed for New York City on April 10, 1912, with 2,223 people on board. Four days into the voyage, on a calm, frigid night, Smith was navigating the ship about four hundred miles south of Newfoundland. Smith had been warned of icebergs via wireless over the past few days and had altered the route accordingly, taking the ship farther south to reduce the risk of collision. That night, the *Titanic*'s radio operators received a number of iceberg warnings but were too focused on relaying messages between passengers to pass the warnings on to the captain. Smith thought that any iceberg that was large enough to do serious damage would be noticed before it was too late, so he ordered the helmsman to maintain a brisk pace of twenty-one knots, just short of the ship's maximum speed. Just before midnight, lookouts spotted a large iceberg directly in front of the ship. They warned the bridge and the helmsman sharply turned left. It was too late. The iceberg raked the ship's starboard side for a mere ten seconds but managed to tear open six compartments. It did not take the crew long to realize that the ship was doomed. Distress rockets were fired, the radio operators frantically signaled for help, and the lifeboats were lowered. Tragically, the nearest ships had turned off their wireless for the night. Those that did respond to the call were too far away to reach the *Titanic* before it sunk.

At first, many of the passengers failed to realize the gravity of the situation and were thus hesitant to board the lifeboats. Many of the first lifeboats to be dispatched were not even filled to capacity. In the first lifeboat to be deployed, only twenty-eight of its sixty-five seats were filled. Under Smith's orders, women and children were given first access to the lifeboats. Men were denied entry to lifeboats even if they were about to be lowered at half-capacity. The result of this was that 74 percent of women and 52 percent of children were saved, compared to only 20 percent of men. There was also blatant classism in the allocation of spots, as first-class passengers were given preference. While 83 percent of first-class and 100 percent of second-class children were rescued, only a third of third-class children survived. There was a similar disparity among women, where a first-class ticket doubled your chances of survival relative to a third-class ticket.

The ship's design slowed down the sinking process, enabling all but two of the lifeboats to be deployed. Various components of the ship began collapsing in its final moments, crushing vulnerable passengers. The ship was completely swallowed by the ocean by 2:20 AM. Captain Smith solemnly went down with his ship, whereas Ismay, the White Star's ranking official on board, managed to secure a spot on one of the later boats. A few lifeboats searched for survivors, but most did not due to overcrowding concerns as well as fears that the suction caused by the ship's sinking might suck the lifeboats underwater. Just 711 of the passengers were still alive when the RMS *Carpathia* arrived four hours after receiving the distress call. She picked up the last lifeboat at 8:30 AM and swiftly made for New York. Officially, 1,514 people died that night, most claimed by hypothermia.

Upon arriving in New York, the survivors received immediate relief from New York–based aid organizations. The White Star Line became embroiled in controversy over its negligence. Ismay was particularly criticized for his role in the accident. A Senate investigation revealed that maritime safety regulations were hopelessly out of date. A number of safety improvements were implemented, including improved hull design, lifeboat requirements, improved life vests, radio communication laws, and mandatory safety drills. As is sadly often the case, it took a tragedy to demonstrate the need for change.

The *Titanic*'s legacy extends far beyond its effect on safety regulations, though. The mistakes of Smith, Ismay, and others have become immortalized in film and print. No captain wants to follow in Smith's footsteps. In fact, the captain of the *Concordia*, Francesco Schettino, specifically stated in 2010 that he never wanted to face a "*Titanic* scenario." As long as the *Titanic* remains the foremost example of maritime ineptitude, any negligent captain who sinks his ship will endure the same comparison. Unlike Smith, Schettino did not go down with his ship or even stay aboard until the passengers were off. So while Smith is a flawed hero who paid for his bad judgment, the captain of the 2012's *Titanic* scenario awaits trial.

44

EXTRAVAGANCE

Useless and Expensive

1916, GERMANY

The World War I Imperial German Navy's construction was begun too soon, and the German navy never had any chance to challenge the Royal Navy on the high seas. Kings, dictators, and emperors want to have the latest and most impressive weapons. Having them is a matter of national and personal pride. You can see this when an African dictator insists he have a few modern jet fighters in his air force when they serve no real purpose, or in Moscow's May Day parade that shows off the Russians' latest weaponry. There was no one prouder than Germany's Kaiser Wilhelm II. One of the things he was most jealous of was his English cousin's Royal Navy. In 1897, he approached Admiral Alfred von Tirpitz and made him secretary of the Reichsmarineamt, the naval office. The admiral was instructed to build a navy that could challenge and defeat that of Britain. At the time, it was decided that Germany would need a fleet of nineteen battleships, eight armored cruisers, and forty-two cruisers to challenge the British. Construction began in 1898. Unfortunately, the English were building more ships too, and by 1900 the English had decided to double the number of ships. Both sides were building as fast as their shipyards allowed, but with more shipyards and greater experience, the Royal Navy continued launching more vessels than Germany. So in 1906 the kaiser determined that another six battleships had to be built, for a total of forty-four. Those ships were never built.

In 1906 everything changed. The British launched the dreadnought, a radically more modern and powerful battleship. Within months, all the battleships Germany had built were obsolete. All of the ships that were under construction were going to become obsolete before being launched. Instead, they had to begin building their own dreadnought-class ships. Those ships were the only type that could stand up to the new British battleships. But Germany could build only two ships per year in the new design. The British were launching four or more each year. More important, the Imperial German Navy was soaking up a good percentage of military spending. This was money that could have otherwise been spent on artillery, machine guns, training, and research by the Imperial Army. No one in the kaiser's government took a step back to look at what they were doing: engaging in a navy-building competition with the world's largest and most experienced naval power.

When World War I started in 1914, the Imperial Army pushed the French and British back for weeks. The reinforcement of the Marne River line and the defensive battle that saved France there is rightfully called "the Miracle of the Marne." The Germans came very close to repeating their feat of 1871 and again capturing Paris. They were close enough that some of their largest cannons could actually fire on the city itself. If the resources that had gone into the German high seas fleet had instead been spent on the Imperial Army, would they have provided the army with just that little bit more? Certainly the tens of millions of marks spent on the ships would have made a dramatic difference. But the government and the kaiser wanted a modern ocean fleet, and once the war had started, the marks were spent.

To call the Germans' World War I Kaiserliche Marine a high seas fleet is a mistake. It was designed to fight in the open waters of the North Sea and the Atlantic. The amount of time that the German battle fleet in World War I actually spent on the open waters of the North Sea was measured in weeks, and not that many. This was because of the disparity in size between the German navy and the Royal Navy. A head-to-head battle was a fight Germany simply could not win. The difference in capital ships is easily shown by a list of the modern battleships that faced each other.

1914 Dreadnought-Class Battleships

GERMANY	BRITAIN
Friederich der Grosse	Iron Duke
Ostfriesland	Marlborough
Thurningen	St. Vincent
Helgoland	Collingwood
Oldenburg	Vanguard
Posen	Colossus
Rheinland	Hercules
Nassau	Neptune
Westfalen	Superb
Kaiser	King George V
Kaiserin	Ajax
Prinzregent Luitpold	Centurion
Koenig Albert	Audacious
	Monarch
	Conqueror
	Thunderer
	Orion
	Bellerophon
	Temeraire

This list does not include the French navy or the American navy.

The German navy began World War I outnumbered in modern battleships by almost two to one and was equally outnumbered in other classes with less than 100 actual warships to the 185 of Britain alone. The British also were more able to continue launching new ships throughout the war.

What happened after the one time both of these fleets met in battle reflects this disparity. The Germans had not planned for the Battle of Jutland to be an engagement between both full fleets. The outnumbered German fleet knew it could not win a head-to-head fight with the British high seas fleet. Their plan was to lure out parts of the British fleet, and then pounce on them with all of their own ships, gaining local superiority. Both side's battle cruisers were heavily gunned but lightly armored. The idea was for this class of warship to be able to outgun anything they could not run from and outrun any ships that were better armored. They sacrificed armor for speed, and so they were vulnerable.

But the aggressive Admiral Maximilian von Spee saw a way to even the odds. If the German battleships could engage just like the British battle cruisers had, a key part of the Royal Navy would be sunk, literally. It was with this in mind that he ordered his smaller battle cruiser squadron into the North Sea to lure out the English battle cruisers. His entire battleship fleet trailed below the horizon ready to spring the trap. The lighter German ships were to lure the larger British battle cruiser squadron into the guns of the German battleships.

It was April 24, 1916, when the Royal Navy heard that the German battle cruisers had sailed. As the Germans had planned, the English wanted a fight and could not resist the challenge. Admiral John Jellicoe did send the British battle cruisers after the enemy ships. But right behind the battle cruisers sailed the rest of the high seas fleet. When, on May 31, the two battle cruiser squadrons met, they fought a running battle in which the German ships fired more accurately. The British took serious damage, but they kept up their pursuit. At first von Spee's plan seemed to have worked. The British main fleet was about fifteen miles behind their battle cruisers and not in sight when the guns of the German dreadnoughts opened fire. Three British battle cruisers were lost. Then Jellicoe and the Royal Navy battleships appeared on the horizon. The outnumbered captains of the German navy found themselves in a battle they did not want and could not win. The fleets clashed twice. After the first exchange, Von Spee turned north to evade the bulk of the English force. This meant he was sailing away from Germany. Rather than follow, Jellicoe sailed south and placed his fleet between the German fleet and the safety of its ports. The two fleets fought again when the Germans broke past the English fleet and finally sailed back to their home ports.

Jutland was one of the greatest sea battles ever fought. But when the Battle of Jutland was over, absolutely nothing had changed. The British lost more ships (fourteen ships and more than six thousand lives) than the Germans (nine ships and more than twenty-five hundred lost), but the Royal Navy could endure their losses better. What the Battle of Jutland demonstrated was that the Kaiserliche Marine could never meet and defeat the much larger Royal Navy's high seas fleet. The German fleet never again sailed into the North Sea. Tens of thousands of sailors and tens of millions of German marks' worth of costly weapon systems sat in port, useless for the rest of the war. When Imperial Germany was forced to surrender in 1918, in a final insult, the German fleet was ordered by the Treaty of Versailles to be delivered by its own officers to the English at Scapa Flow. Many of the German commanders scuttled their ships in protest, but the boats were eventually raised.

From the beginning, Imperial Germany spent money and wasted manpower on a navy that could never defeat that of the British. There was never a mission that a fleet half the size of the Royal Navy could accomplish that could justify its immense cost. Had those resources, effectively wasted on the Kaiserliche Marine, been better spent, the outcome of World War I might have been very different.

THE VERY WRONG THING TO SAY

Zimmermann Telegram

1917, MEXICO

IIIIIIIIIIIIIIIIIIIIIIIIIIIIIIIIIIIIIIIIIIIIIIIIIIIIIIIIIIIIIIIIIIIIIIIIIII

I t is a rare situation when a single blunder on the battlefield results in the loss of a war; rarer still are cases in which a single political blunder has that effect. That may have been the case, however, with the Zimmermann Telegram. In 1917, Germany had been fighting with France and Great Britain for several years in the bloodiest war the world had ever seen. Dubbed the Great War at its conclusion, World War I left millions dead in the terrible trenches that gouged France's countryside. The war had dragged on far longer than anyone had anticipated, and the Allies were feeling the fatigue of extended bloodshed. The United States had pursued a fairly isolationist policy during the war, seeking to avoid using its considerable might to support either side. Then it was revealed that German State Secretary Arthur Zimmermann had approached Mexico with a proposal to ally against the United States. Around the same time, German submarines sunk a passenger ship with a large loss of American lives. The United States subsequently entered the war on the side of Britain and France.

Germany paid the price for this diplomatic blunder in lives and defeat.

Preceding the United States' entry in the war, Allied prospects seemed grim. Russia, an instrumental ally at the start of the war, was suffering the Communist revolution. As a result, Germany could pull large numbers of soldiers to the western front. England and France had basically exhausted their reserves and had no new manpower to counter the German arrivals. The nature of trench warfare and the advent of several technological gains in artillery and machine guns had dramatically increased casualties. Both sides had lost countless soldiers in the combat, and their forces were becoming depleted. France was facing mutinies in its ranks and desertion was a significant problem. It was unclear which side would emerge victorious, but the Allies knew that their chances would be greatly enhanced were the United States to enter the war. The United States had maintained a policy of hesitant support for the Allies throughout the war. It engaged in regular munitions deliveries to Britain and tacitly supported the British blockade of Germany. However, Woodrow Wilson had been reelected principally on a platform of staying out of the war. His campaign slogan in 1916 was "He Kept Us Out of War." The war in Europe just was not a personal thing to the average American.

In this area, Germany sowed the seeds of its own demise. Tensions between Germany and the United States first escalated as a consequence of Germany's policy of unrestricted submarine warfare. Germany warned the United States that American merchant ships in war zones would not be spared. Germany understandably desired to short-circuit American shipments to Great Britain, but its policy resulted in heavy anti-German sentiment among the American public. One high-profile example involved the RMS *Lusitania*, a luxury ocean liner that was torpedoed eleven miles off the coast of Ireland. Though it was a British ship, enough Americans were on board to greatly dismay Wilson and the American public. Despite this, President Wilson did not enter the conflict, declaring, "There is such a thing as a man being too proud to fight. There is such a thing as a nation being so right that it does not need to convince others by force that it is right." Several other liners were sunk in subsequent months with less significant American casualties. For fear of American entry into the war, Germany temporarily reversed its policy and established a rule of firing only on ships that were unequivocally British. Wilson and the American public were placated, albeit briefly.

Eventually, however, Germany was forced to resume its policy of unrestricted submarine warfare. The strategic advantage of disrupting the British blockade that was crippling the German economy and of preventing Britain from being resupplied was too attractive to German decision makers to avoid resumption. Fearing that this act would inevitably draw the United States into war, Zimmermann calculated that he should prepare for this eventuality. He did so by offering Mexico financial assistance and a formal alliance if it were to attack the United States; Germany was counting on Mexico's desire to reclaim lost areas such as Texas and California, whose sale had been forced by the United States.

The message was dispatched on January 16, 1917, to the German ambassador in Washington, Johann von Bernstorff. Per Zimmermann's requests, Bernstorff was to then forward the telegram to the German ambassador to Mexico, Heinrich von Eckardt. He would offer the proposal to the Mexican president. To add insult to injury, Germany sent the telegram along American telegraph routes, as they were the only secure ones because Britain had cut German cables in the Atlantic and shut down German stations in neutral areas. Zimmermann calculated that the United States would not decipher the message and Great Britain would not have the gall to intercept a message on an American route for fear of reprisal. He calculated incorrectly.

As soon as the telegram was sent, British code breakers in Room 40 at the admiralty intercepted it. The British had seized a codebook in a previous battle and swiftly decoded the message. Britain was faced with a dilemma, however. While it was tempting to reveal the telegram to the American public, doing so would reveal to the United States that Britain had been monitoring its telegrams. Exposing the message would also demonstrate to Germany that Britain was capable of decoding its messages. Britain elected to bribe a telegraph company employee in Mexico to purchase the original telegraph. This employee stated officially that he had intercepted the message with the assistance of a British mole in the German embassy in Mexico. The plan succeeded: America was not upset that Britain had been monitoring its telegraph communication and Germany went on a witch hunt in Mexico to find the phantom spy.

Meanwhile, American popular sentiment roared against Germany. Many initially doubted the authenticity of the document and believed it to be a forgery. However in a diplomatic blunder that was practically on a level of its own, Zimmermann personally admitted to the legitimacy of the telegram. Britain then turned over the original cipher text to important U.S. officials. Zimmermann resigned from his position as German state secretary.

An America that had been tilting toward supporting the Allies was now ready to commit. It was not long before Wilson called on the American public and Congress to declare war on Germany. Thousands of American troops were shipped overseas daily. The fresh and enthusiastic Americans arrived in the nick of time. In Germany, General Erich Ludendorff had mounted a substantial offensive hoping to force a peace before the U.S. Army was a factor. While it failed, the strain on both sides pushed Germany to the edge of collapse. There had already been mutinies among the weary French units. American troops revitalized the depleted Allied forces and helped mount the first really successful Allied offensive. Germany was pushed back and eventually surrendered.

An ironic element to the entire situation is that Mexico did not even desire an alliance with Germany. Germany had sought the strategic benefit of distracting the United States on its southern border while it pushed against France. Mexico determined, however, that the likelihood of a successful offensive against the United States was slim. Though Mexico received a share of the American public's outrage, it never had any realistic designs against the United States. Mexico formally declined Germany's overture shortly after the United States declared war against Germany.

The Zimmermann Telegram was perhaps the single most important factor in compelling American involvement in World War I. Germany might have lost regardless of American involvement, but the United States' entry certainly hastened its defeat. Had the United States not been involved and Germany and the Allies reached a ceasefire or some less punitive agreement (the Treaty of Versailles was, after all, a mistake in its own right), World War II might never have happened. Or it might have started years earlier. But by angering the American public, Arthur Zimmermann's political mistake was war-changing.

46

PUNISH BUT NOT PREVENT

Treaty of Versailles

1918, FRANCE

I n the wake of World War I, the leaders of the Allied forces would have done well to heed the wisdom of one Abraham Lincoln: "Am I not destroying my enemies when I make friends of them?" Lincoln believed that punishing Southerners after the Civil War would merely alienate them and sow the seeds of future conflict. The victors of the Great War should have adopted a similar attitude toward Germany. Instead, they installed punitive measures that bred resentment in the German public. French Premier Georges Clémenceau argued that Germany should be militarily and economically crippled as punishment for its belligerence. U.S. President Woodrow Wilson and British Prime Minister David Lloyd George acceded to his demands. Their problem was that Clémenceau's plan worked. Germany's economy was battered by the reparations the nation was forced to pay and suffered from runaway inflation. Germany was humiliated by the terms of the treaty. Their troops had still been on French soil when the kaiser's government surrendered. Just how far the German army was stretched and how low their supplies had gotten were not generally known even after the war. Rumors immediately arose that they had lost because of some sort of betrayal. This was a myth the Nazis would use to full advantage. The Treaty of Versailles treated Germany as if it had been conquered and occupied. To a people who had suddenly been told they had lost the war, this was just too much to accept. This resentment would simmer within the German public until the onset of World War II.

France and Germany had a rocky history. Fifty years earlier, in 1871, Germany had crushed France during the Franco-Prussian War. German Chancellor Otto von Bismarck forced France to pay reparations despite the fact that Bismarck had, more or less, artificially engineered the conflict to energize German nationalism. Germany also annexed the valuable Alsace-Lorraine region, along with its thriving mining industry. France remained sore over the conflict in the ensuing decades. When World War I erupted, their rivalry was renewed. This time the war lasted four years rather than five months. There were heavy casualties for the British, Germans, and French. The battle was fought on French soil. The French countryside was ravaged by German artillery and trench warfare. France incurred more casualties than any other country apart from Germany and Russia. It had lost a generation of young men and a decade of economic growth, and felt that Germany was to blame.

In light of this, it is not surprising that Clémenceau felt so vindictive. Like any politician, he was beholden to the will of the public. He would face electoral repercussions if he appeared too soft on Germany. Clémenceau wanted France to be the political and economic leader of the European mainland, and he believed that Germany was France's primary obstacle. If he could weaken Germany, he would pave the way for undisputed French dominance on the Continent. The English prime minister was leery of steep reparations, but France and Britain had endured too much together to break rank now. Wilson was also easy to convince; all Clémenceau had to do was condition his approval of the League of Nations on Wilson acceding to his demands. While Clémenceau did not get everything he wanted (indeed, many French observers harshly criticized Clémenceau for not pushing the envelope further), he did manage to establish a number of provisions constraining Germany's military and economy.

In its final form, the Treaty of Versailles was heavily flawed. It contained few provisions for preventing future aggression except by Germany. Its main way of dealing with conflict was the feeble League of Nations, and the United States never even joined that organization. The treaty harshly punished Germany in many ways. First, it put a number of restrictions on Germany's military. Germany was forced to substantially downsize its army and navy; it was also banned from producing tanks, submarines, and warplanes. The Rhineland, an area between Germany and France, became a demilitarized zone to provide a buffer along the entire border with France. This was also one of the major manufacturing regions in Germany, now effectively a defenseless hostage to the French army. Germany was not allowed to move any troops into the region, but the Allied forces were allowed, by Versailles, to maintain an army inside Germany on the west bank of the Rhine.

Germany also received many economic penalties. The Alsace-Lorraine region was restored to France. In addition, France and Britain divvied up Germany's colonies between them. Germany was deprived of a number of economically valuable locations in an effort to undermine its industries. The treaty also imposed hefty reparations on Germany. The bill was astronomical, amounting to about $31.4 billion (equivalent to $385 billion in 2012). The sum was criticized heavily by the era's most famous economist, John Maynard Keynes. Keynes argued that Germany would not be capable of paying the amount and that the demand would destabilize the nation. He called it "one of the most serious acts of political unwisdom for which our statesmen have ever been responsible." His predictions stood the test of time. Germany did not fully repay the debt until 2010. In comparison, the French reparations to Prussia in 1870 took only three years to pay. Keynes's predictions of instability also proved to be prophetic.

Growth stagnated during the 1920s as Germany struggled with its massive debt and inflation. This was the era of the Weimar republic where the story was told that it took so many marks to buy a loaf of bread that one man needed two baskets full of bills to shop. Tiring, the German forgot one of the baskets of money just outside a store while he rushed in. When he went back out, the money was in a pile but the basket had been stolen. The penalized and battered German economy was too fragile to withstand the impact of the Great Depression. Adversity breeds extremity, and it was from this turmoil that the Nazi Party was born.

France justified this harsh punishment via Article 231 of the Treaty of Versailles. This article was called the War Guilt Clause. It assigned 100 percent of the blame for the onset of the war to Germany and stipulated that the central powers were accountable for all damages to the Allies. This was an affront to the German people; German Foreign Minister Ulrich Graf von Brockdorff-Rantzau responded by saying: "You demand from us to confess we were the only guilty party of war; such a confession in my mouth would be a lie." Germany was correct, but it didn't matter. As the defeated party, they were subject to the draconian terms of the Allies.

The treaty was unhappily approved by the German National Assembly in June 1919. Conservatives in Germany sharply criticized what they viewed as willful capitulation. They regarded left-leaning signatories as traitors. The German public felt humiliated that their leaders had been trammeled by, of all people, the French. A burning resentment festered over the next few decades. French Field Marshal Ferdinand Foch put it best: "This is not a peace. This is an armistice for twenty years." Twenty years later, Hitler's army invaded Poland to begin World War II.

Over the next few decades, the Treaty of Versailles proved almost useless. The League of Nations, for which American President Woodrow Wilson traded his support of the harsh terms, proved an abysmal failure. The restrictions on German militarization were circumvented via underhanded deals with fellow pariah nation Russia. Hitler would eventually flout the terms of the treaty with an aggressive remilitarization program to the cheers of the German public. Clémenceau's punitive measures proved to be ineffective at containing German military and economic growth. They merely incensed the German public, stoked German nationalism, and paved the way for extremist leaders like Hitler to assume power. France should have sought to make an ally of Germany; instead, it made an enemy who took revenge in 1939.

||||||||||||||||||||||||||||||||||||||||||||||||||||||||||||||||||||||||||

47

FORM OVER SUBSTANCE

Failure of the League of Nations

||||||||||||||||||||||||||||||||||||||||||||||||||||||||||||||||||||||||||

Woodrow Wilson was one of the most idealistic men to ever become president. He had spent most of his life as a professor or college president. After helping to win World War I, Wilson believed that he was in a position to forge a new world order. He envisioned a world without colonialism, made up solely of democracies, where disputes, both regional and global, could be settled by international bodies devoted to maintaining the peace. Yet Wilson had to deal with obstinate forces at both home and abroad, and he was ultimately unable to actually secure any of his goals.

After World War I Wilson became obsessed with the idea of establishing what he called the League of Nations, which would become the steward of the harmonious new world. Wilson's mistake was twofold. In dealing with Britain, and especially France, Wilson made far too many concessions to get the League of Nations approved. His expressed opinion was that the league could rectify any problems. The result was the flawed Treaty of Versailles, which proved more of an armistice than a peace. Having conceded too much, the American president then did the opposite. When he returned from the United States, Wilson showed a rigid unwillingness to compromise with Republicans.

In the wake of World War I, the United States was more powerful and well respected than it had been at any point in its relatively short history. American entry into the war had helped turn the tide against Germany. Wilson was regarded by many Europeans as their savior. He was admired and respected for his Fourteen Points, a collection of ways Wilson wished to tweak the world. They ranged from general prescriptions (no secret treaties) to specific (Polish independence) and from economic (greater international trade) to political (broad decolonization); it was an idealistic, liberal appeal to combat injustice and better the planet. The fourteenth point was Wilson's favorite, calling for the formation of a general assembly of nations that would guarantee political independence and territorial integrity for all nations. This assembly was to be called the League of Nations. It was Wilson's greatest aspiration to see a functioning league in his lifetime.

Wilson had a harder time selling the league to the other parties involved in the peace negotiations. The most important men he had to convince were British Prime Minister David Lloyd George and French Premier Georges Clémenceau. Lloyd George and Clémenceau had a very different perspective on how the peace should proceed. Britain and France suffered far more from the war than did the United States. France was particularly devastated, as it was the French countryside that had been ravaged by trench warfare. Having paid for the war with blood and money alike, France and Britain felt rather vindictive toward Germany. They desired harsh punitive measures toward Germany that would curtail its ability to remilitarize.

This was not the only place where their views differed, however. France and Britain both held significant colonial possessions and thus were wary of endorsing Wilson's message of self-determination for all. If they agreed to the principle that all people should be able to govern themselves, they would be forced to relinquish valuable colonial possessions in Africa, Asia, and elsewhere. As the winners of the war, neither country felt particularly inclined to give land away.

Wilson should have been the one demanding concessions, not granting them. There is nothing wrong with being willing to compromise, but Wilson hyperfocused on securing the League of Nations at the expense of his other goals. He allowed France and Britain to lay the blame for the war completely at the feet of Germany. He failed to dissuade France and Britain from imposing harsh sanctions on Germany. He also was unable to convince them to decolonize; in fact, France and Britain acquired more territory by partitioning up Germany's colonial possessions.

Clémenceau and Lloyd George tried to delay the issue of establishing the league. They told Wilson that they ought to establish the league in a separate measure, so as not to delay the peace treaty. Wilson was insistent, though, for he feared that the league would never get approved without being attached to the treaty. Because Wilson had been so accommodating on everything else, Lloyd George and Clémenceau humored him. They signed on as supporters of the league. Wilson was delighted despite failing on almost every front, for in his eyes, he had won the greatest battle of all.

Unfortunately for Wilson, securing the league as part of the Treaty of Versailles was only half the battle; in fact, it was the easier half. Wilson's treaty still required Senate approval. Many of the senators were skeptical of the League of Nations. There were many isolationist politicians who felt uncomfortable allowing the United States to be beholden to the rules of an international organization. Senators were particularly nervous about Article X, which opponents argued would obligate America to use military action whenever the league saw fit. For these "irreconcilables," no compromise could earn their vote. Another faction sided with Wilson, supporting the treaty without any modifications. A third group of Republicans, led by Senator Henry Lodge, supported the treaty if it were altered. Wilson was able to convince a majority to his view but not enough to secure the two-thirds vote required to ratify a treaty.

Instead of compromising, Wilson tried to sell the treaty to the American public. He traveled across the United States in an attempt to rally support for his cause. During his tour, he experienced a series of debilitating strokes and was forced to return to Washington. Wilson changed after his stroke. Physically, he was an invalid, constrained to his bed in the White House. Yet his personality also was altered. He was more paranoid and refused to interact with the press. And although Wilson had been willing to compromise with Clémenceau and Lloyd George extensively in Europe, he was completely intractable at home. Lodge formed a coalition with pro-treaty Democrats and almost secured ratification of an amended treaty, but Wilson marshaled enough Democrats to torpedo the attempt. Wilson was tired of watering down his principles; his unwillingness to compromise meant he never saw his dream realized.

The United States did not join the league despite being responsible for its creation. The league was weakened by not including one of the world's premier powers. It was already a toothless institution, but without the United States, it was nearly useless. Wilson sacrificed so much on the league's behalf, hoping it would usher in global peace. During its short existence, the league had no major successes. It was a complete failure in preventing World War II; in fact, the league proved most useful as an example of what *not* to do when creating an international institution.

Wilson was a man of high principles, but he was not able to see those principles realized. It is hard to completely blame Wilson, because his behavior toward the Senate might have been different had he not been mentally compromised by the strokes. Yet the treaty was flawed from the start because Wilson made too many concessions to his allies. His league might have been successful if the United States were involved. Wilson was more professor than politician, better suited for lectures back at Princeton than the knock-down, drag-out battles in Congress. Had he been more willing to compromise with Lodge or less willing to compromise with Clémenceau and Lloyd George, the postwar era may have looked very different, and the next war might not have been fought at all.

||||||||||||||||||||||||||||||||||||||||||||||||||||||||||||||||||||||||||

48

FORCED SOCIAL CHANGE

Prohibition: The Failed Experiment

1919, UNITED STATES

||||||||||||||||||||||||||||||||||||||||||||||||||||||||||||||||||||||||||

When Senator Morris Sheppard retired, no one doubted that he was a man of principle. He had been an ardent supporter of suffrage for women and for limitations on child labor. His legacy was marred, however, by his support for one of the United States' most well-meaning failures: Prohibition of alcohol. Dubbed the "Noble Experiment," Prohibition sought to ameliorate many of society's ills. Instead the amendment ended up making problems much worse and creating new problems.

Prohibition was an anti-alcohol movement that gained steam throughout the nineteenth century and became a staple of the twentieth-century Progressive movement. By 1900, half of the states were "dry," meaning they did not serve alcohol. The problem with such haphazard prohibition was that denizens of dry states could easily acquire alcohol from wet states. This meant that the proponents of Prohibition desired national regulations. They started with the Interstate Liquor Act of 1913, which criminalized even personal interstate liquor transactions.

Though Prohibition was not a big-ticket item during the 1916 election between Woodrow Wilson and Charles Hughes, congressional leaders were more sympathetic to the cause. Sheppard proposed a Senate resolution in favor of a constitutional amendment to ban selling and drinking alcoholic beverages across the United States. In 1917, this desire resulted in a proposed amendment to ban the sale and manufacture of alcohol throughout the United States. It was a divisive issue that was debated for two years. The anti-alcohol movement earned support from an array of groups, including the Women's Christian Temperance Union and the Ku Klux Klan. Its opponents included immigrant groups and Catholics. This was not a partisan issue. The Prohibition amendment had supporters and detractors among both Democrats and Republicans.

Having passed the Congress, the Eighteenth Amendment was narrowly ratified on January 29, 1919. It banned all drinks with an alcohol content greater than 40 percent. It was supplemented by the Volstead Act in October, which passed Congress over Wilson's veto. It prohibited the sale and manufacture of all drinks with an alcohol content more than 0.5 percent. Due to the small amount of alcohol triggering the limit, this was a de facto ban on all alcohol. Even the lightest beer was illegal.

Proponents of the amendment had grandiose expectations for post-Prohibition America. The Reverend Billy Sunday summed up his expectations as such: "The reign of tears is over. The slums will soon be a memory. We will turn our prisons into factories and our jails into storehouses and corncribs. Men will walk upright now, women will smile and children will laugh. Hell will be forever for rent." Sunday and Sheppard were to be disappointed, however. Prohibition failed at meaningfully reducing alcohol consumption; instead, its legacy was increased crime and corruption.

When unfair laws force good men to perform criminal acts, the distinction between citizen and criminal is blurred. And where there is no agreement that something illegal is wrong, the laws will be broken and those who break the laws will prosper.

Prohibition was active from 1920 to 1933. During that era, the United States experienced a dramatic increase in violence and organized crime. Prohibition created a lucrative black market that appealed to men like Al Capone. The Mafia expanded in influence and size during Prohibition. Robbery and homicide rates shot up, the latter by 78 percent. Speakeasies, illegal distributors of alcohol that were often run by crime syndicates, cropped up in most major cities. Violent crime peaked in 1933, but has declined annually since Prohibition was repealed. Before Prohibition, crime had been a local problem. By 1933 it was organized on a national level.

Prohibition did manage to put a small dent in alcohol consumption early on, but consumption ticked back up to above pre-Prohibition levels within a few years. Drunk driving arrests actually increased by 81 percent during Prohibition. Moreover, alcohol began to be adulterated by toxins due to lack of regulation. Beverages were, on average, 50 percent more powerful during Prohibition; substances like moonshine were brewed, with hazardous consequences for the health of their drinkers. The result was that the rate of alcohol poisoning nearly quadrupled during Prohibition. Moreover, drinkers were younger: The average age of individuals dying from alcoholism fell by six months during Prohibition. Use of marijuana, opium, and cocaine also increased because they were viewed as substitutes for alcohol.

Public opinion turned against Prohibition thanks to events like the Saint Valentine's Day Massacre: the 1929 murder of seven mob associates in Chicago. City dwellers were tired of spending exorbitant sums on law enforcement as well as dealing with the corruption of police and politicians. The crime lords held a stranglehold on city life. Eventually, the thrust of the opposition was made up of people who witnessed Prohibition's costs on a daily basis. Despite congressman and leading Prohibitionist Morris Sheppard's assertion that "there is as much chance of repealing the Eighteenth Amendment as there is for a humming-bird to fly to the planet Mars with the Washington Monument tied to its tail," support for repeal steadily increased until Franklin D. Roosevelt felt compelled to ease restrictions. Quipping, "I think this would be a good time for a beer," Roosevelt allowed the brewing of certain beers and light wines. A full-fledged repeal occurred in December 1933. States were still permitted to prohibit alcohol, and many chose to. Crime syndicates remained, though they were weakened by the repeal. Drug use also persisted. Unfortunately, the negative consequences of Prohibition could not be completely eradicated by its repeal.

The Noble Experiment was a self-inflicted wound. The federal government sought to expunge a vice but underestimated its significance in American society. By criminalizing the common man, crime became common; it was a lesson that modern Prohibitionists sometimes forget.

DOUBLE-DEALING

Britain's Promises

This is the story of two promises, neither of which should have been made. Without these two mistakes, the Middle East would be a very different and perhaps much better place today. But in a time of war, long-term thinking is often sacrificed to short-term needs. In this case, the British made that mistake twice, and in contradictory ways, and today two very different peoples are paying the price for those mistakes.

When examining the Israeli-Palestinian conflict of today, it's easy to assume that Jews and Muslims have been warring in the Middle East for hundreds of years. In actuality, the conflict over Palestine is only about a century old. Its roots lie more in British imperialism than in historical animosity. Britain sought to gain any advantage it could during World War I. In the process, it promised several groups the same prize: the Holy Land, Palestine, a region coveted by Jews and Arabs alike. Britain tried to balance Zionism for the Jews and self-determination for native Arabs, but to no avail. The bloodshed of the last century thus began with Britain, yet its end lies nowhere in sight. The leaders of Britain should have formulated a coherent strategy rather than committing themselves to contradictory positions.

During World War I, the Ottoman Empire, which had ruled the Middle East for centuries, allied with the central powers. Britain was at war with Germany and desired a means of undermining its enemy. The Arabs were already discontented with Ottoman rule, and it took little convincing by the British for them to revolt. In a series of letters between Sir Henry McMahon, the British high commissioner in Egypt, and Hussein bin Ali, the sharif of Mecca, McMahon exhorted Hussein to rise up against the empire. In 1915, McMahon promised Hussein an independent Arab state ruled by his own Hashemite family, so long as Hussein led a revolt and supported Britain in the war. Hussein was true to his word. With the help of T. E. Lawrence, a British agent who would be immortalized in the film *Lawrence of Arabia*, Hussein's son Faisal successfully led an insurgency against the Ottomans.

Meanwhile, there was growing sympathy in Britain for a political movement called Zionism which sought to establish a sovereign Jewish state. The movement was born near the end of the nineteenth century in response to rising anti-Semitism in Europe. Growing pressure from leading Zionist Chaim Weizmann compelled British Foreign Secretary Arthur Balfour to issue the Balfour Declaration of 1917, which stated Britain's hope to create a national home in Palestine for the Jewish people without prejudicing the rights of non-Jews already in the region. Balfour's decision was largely strategic. President Woodrow Wilson had two Zionist advisers, and Balfour hoped that the declaration would strengthen a tentative alliance. Balfour also hoped that Russian leaders of Jewish descent, like Leon Trotsky, would feel compelled to stay in the war. Russia was in the middle of a revolution and did stop fighting the kaiser.

Unbeknownst to the Arabs or the Jews, the British and the French had secretly agreed to divide Arab territories into British and French spheres of influence after the war in what was called the Sykes-Picot Agreement of 1916. Then Hussein heard about

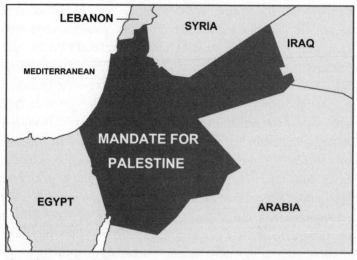

The Palestine Mandate

this agreement. Britain reassured him that it was not a formal treaty and that they would uphold their agreement. In response to the Balfour Declaration, Hussein called on Arabs in Palestine to welcome the Jews and cooperate with them. Hussein was unaware that Britain intended to give the Jews an independent state separate from the entity agreed on with McMahon. When the Ottomans were defeated, Prime Minister David Lloyd George insisted that the McMahon-Hussein correspondence was a treaty obligation and that France could not occupy the territories in question. France obtained a mandate over Syria, whereas Britain gained control over the area that is now Israel, the West Bank, the Gaza Strip, and Jordan. At the ensuing peace accords, Zionists and Arabs signed the Faisal-Weizmann Agreement, which tentatively outlined cooperation between the two groups.

In 1921, Britain divided its mandate into two regions. East of the Jordan River was the emirate of Transjordan, ruled by the Hashemite family. West of the region became the Palestine Mandate. This angered Arabs, as they had not expected the region to be splintered into two parts. McMahon insisted that he had never mentioned Palestine and that the expectation was based on miscommunication. While McMahon was correct that Palestine was not specifically mentioned in the correspondence, the proposed boundaries would have included the region. His wording was ambiguous at times, but Britain's interpretation of the agreement had little basis in the earlier discussions. Some, like Balfour, freely admitted that Britain had made contradicting pledges. In Balfour's own words, "Zionism, be it right or wrong, good or bad, is rooted in age-long traditions, in present needs, and future hopes, of far profounder import than the desire and prejudices of the 700,000 Arabs who now inhabit that ancient land." In essence, Balfour considered the needs of European Jews to be more important than those of indigenous Arabs. Balfour believed fervently in the Zionist cause, and his view was shared by the four great postwar powers, Britain, France, Italy, and the United States.

Many Arabs professed sympathy for persecuted Jews, but they believed that Britain intended to create a ruling Jewish class that lorded over the Arab population. This concern was aggravated by the influx of Jewish immigration from Europe. The proportion of Jews in Palestine would rise from one sixth to one third over the following couple of decades. Riots occurred in the early 1920s and again in 1929 over religious disagreements, resulting in several hundred deaths and intensifying the conflict. After Hitler's rise to power, European immigration to Palestine dramatically increased. As Jews flooded into Palestine, they purchased large parcels of land from absentee landlords, causing Arab tenant farmers to be replaced with Jewish settlers. In 1936, the Supreme Muslim Council revolted in Palestine, rioting and murdering Jews. At first the rebels were placated with political concessions. When violence resumed, it was suppressed by the British army.

Britain decided that it needed to reevaluate its governing strategy. It released a new policy paper that established a quota on Jewish immigration and restricted the ability of Jews to purchase land. It was horrible timing for such a move, as it blocked many

Jews from fleeing Europe during World War II. The Zionists regarded this as betrayal. The restrictions would stay in place until after the war, at which point the United Nations, horrified by the Holocaust and feeling an obligation to European Jews, would establish Israel.

Israel has stood ever since as a pocket of Western influence in the Middle East, surrounded by hostile Arab nations. Despite its ramifications, creating Israel was not the mistake. The mistake lay in the hands of Balfour, McMahon, and their superiors, who cobbled together an incoherent, contradictory array of promises in a shortsighted attempt to sway the war. The Arabs were content to welcome persecuted Jews. They merely feared becoming a minority. Britain stoked that fear with its apparent Zionist favoritism. By making promises they simply couldn't keep, Balfour, McMahon, and the British government sowed seeds of discontent that have grown into the perpetual conflict of today.

51

POORLY CHOSEN
FRIENDS

With Friends Like
These . . .

Warren Gamaliel Harding is often considered one of the worst presidents of all time. His administration was rife with scandals that were unequaled in U.S. political history until Watergate in 1972. Yet Harding's fatal flaw was not that he was inept, rather that he was loyal—and possibly indebted—to the wrong friends.

The president loved poker. He did not particularly like administrating or working with details. Elected in 1920, Warren Harding immediately appointed his friends and poker buddies to powerful government positions. For the most part, the appointments had little to do with the welfare of the country. Harry Daugherty, the man responsible for guiding Harding's political rise, was rewarded by becoming attorney general. He also had a side business selling illegal alcohol. Thomas Miller, chairman of the Office of Alien Property, accepted bribes. Charles Forbes, the head of the Bureau of Veteran's Affairs, was an embezzler. Edwin Denby, secretary of the navy, participated in cronyism. However, perhaps the most damaging of Harding's appointments was that of Albert Fall as secretary of the interior.

Though charged with protecting the country's public lands and resources, Fall had no interest in conservation. He had spent most of his law career representing mining and timber interests and held mining investments. Harding apparently did not realize it at the time, but Fall's appointment was the equivalent of hiring the fox to protect the hen house. Once in office, Fall attempted to open Alaska's reserves to commercial oil, coal, and timber mining, only to be stopped by conservationists. Then he tried to gain control of the national forests by transferring control of the forests and the Forestry Service to the Department of the Interior. Conservationists managed to block him again, with the help of progressives in Congress. Not one to give up, he focused on the rich oil fields of Elk Hills and Buena Vista in California, and the vast Teapot Dome oil field in Wyoming. He knew oilmen who would do anything for access to such rich deposits. Unfortunately, all three sites had been set aside as part of the Naval Reserve, under the control of Secretary of the Navy Denby. However, Denby was part of Harding's inner circle, the Ohio Gang, as they were later called.

Fall managed to convince his friend Denby that the Interior Department could do a far better job of managing the reserves than could the navy. If he controlled the oil fields, he would make certain the navy received a store of refined oil rather than leaving the profits to Congress or, worse, leaving the oil underground, where it would benefit no one. They both convinced President Harding to transfer authority for the reserves to Fall because Fall had so much more experience with land management. Harding trusted both men, so in 1921 he signed Executive Order 3474, transferring the oil fields to the Department of the Interior.

Once he had control, Fall immediately arranged secret leases for the oil fields. One set of lease agreements gave his old prospecting pal Edward Doheny, of the Pan-American Petroleum and Transport Company, access to the Elk Hills and Buena Vista reserves in California. In exchange, Doheny would build storage tanks for the navy at Pearl Harbor, a refinery in California, and a pipeline from the reserves to the refinery. Of course, Pan-American Petroleum gained exclusive rights to exploit approximately thirty thousand acres of oil lands. Doheny himself estimated the profit potential to be at least $100,000,000.

On February 3, 1922, Fall negotiated the lease of the vast Teapot Dome reserve in Wyoming, considered the richest of all, to Harry Sinclair of the Mammoth Oil Company. The lease also required Sinclair to pay the navy in refined fuel and storage rather than cash because any cash would have to go to the U.S. Treasury. Once the money was there, the navy would be at the mercy of congressional appropriations to get any of it back. On April 7, Secretary of the Navy Denby and Harry Sinclair secretly signed a lease for all of Teapot Dome, which Fall then locked in his desk drawer.

For his part, Fall later claimed he was just doing his job, making sure the navy didn't lose its oil reserves by having them drained off by outside wells. He claimed that he never took bribes or kickbacks; he was just given several, er, loans. Yet curiously, during the lease negotiations, Edward Doheny had his son pull $100,000 out of his account, wrap the cash in paper, put it all inside a black bag, and deliver it to Fall's apartment in the dark of night. Of course, it was a loan, albeit interest free. Yet the only paperwork that ever surfaced to prove it had the signature portion torn off. In December 1921, while entertaining Sinclair at his ranch in New Mexico, Fall discussed the possibility of Mammoth Oil leasing some of the Teapot Dome lands. The men also discussed Fall's need for additional cattle on his ranch. Shortly after Sinclair returned home, he sent Fall six heifers, a yearling bull, two six-month-old boars, four sows, and a fine horse for his foreman. Later, Sinclair gave Fall's son-in-law $233,000 in Liberty Bonds. After Congress started asking questions, the son-in-law gave Sinclair a check for $1,100 to pay for the previously gifted livestock, but during the same meeting he requested and received a $36,000 cash loan for Fall. Fall eventually received over $400,000 in gifts and loans from the oilmen.

However, the secret leases did not stay secret for long. Oilmen in Wyoming and Colorado discovered they had been shut out of Teapot Dome. They started asking questions. Fall's neighbors in New Mexico could not help but notice the sudden increase in the size of Fall's ranch and the drastic improvement in his lifestyle. On April 14, 1922, the *Wall Street Journal* broke the story, announcing that Teapot Dome had been leased to Harry Sinclair's company Sinclair Oil.

Congress started asking their own questions, demanding to know how navy reserves could be leased without bids or congressional approval. Were these actions part of administration policy? President Harding stood behind his poker buddies, Fall and Denby. He stated that "the policy which has been adopted by the Secretary of the Navy and the Secretary of the Interior in dealing with these matters was submitted to me prior to the adoption thereof, and the policy decided upon and the subsequent acts have at all times had my entire approval."

With President Harding vouching for the deal, or what little he actually knew of it, Fall probably felt fairly safe. Harding resisted senatorial pressure to launch an inquiry into his friend's actions. Then long before the end of his term in August 1923, President Harding died. Without Harding's protection, Fall had little chance of keeping his deal secret. President Calvin Coolidge felt no loyalty to Harding's cronies. Determined to prove the integrity of his administration, he appointed two special prosecutors to investigate the entire matter. Eventually, after tireless investigations, two civil trials, and six criminal trials, the naval reserves were restored to the United States. Sinclair went to jail for nine months, Secretary of the Navy Denby and Attorney General Daugherty resigned, and Albert Fall, convicted for bribery, became the first cabinet member convicted of a crime committed while in office. Before his death Harding said, "I have no trouble with my enemies. I can take care of my enemies all right. But my damn friends. They're the ones that keep me walking the floor nights!" Those friends made Harding's administration the most corrupt in U.S. history.

52

DID NOTHING

Herbert Hoover and the
Great Depression

||||||||||||||||||||||||||||||||||||||||||||||||||||||||||||||||||||||||

Herbert Hoover was elected the thirty-first president of the United States as the country was coming off of a decade filled with massive social and cultural changes. It was the time for the emergence of new and exciting technologies. At the end of a brutal world war, Americans had embraced moving pictures, automobiles, radio, women's rights, and jazz. The country was in a good mood during the Roaring Twenties, and they went on a collective spending binge. Shortsighted consumers overextended their credit, not realizing they were setting the stage for a crash at the end of the decade. Banks lent money freely, and Hoover himself declared that "We in America today are nearer to the final triumph over poverty than ever before in the history of any land." The president's naive optimism may have contributed to Hoover's failure to take early action necessary to stop the economic hemorrhaging that ushered in the Great Depression.

Less than a year after Hoover made that bold remark, the country was in the throes of a depression precipitated by a cyclical downturn in the market but later exacerbated by two presidents' misguided economic policies. Many historians have claimed that Hoover did nothing during the Great Depression and that inaction caused the depression to worsen. While it's true that he took no meaningful early action, if he had continued to do nothing, the depression might have been milder and shorter. Instead, Hoover did something much worse. At first he didn't act, and then when he realized his inaction was causing catastrophic economic events, the president pushed for policies that actually deepened and lengthened the depression.

Hoover secured the Republican nomination for the presidency in 1928 despite never having run for any form of public office. At the start of World War I, Herbert Hoover had personally assisted hundreds of Americans, trapped in Europe, to return home. He had organized the country's food-rationing during the war and orchestrated humanitarian efforts for those lacking food after the war. He was also famous for serving as secretary of commerce in the Harding and Coolidge administrations. This allowed Hoover to claim he had helped create the economic growth of the 1920s. He portrayed himself as an economic guru who would safeguard voters' wallets into the next decade. While his success as commerce secretary certainly helped put the *Roaring* into the twenties, it also may have given him a false sense of the country's economic resilience. This caused him to gravely underestimate the need for government intervention during the first weeks of the Great Depression.

In October 1929, on a day forever remembered as "Black Tuesday," the stock market experienced a monumental collapse. The burst of the investment bubble precipitated the most severe economic downturn of the twentieth century. The stock market rebounded modestly in the following months, but consumer confidence was shattered. Bank runs began in earnest. And many lenders went bankrupt as the Federal Reserve did nothing. The Fed's inaction in allowing the banks to collapse deepened the crisis. Many economists believe that if Hoover and Congress had pressured the Fed to ease the money supply, the period after the stock market crash would never have deepened into a depression.

Instead Hoover rejected his treasury secretary's advice to intervene before it was too late. Perhaps his unwillingness to acknowledge that the party was over stemmed from the years of prosperity he presided over as commerce secretary. Or perhaps he thought he could calm the panic by reassuring Americans that this was just a temporary downturn that required no action on his part. As he often stated, Herbert Hoover had faith that the free enterprise system would solve its own problems without government intervention. So as president he took a mostly laissez-faire response to the crisis, treating it as a cyclical event. Proponents of such a view believed that the economy would naturally rebound regardless of government behavior. But as economic reality set it and it became apparent that the economy was not going to rebound on its own, Hoover decided he better get off the bench and play the game. Unfortunately for the country, he played like a rookie who had been locked out during preseason.

An economic crisis is the worst time to become protectionist, but this didn't stop Hoover and his buddies in Congress. In June 1930, Congress passed the Smoot-Hawley Tariff Act. Hoover initially came out in opposition to the bill, correctly predicting that it would undermine international economic cooperation; nonetheless, he eventually signed the bill against the advice of a coalition of prominent economists as well as industrialists such as Henry Ford. The tariff imposed duties higher than at any other point in American history (narrowly less than the 1828 "Tariff of Abominations"), weakening banks and undermining trade.

Hoover's miscalculations extended well beyond the tariff, however. Various policies aimed at encouraging job sharing and propping up wages were responsible for close to two-thirds of the drop in gross domestic product. Due to elevated industrial wages, unemployment became rampant.

Hoover's presidency witnessed unemployment tick up to almost 25 percent. Homelessness increased as well, resulting in a proliferation of shantytowns across the country, derisively referred to as "Hoovervilles." Hoover attempted to combat this via the Federal Home Loan Bank Act, a policy that was intended to spur new home construction. The act was too little, too late. Secretary of the Treasury Andrew Mellon oversaw a tremendous decrease in taxes on high earners—from 73 to 24 percent—in the prerecession years. This meant the Federal Home Loan Bank Act lacked the finances to have a meaningful impact. Hoover sought to recoup this revenue by reversing the tax cuts. Such a dramatic tax increase during an economic contraction is a deadly economic sin; his decision adversely affected growth.

Hoover wasn't done dealing damage to the economy, though. In 1931, he urged major banks to form a consortium called the National Credit Corporation (NCC). While Hoover encouraged the banks to loan money to smaller banks, the policy wasn't mandatory. The result was that such loans were very rare, as the NCC was leery of such risky lending. While the NCC acted in its own best interests, the economy overall would have benefited by such a requirement.

In the 1932 election, Hoover stood little chance against Franklin D. Roosevelt. The election was one of history's most important in that it ushered in a political realignment. Republicans had been dominant in American politics since Reconstruction, but the elections of 1932 were the beginning of an era of Democratic domination. Roosevelt would be elected four consecutive times and Democrats would control Congress, with little interruption, until 1994.

Roosevelt often earns admiration for his handling of the Depression, but he looks good only when stacked up against the ineptitude of Hoover. In fact, Roosevelt continued many of Hoover's economically ruinous policies. Unemployment remained high in the face of his New Deal, and thus Roosevelt's first two terms saw little economic progress. It wasn't until World War II energized the economy that the United States really returned to prosperity.

Hoover's lack of action during a time when the country was at the precipice of economic disaster made him the electoral scapegoat in his day. After all, Hoover had been the steward of the economy when it tanked. Whether due to his own ego, naïveté, or overall ineptitude, this inaction made the economy free-fall. Perhaps it was the combination of those qualities that compelled Hoover to make one ruinous policy decision after another. Regardless, the country paid a heavy price for Herbert Hoover's mistakes, for many years after the president left office.

53

LEADERSHIP
DECISIONS BASED
ON FEAR

Hitler's Rise to Power

1932, GERMANY

The two men who actually put Adolf Hitler in power were not Nazis. One was an honored and respected World War I commander and war hero, Field Marshal Paul von Hindenburg. Hindenburg was not a young man. He had risen to be president of the democratically elected German government. He was the most trusted figure in Germany. Both the people and the army trusted him. Hindenburg also took the actual step that put the Nazis and Adolf Hitler in power. The second figure was Franz von Papen, a centrist politician who made too many compromises.

Times were hard for Germans and Germany, with inflation eating up wages and the allies still demanding reparations. There was little cause for any national pride and a lot of bitterness. Rising in the discontent were two radical and opposed factions. One was the National Socialist Party and the other the German Communist Party. They were just the two largest and most powerful of more than a dozen parties who contested and competed in the Reichstag. Each was sure they had the only solution for Germany's problems. The result was a government that could accomplish little.

In 1932 an election was held. The vote was for president and the members of the congress, or the Reichstag. For president the results were Hindenburg 49.6 percent, Hitler 30.1 percent, Ernst Thälmann 13.2 percent, and Theodor Duesterberg 6.8 percent.

If Hindenburg had gotten 0.5 percent more of the vote, there might never have been a World War II. But he did not, and this forced a runoff between the top three candidates held that April. The second round of voting gave Hindenburg 53 percent of the vote and victory. Adolf Hitler got 36 percent. The Nazis reacted by fostering chaos and violence in the streets. Any meeting or gathering by another party, especially the Communists, was attacked by uniformed Nazis. Many of the police refused to intervene or supported the fascists. They saw them as the only force capable of countering the Communists, whose first loyalty was to Stalin. Opposition leaders were murdered or publicly beaten. All this was happening in the weeks after the Nazis had lost badly in the election. The violence finally got so severe that the army felt threatened and any gathering of the Sturmabteilung (the SA or Brown Shirts) was banned.

Still Hindenburg resisted the call to appoint a strong leader, Hitler, to take control of the situation. He confided in one aide, Otto von Meissner, that things were so bad he could not place the government in the hands of a new and inexperienced party that did not have majority support.

Hindenburg then made his first crucial mistake. He appointed Franz von Papen, a Catholic Centre Party politician with little support but few enemies, to be the new chancellor. The German chancellor ran the day-to-day workings of the government. Papen soon found himself pressured from all sides and particularly by the Nazis. In an effort to appease Hitler, Chancellor Papen lifted the ban on the SA. Then he allowed the Social Democratic Party's elected government in Prussia to be forced out by the Nazis. This move toward the Nazis drove the moderates in the Reichstag, still the majority, away from Papen, and he was forced to give up his chancellorship. This drove the former chancellor into a personal alliance with Adolf Hitler.

The new government was formed behind an army general named Kurt von Schleicher. But even with the active support of the German army, Chancellor Schleicher was unable to gain a majority vote in the Reichstag, much less deal with the Nazis' choreographic chaos. A third election was called, and the Nazis actually lost thirty-four of their seats in the Reichstag. Unfortunately, this made no difference because the Reichstag continued to be deadlocked while inflation ran wild and violence spread. Fifty-seven days after he was appointed, Schleicher resigned as chancellor. The army was concerned, people felt threatened, and partisanship continued to grind the legislature to a halt.

At this point Franz von Papen, now himself a National Socialist adherent, convinced Hindenburg that only the strong hand of Hitler and the Nazis could save Germany from collapse. He promised that as vice chancellor he would be able to moderate Hitler's policies. He was not. On January 30, 1933, Hitler was appointed chancellor of the German government. From that position he began to consolidate all power in his own hands. After the German congress's Reichstag building was destroyed by a February 27 fire, which was set by the Nazis and blamed on the Jews, Hitler convinced Hindenburg to issue a decree titled "For the Protection of the People and the State." The decree basically suspended civil liberties and asked the Reichstag to grant Hitler dictatorial powers. Under extreme pressure and with several of the measure's opponents suddenly missing, the measure passed on March 23, 1933. The vote was 441 yes and only 84 no. After being defeated in three elections, Hitler was in complete control of all of Germany.

Paul von Hindenburg died soon after that. With his death, the last possible balance to Hitler's power was lost. Franz von Papen became the ambassador to Austria and then Turkey. He was tried and acquitted at Nuremberg in 1945. His personal wealth was returned, and he lived comfortably until dying in May of 1969.

The Nazi Party never had more than 230 of the 608 elected seats in the German legislature. Nor at his peak did Adolf Hitler get much more than a third of the votes in any free election. But because of the decisions made by Hindenburg and Papen, he was able to seize total control of Germany.

APPEASEMENT

Fool Me Once,
Shame on You

1936, THE RHINELAND,
GERMANY

On March 7, 1936, Germany unquestionably broke the Versailles Treaty that had been imposed on them after their defeat in World War I. Adolf Hitler has been chancellor since 1934. Since his election he had threatened to ignore the terms imposed on Germany after the war, and this was the first time he had actually done so in a way that could not be ignored. After World War I, the industrially rich western part of Germany, running from Switzerland to the Netherlands, was declared a demilitarized zone. It was to be a buffer into which the German army could not enter. This protected all approaches to France and Belgium from a surprise attack. The zone was a constant reminder to the German people that they had been defeated and were still being punished.

It was 1936 and Hitler was a virtual dictator, but still he had to prove himself to most of Germany, and particularly to the German army. On March 7, 1936, he took his boldest action to date by ordering units of the German army and police to reoccupy the

Rhineland in violation of the Treaty of Versailles. The force he sent in was small, less than fifteen thousand soldiers and twenty-two thousand police supported by a few planes. They were all under orders to not fire back and to flee the Rhineland at the slightest sign of any French military reaction. There was none. The reaction, for different reasons, of both England and France was to do nothing. The cost of doing nothing can now be measured in the millions of lives that were later lost.

France and Britain were both unprepared and understandably hesitant to relive the horrors of the Great War. Both nations had lost a generation of their young men in the trenches. The English government was also reluctant to react because most of the ministers felt that Germany had been punished enough. Many publicly stated that the treaty was unfair. Most correctly observed it did more harm to peace than it did anything to preserve it. Some described the Rhineland as Germany's "backyard." It was also agreed that Germany had been a good neighbor for twenty years and had earned the right to be treated like other nations. Evidently none of them realized that by being fair to Germany, they were boosting Hitler. Britain was also in the beginning of an expansion and re-equipping of the Royal Air Force and felt unprepared for war.

France also was unready to fight a war, or at least felt that way. The Maginot Line had just been completed and so a buffer zone that would warn of a German attack seemed no longer needed. The French top commander, General Maurice Gamelin, massively overstated the size of the German army when he reported to the French government. Then he insisted that France could not match Germany in the field until it was fully mobilized. Mobilization would take weeks and hurt their struggling economy. In reality, the German army had less than three hundred thousand soldiers and France had three times that, although two hundred thousand of those men were stationed in the French colonies. The French air force was well equipped and outnumbered the Luftwaffe two to one. But this was not the French perception. There was a political crisis distracting the Paris government as well. As a result, the French also accepted Hitler's action without protest.

Adolf Hitler later described the reoccupation of the Rhineland as his greatest gamble. Never was he to be weaker and more vulnerable in Germany and not again until 1945 was Germany as vulnerable militarily. He is often quoted as saying, "If France had then marched into the Rhineland, we would have had to withdraw with our tails between our legs." Had Germany and her general staff been embarrassed, the consequences for Hitler would have been grave. Active opposition by the same army that helped put him in power would have likely resulted in his removal and the downfall of the Nazis. He was tolerated and supported by the army because of his successes and ability to maintain order. At worst, Hitler's near-dictatorial powers as chancellor would have been moderated. World War II might never have begun. Hitler's success in flaunting the Treaty of Versailles raised his stature with the German people to such a level not even the army could resist his will.

56

MORE APPEASEMENT

Fool Me Twice, Shame on Me

1938, SUDETENLAND AND GERMANY

The extortion started in 991. The Vikings had laid siege to London. To get them to leave, the residents and merchants of the city gave them a large payment in silver and gold. The Norsemen returned in 994 and again extorted another massive payment. The fact that they were paid so much silver to leave simply whetted the appetites of other Vikings. They returned again and again, demanding larger payments each time in 1002, 1007, and 1012. This was called the Danegeld, and it was basically extortion using the threat of war. It was the cost of peace.

In 1938, Adolf Hitler demanded his own price for peace. After his successful militarization of the Rhineland, the Nazis had occupied and annexed Austria. They then turned to the next largest concentration of German speakers outside of Germany, eastern Czechoslovakia. This was the Sudetenland. Between 30 and 40 percent of those living in the Sudetenland were German speakers. While in theory Czechoslovakia was protected by treaties with England and France, the reality was that once again neither of those countries was willing to risk a war with Germany.

The Sudetenland

In their eyes, the leaders of the two powerful western European nations had no choice but to once more pay off Hitler. This time it was with part of another country. Most of Europe had been scarred by World War I. England became insecure and cautious, France poured wealth into the Maginot Line, and Germany was bitter and frustrated. All hoped that Woodrow Wilson's League of Nations would create a lasting peace. That illusion was destroyed in 1931 when Japan invaded Manchuria. The league voted to condemn Japan and ordered her soldiers to leave. Japan simply quit the League of Nations. The remaining members, most of the world's nations, then realized that there was nothing the league could do. By 1938, the League of Nations was a hollow debating society ignored when convenient. So in the name of peace, Czechoslovakia's own allies forced that nation to give its richest province to Germany.

The main advocate for this appeasement was the British prime minister. Just after signing the treaty dismembering Czechoslovakia, he addressed the British Parliament. Here is how Prime Minister Neville Chamberlain explained why they had betrayed Czechoslovakia and signed the Munich Agreement.

When we were convinced, as we became convinced, that nothing any longer would keep the Sudetenland within the Czechoslovakian State, we urged the Czech Government as strongly as we could to agree to the cession of territory, and to agree promptly. The Czech Government, through the wisdom and courage of President Benes, accepted the advice of the French Government and ourselves. It was a hard decision for anyone who loved his country to take, but to accuse us of having by that advice betrayed the Czechoslovakian State is simply preposterous. What we did was to save her from annihilation and give her a chance of new life as a new State, which involves the loss of territory and fortifications, but may perhaps enable her to enjoy in the future and develop a national existence under a neutrality and security comparable to that which we see in Switzerland to-day. Therefore, I think the Government deserve the approval of this House for their conduct of affairs in this recent crisis which has saved Czechoslovakia from destruction and Europe from Armageddon.

Does the experience of the Great War and the years that followed it give us reasonable hope that, if some new war started, that would end war any more than the last one did?

One good thing, at any rate, has come out of this emergency through which we have passed. It has thrown a vivid light upon our preparations for defense, on their strength and on their weakness. I should not think we were doing our duty if we had not already ordered that a prompt and thorough inquiry should be made to cover the whole of our preparations, military and civil, in order to see, in the light of what has happened during these hectic days, what further steps may be necessary to make good our deficiencies in the shortest possible time.

Parliamentary Debates, House of Commons, session 1937–1938, pp. 12:361–369, 373

Chamberlain still believed that Germany had been mistreated by the Versailles Treaty. History tends to agree with him, blaming its stringent terms for many economic and social problems in Germany. This tended to affect his treatment of the Nazis. Some of the ministers objected to appeasing Hitler. Anthony Eden, Chamberlain's foreign secretary, resigned in protest. Most of England approved. After the bloodbath of World War I, any alternative to war had appeal.

The irony is that captured records and interviews after World War II showed that Germany was in no position to start a war in 1938. Some highly placed generals were actually organizing to overthrow the Nazis if Hitler did begin to start one. Chamberlain even refused to give any assurances of support to a group of influential German business and military leaders, known as the Schwarz Kappel, who were ready then to imprison the Nazi leaders and take over the government. But when France and England chose again to appease Hitler rather than oppose him, the Schwarz Kappel were unable to act. The Sudetenland success made Adolf Hitler unassailable. With its natural defenses gone, the rest of Czechoslovakia was quickly occupied by the Nazis when the war began. Chamberlain's appeasement in 1938 bought England barely a year of peace and guaranteed the start of a new world war.

||||||||||||||||||||||||||||||||||||||||||||||||||||||||||||||||||||||||

57

PARANOIA'S PRICE

Officer Corpse

1935–1939, RUSSIA

||||||||||||||||||||||||||||||||||||||||||||||||||||||||||||||||||||||||

n 1935, the Red Army was an effective military force. Many of its older officers had fought in the Russian Revolution and against the White Armies or in the war with Poland. It was one of the areas in Stalinist Russia where you could advance based on merit. That was the problem. There is no question that Joseph Stalin was paranoid. He saw any type of real competence as a threat to his absolute control of the Soviet Union. From 1935 to 1939 he purged, had killed, or exiled to Siberia millions of Russians from all levels and occupations.

Two years before the military purges, in 1933, Hitler was elected chancellor of Germany. One of the main reasons he was elected to this position was his hard-line stand, including violence, against the German Communists. In Hitler's book *Mein Kampf*, he clearly states that his intention is to conquer, depopulate, and open the Russian lands to Aryan settlement. Stalin's spies told him this. The British warned the Soviets on several occasions. Hitler made no secret of the disdain he had for all Slavs, including the Russians. There was no question that someday Germany and Russia would be at war.

But despite the rearming of Germany, the occupation of Austria and the Sudetenland, and the rise of fascism in Italy and Spain, Stalin still felt compelled to eliminate any possible threat to his personal rule that might come from the Red Army. He did this by having shot virtually any officer who showed initiative, appeared to be able to think for himself, or simply seemed competent. By 1939, he had purged three of five marshals, thirteen of fifteen army commanders, eight of nine admirals, fifty of fifty-seven corps commanders, and 154 of his 186 division commanders. He even executed most of the top commissars attached to the army, whose sole purpose in being there was to ensure Stalin's wishes were followed.

By eliminating the best of his officers and most of his experienced commanders, Stalin badly degraded the ability of his army to fight a war. So just when Stalin needed a strong army the most, the Red Army was weak. This was emphatically demonstrated when 450,000 Soviet troops attacked Finland on November 30, 1939. The Finns had barely over 150,000 men in their entire army and no reserves. The Finnish army also lacked just about everything needed to fight a modern war except courage. The Finns had few tanks, comparatively little artillery, a minute air force, and a shortage of ammunition. The Finns did have skis, which proved to be decisive in what was later named "The Winter War."

Due to an incredible level of incompetence at the higher ranks of the Russian commanders, the Finns were able to first slow then stop the Soviet invasion. The world was astonished. The Soviets reorganized and re-formed to attack again. This time tanks led the way, followed by tens of thousands of fresh soldiers. There was little the Finns could do to stop them. The Red Army again took massive losses but finally broke the Mannerheim Line, which was mostly made of just trenches and log redoubts. It still wasn't until March 5, 1940, that Finland was forced to concede defeat. The Soviet Army suffered an astonishing 126,000 dead or lost in the three-month war. That is almost as many soldiers killed or missing as there were men in the entire Finnish army. The outnumbered and outgunned Finns suffered only 22,000 dead or missing in action.

The disaster did cause reforms and a major effort at retraining the Soviet officers at all levels. Making up for the purged military leadership was a slow process begun only when it was too late. In Stalin's purges, the Soviet Union lost its officers most capable of reacting to the German invasion in 1941. With anyone who once showed initiative killed, there were few officers willing to act without direction from above; they had seen the fate of those who had. Russia lost hundreds of thousands of soldiers in the first weeks of the war. So when the Soviet Army needed leadership the most, there was none available. It had been purged out of the Red Army.

There is no question that the weakness of the Red Army was a major factor in Hitler's decision to invade in 1941. The Red Army had shown itself to be hollow and incompetent. It would never be weaker than it was that year, although it was in the process of rebuilding. Had Joseph Stalin not crippled his forces, there is a good chance that the Nazis would have been much more hesitant to invade. Hitler would not have needed to act before the Russian army improved. Because of his own paranoia, Stalin's purges did such serious damage to his army that they brought on the war he most feared.

58

||||||||||||||||||||||||||||||||||||||||||||||||||||||||||||||||||||||||||

WHAT WORKED
ONCE WILL NOT
ALWAYS WORK
AGAIN

Hitler's No-Retreat Orders

1940–1945, GERMANY

||||||||||||||||||||||||||||||||||||||||||||||||||||||||||||||||||||||||||

This is a mistake that Adolf Hitler made over and over even when his top general protested or resigned. In the last two years of the war, Hitler's insistence on holding every inch of soil and never retreating cost the German army dearly. Tens of thousands of experienced soldiers were lost on pockets all across the Soviet Union. Hitler, even after Stalingrad, refused to change his policy and regularly threatened or even fired commanders who disagreed or acted on their own. Fifty-seven thousand men were lost in the Korsun Pocket in February 1943. Even in 1944, he forbid the army that had been besieging Leningrad to retreat. Only General Walter Model's disobedience saved his army.

There may be many reasons for Hitler refusing to allow any retreats or breakouts. Among them were likely Hitler's deteriorating mental condition and his growing distrust of his General Staff. There had been at least one assassination attempt by his own generals. Another of the reasons that Adolf Hitler held firmly to his no-retreat policy was that in the winter of 1941 it had worked.

After Army Group Center's 1941 offensive stalled in front of Moscow, the Russians began their winter counterattacks. The Wehrmacht was overextended and suffering severely from the cold. The General Staff insisted that the army pull back to regroup on a shorter, more defensible line. Hitler said no and enforced his order harshly. That winter the German line did hold, and future experience showed that if the German infantry had tried to retreat, it would have either perished in the cold or been overrun. By the spring, the generals had to concede Hitler had been right. Unfortunately, the Führer held on to this success and refused to change his no-retreat order no matter what the circumstances.

By the end of World War II Germany had lost over two million soldiers in pockets, many caused by the no-retreat policy. Rather than writing off North Africa and withdrawing troops as advised, Hitler chose to reinforce his army and then ordered two hundred thousand men to stand. Stalingrad was the worst example, but tens of thousands of veteran German soldiers were also lost to no purpose in Kiev and the Crimea.

59

OVERCONFIDENCE

Fatal Delay

MAY 1940, CRETE

||||||||||||||||||||||||||||||||||||||||||||||||||||||||||||||||||||

There is a myth that Hitler, having to invade Greece, caused a fatal delay in the launching of Operation Barbarossa. This places the blame for the results of that delay on Mussolini. Certainly Benito Mussolini was guilty of many mistakes, but the delay that cost the Nazis Moscow was not his fault. Mussolini had invaded Greece from Albania for many reasons. Among these was that it appeared to be an easy victory from the Italian bases in Albania. There also was an element of jealousy. Adolf Hitler had been going from victory to victory, while Italy's army failed in Ethiopia and Africa. It was a sign of this jealousy that the Italian dictator never notified the Germans of his plans. The Italian invasion failed. It failed so badly that within weeks there was a Greek army occupying part of Albania and a humbled Mussolini had to ask Hitler for help. But the decision that changed history here was not bailing out the bumbling Italians, but one Hitler made afterward.

There is no question that the postponement until June 22 of the launch of Operation Barbarossa, the invasion of Russia, had major repercussions the following winter. That December, the final push toward Moscow was stopped by two things. One was the weather and the other was the arrival of several divisions from Siberia that were rushed east just in time to reinforce the Russian capital's defenders. The weather deteriorated badly in the last two weeks of the German offensive. Without the delay, this would not have been as significant a factor. An earlier attack also would have met with fewer well-built defenses and fewer Siberian divisions.

So what caused the postponement that actually mattered? Why did Barbarossa begin on June 22, 1941, and not its original start date of the end of April? The answer is that there were really two delays. The first was caused by Mussolini's failed invasion of Greece. The second delay was caused not by Mussolini, but by Hitler himself.

It began the year before. Italy was an ally of Germany. Unfortunately for Hitler, they fell into the "with allies like these who needs enemies" category. Having been defeated in Ethiopia, the kingdom of Italy, under the fascist Benito Mussolini, decided to take on the much smaller British army that was defending Egypt. The Italian forces were far more numerous but were short on artillery, suffering from poor officer training, and lacking trucks. But the British were in no position to send reinforcements from England. By mid-September, ten Italian divisions under Marshal Rodolfo Graziani had advanced along the coast until they were just eighty miles from the British main defense line at Mersa Matruh. Even though Graziani had more than four times as many soldiers than Archibald Wavell's thirty-six thousand, he stopped and began digging in. He was short on just about everything from shells and food to gasoline and medicine. He chose to dig in and dispersed his army into a number of fortified camps and towns until he had enough shells, tanks, and supplies to launch an overwhelming attack. The British did not wait and began attacking one Italian camp after another, gaining local superiority each time. The entire Italian army began to pull back, but not in time. When the only British tank division, the Seventh Armored, cut the coast road at Beda Fomm, it cut off the only line of retreat. Graziani's entire army surrendered. The thirty-six thousand British captured 130,000 Italians at the cost of a few thousand casualties. This loss is why Germany felt it necessary to send Erwin Rommel and the Afrika Korps to Africa. They were needed to reinforce what Italian forces remained.

So Mussolini was smarting at a massive defeat and looked to find somewhere to invade where his army could win. He settled on Greece. The choice was appealing because Italy already controlled Albania, which shared a long border with Greece. The Italian fascist was so sure of victory that he did not even warn the Germans of his invasion. "Hitler always faces me with a *fait accompli*. This time I am going to pay him back in his own coin. He will find out from the papers that I have occupied Greece," Benito Mussolini told Count Ciano, his foreign minister.

The invasion failed. It was worse than just a failed attack. The Greek army not only defended their passes but also pushed the Italians back, pursued them, and occupied part of Albania. Eventually, the Italians even abandoned Albania. The British used this as an opportunity to occupy the islands of Crete and Lemnos. The British intervention seemed to have been what actually forced Hitler to intervene. Greece was no threat, but the English landings were. He could not afford to have the British poised on his southern flank when he invaded Russia. Churchill had always favored attacking "the soft underbelly" of Europe. He had been behind the Gallipoli landings in World War I.

On November 4, 1940, the Germans attacked from Bulgaria and Yugoslavia. Operation Marita was a success, though fierce resistance by the Greeks and British units slowed even the overwhelming German forces. Greek units defended the mountain passes, often to the last man, but courage could not overcome the Germans' superiority in men, tanks, and aircraft. The Wehrmacht began Operation Marita with almost 700,000 well-equipped and experienced soldiers who had never been defeated. They were supported by seven hundred aircraft and twelve hundred panzers. There were exactly twenty tanks in the entire Greek army and about 430,000 soldiers. But many of their best units were in Albania. And reluctant to give back the place the Italians invaded from, they remained there too long. The British sent what they could from Egypt but that came to just over 60,000 soldiers, one hundred tanks, and a few hundred planes. Eventually the Germans defeated the defenders in detail, taking each area of mountainous Greece. By the end of April, 50,000 British soldiers had been evacuated and all of Greece was in German hands.

At this point, the end of April, the bulk of the German units could have been shifted toward Russia. Operation Barbarossa could have easily begun in May. Instead Hitler made one of those seemingly logical decisions that later are called fateful. Parts of Yugoslavia were resisting the fascists, and the bulk of the escaping British were just a short distance offshore on the island of Crete. Because the army was next to the resisting areas, Hitler chose to have them pacify Yugoslavia. The German dictator also decided to trap and capture the British on Crete. Both objectives were partially achieved. Most of Yugoslavia was at least occupied and an airdrop gained Crete, though the Royal Navy managed to save the bulk of the soldiers there with yet another heroic evacuation. The last part of the island was captured on May 29, a full month after Greece had surrendered: a month that hundreds of thousands of German soldiers were not in place for Barbarossa.

The resistance in Yugoslavia actually posed no direct threat to Germany. Nor were the British forces on Crete, who had lost most of their heavy weapons. By making the decision to attack both of them, Hitler himself delayed the start of Operation Barbarossa almost a full month longer than was necessary. Four more weeks of good weather and less time for the Siberian units to reinforce the Moscow defenses would have almost certainly meant the capture of the administration and transport heart of Russia. Pushed behind the Ural Mountains, there is some question as to whether Russia would have been able to turn their defeat into eventual victory or even have kept fighting. But while Mussolini blundered first and had to be bailed out in Greece, it was Hitler's decision to do more, after turning the Italian defeat into a German victory, that made all the difference.

60

A TWISTED CHAIN OF COMMAND

Stop Order

1940, DUNKIRK

T his is a mistake that you cannot blame only on Adolf Hitler, though his personal style guaranteed that it would occur. In the last week of 1940, to the astonishment of even the panzer commanders, the Blitzkrieg tactics worked and France was in trouble. The German army had pushed through to the Channel and trapped the entire British Expeditionary Force (BEF) in what is now called the Flanders Pocket. The bulk of the French army was falling back toward Paris in growing disarray. France was falling, though still resisting, and it was likely that soon the only nation standing against the Nazis would be Britain.

The Flanders Pocket, centered on the port city of Dunkirk, was surrounded. Trapped in it were not only the majority of the BEF, but also what remained of the Belgian army and considerable French forces (French First Army). More than four hundred thousand soldiers were trapped against the Channel. By May 23, their situation was dire. Thousands of men were completely surrounded and far from the rest of the French army. They could not be resupplied and were unable to break out against the more mobile panzer divisions.

Without the core of trained and experienced men who were trapped in the Flanders Pocket, rebuilding the British army would have required not only reequipping the entire force but training a new one. This would have taken months or even years, time Britain would not have. Churchill was determined to fight on, stating that a truce with Germany was a betrayal of England's values. If the BEF had been lost, then even a small Wehrmacht force could have successfully invaded the island. The very negative attitude of the German general staff, who controlled all of the Nazi land forces, toward Sea Lion, the invasion of the British Isles, would have instead been enthusiasm. An invasion of Britain would have been inevitable, even if the Royal Air Force (RAF) and Royal Navy had made the landings expensive. Half a dozen panzer and mobile divisions would have been unstoppable once they landed. Contingency plans were being drawn up for Churchill's cabinet to continue the war from Canada.

The German Armor had pushed hard and was suffering from it. Mechanical problems were common and repairs were needed. The commander of the Fourth Panzer Army, Günther von Kluge, ordered a halt. He was concerned about the condition of his tanks and may well have felt no time pressure because the Flanders Pocket had been sealed and the British Expeditionary Force was separated from the bulk of the French army and trapped against the sea. His superior at Army Group A, Colonel General Gerd von Rundstedt, agreed with the halt in the offensive against Dunkirk, and on May 24 the panzers pulled back. Such a decision had to be approved at the highest levels. Army Supreme Command (OKW) disagreed and reacted by putting all of the forces in Army Group B under the command of Army Group A, with the intention of immediately renewing the attack. But the next day, Adolf Hitler arrived at Army Group A and overrode the OKW order, restoring control of Army Group A, including the Fourth Panzer Army, to Rundstedt. This meant the stop order for the panzers stood and without them the German infantry was forced to hold as well. As a result of Hitler overriding the OKW, the attack on the Flanders Pocket did not get back under way until the 27th. Those few days made all the difference. Instead of a ground assault, Hitler ordered the Luftwaffe to punish the pocket and isolate it. They were to bomb the British into submission. There seems to have been little expectation that the Royal Navy could evacuate any measurable portion of the BEF. This almost was the case.

By May 23, it was obvious that France would be lost. The Royal Navy began planning to evacuate the BEF, but it lacked the ships. Dunkirk was also a small port, incapable of handling the mass of men involved. In addition, the docks were so damaged as to be unusable. The BEF would have to leave from the beaches, but two moles (seawalls that extended out to sea) were slowing the process even more. The decision to pull the BEF out was finalized on May 25. Destroyers and other naval vessels were sent, and the evacuation actually began on the 27th, the same day that pressure on the pocket was renewed.

Initially, it looked as if the task would be impossible. On the first day only eight thousand soldiers were evacuated. But the word went out that Britain needed almost anything that floated to converge on Dunkirk. At its peak, naval and civilian ships took off sixty-one thousand men in a single day. The RAF flew constantly over the beaches and lost at least 150 planes. The Luftwaffe lost slightly more, many to naval and ground fire. They were assisted by clouds and storms that made attacking Dunkirk from the air difficult.

By June 3, the entire BEF was off. Churchill insisted the naval ships return one more time, and they were able to take out almost thirty thousand more French soldiers. Even so another twenty-six thousand Frenchmen, who were holding the final line against overwhelming odds, were captured.

Had Hitler not felt the need to take charge of the Army Group A headquarters and change the OKW order, the BEF would have been unable to disengage and pull back to the beaches. There would have been no miracle of Dunkirk. The evacuation would have been slower, and tens of thousands of British soldiers, if not the bulk of their army, would have become prisoners of war: prisoners who would have themselves been leverage that might have forced a treaty on Britain. But Hitler wanted to show that he was in charge, not the OKW, which he distrusted. In doing so, he may have missed his best chance to have knocked Britain out of the war along with France.

61

REVENGE IS NOT WAR

Call Me Meier

Dunkirk had been a miracle and the end of a disaster. In England the British army was in disarray. Almost all of its armor, most of its artillery, and even a majority of its machine guns had been left behind. All Britain could muster for the defense of the home islands were three understrength armored and fifteen infantry divisions, all short of heavy weapons. Poised to invade England as part of their Operation Sea Lion, Germany had thirty-nine divisions, including panzer and mechanized divisions.

All that protected Britain was the English Channel and the Royal Navy. Germany simply did not have a surface navy. The *Bismarck* had not even been launched, but even that great ship could not have defended barges and transports against the British battleships.

But the Royal Navy was itself threatened. By 1940 it had become painfully apparent that even the most powerful ship was vulnerable to attack from the air. If her navy protected Britain, then the Royal Air Force (RAF) protected the Royal Navy. The

Germans knew this and the admiralty and British government were painfully aware of it as well. So once it became apparent that Churchill's England was not going to accept peace on German terms, the Luftwaffe was ordered to destroy the RAF. They had to in order to open the way for Operation Sea Lion. While designed more for supporting their army than as an air assault, the Luftwaffe had thousands of experienced pilots and aircraft based just a few minutes of flight time across the Channel. Defending England from over three thousand planes were the RAF's 650 fighters and pilots.

When the sparring near the coast ended and the Battle of Britain really began, on August 8, the Germans opened the air battle by launching more than fifteen hundred missions against England on the first day alone. That was more than two planes for every defending British fighter. Outnumbered and desperate, the pilots of the Royal Air Force stood against an onslaught. They had no choice. Often a pilot would fly five or more interception missions beginning at dawn and would be completely exhausted by sunset. Then those same pilots would awaken and do it again the next day, and the next, without a break.

The German battle plan was well thought out. Its target was correctly determined to be the RAF bases, factories, and related defenses. They even hit the new radar stations with Stuka dive-bombers early in the battle. The idea was to force the British fighters to engage the more numerous German fighters or see their aircraft destroyed on the ground. It worked. The Luftwaffe went after the coastal bases mercilessly. They lost more pilots than the British, even though they had a much larger force to begin with. Every day in August, fewer fighters rose to contest the German formations.

After a little over two weeks, virtually all of Britain's coastal airfields had been destroyed or rendered inoperative. Their runways were cratered, and their hangars and petrol tanks smashed. Then starting on August 24, the Germans turned their attention to the major air bases farther inland, such as Biggin Hill and Andover. These key fields, where all of the aircraft staged from and were serviced, were irreplaceable. The German attacks on these bases continued daily and grew larger with more fighters escorting more bombers. The central airfields were overwhelmed, and British losses mounted. Pilots too were near collapse, and losses were leaving gaps in the squadrons. There was no time for replacements to adapt, and the loss rate for new pilots was excessive. It was becoming impossible to repair the damage to the bases each night or to send up enough fighters to defend them all. If the central air bases had been knocked out, then the south of Britain and the English Channel would have been defenseless.

For a while, Lord Dowding hoped to implement a policy of gathering several squadrons together before tackling the large German formations. This meant more aircraft would get through to the bombers. But at first logistics and limited fuel made gathering enough aircraft difficult. Then the British pilot losses were so great there simply were not enough fighters left for Dowding to create a large formation. The British air marshal notified Winston Churchill that if the battle continued, within weeks there would be no pilots or bases left to defend southern England.

The Germans were winning the Battle of Britain.

And if the RAF had been knocked out, then the Royal Navy would have been unable to stand in the Channel against an unhindered Luftwaffe attack. Operation Sea Lion would have happened and a near-defenseless England would have been invaded. Germany seemed about to win the war and conquer the last European nation resisting the Third Reich. Tentative discussions about asking for a truce occurred even in Churchill's cabinet. Winston Churchill rejected a truce, stating that even if they had to fight from Canada, Britain would never make peace with the Nazis. By the start of September, there seemed little hope. Then Hitler and Hermann Göring made a mistake.

It began on the night of September 5 because three German Heinkel bombers did not know that they were over a blacked-out London. Since the German bombardment of Rotterdam that forced a Dutch surrender, there had been an unstated truce that neither side attack the other's cities. But these three bombers jettisoned their bombs. They did this just to be lighter and able to fly faster back to France. They had been unable to see a worthwhile target and were turning back. They were just dumping their bombs over what the pilots thought were empty fields. In reality, the bombs fell on London's East Side. But the three German pilots did not even know what they had done.

At the start of September, Reichsmarschall Hermann Göring was feeling good. His Luftwaffe was doing well over England, and he was now Hitler's second in command and heir. The propaganda minister, Heinrich Himmler, put him on the national radio to brag about the Luftwaffe's air victories and the superiority of the German pilots. Göring was exuberant. When asked if he feared that the British might bomb Berlin, he responded that his Luftwaffe was so powerful it could never happen. In fact, he added, if they do that, "you can call me Meier," which meant you could call him a Jew.

Only a few days after Göring's national radio interview, Winston Churchill ordered the Royal Air Force to bomb Berlin in retaliation for the bombing of London. Around fifty British bombers flew in darkness over the North Sea and dropped their bombs on Berlin. The attack was not very effective. Night attacks are by their nature inaccurate. Only one life was lost and that was an elephant in the Berlin Zoo. But Göring was embarrassed and Hitler enraged. Hitler immediately ordered the entire air strategy be changed. Instead of attacking the RAF, the Luftwaffe was to destroy London and the other British cities. It was the beginning of the Blitz. Operation Sea Lion, once thought imminent, was delayed.

With the Germans no longer attacking their bases, the RAF pilots could rest and new flyers could be hurriedly trained. Runways were repaired and maintenance was done on worn-out Hurricanes and Spitfires. Within a few weeks, the RAF was revitalized and rising up in ever greater numbers. The tide of battle turned, and the Luftwaffe began taking unacceptable losses. Sea Lion was delayed, delayed again, then postponed until the next spring.

In the fall of 1940, Germany almost won World War II. They had not yet attacked Russia. The United States was not yet in the war. But just when they had almost won, when England was almost down and out, Hitler and Göring made an emotional mistake. And by doing so they alone lost what may have been Germany's first and best chance to win the war.

62

SELF-DECEPTION

Yes-Men

SEPTEMBER 1941, RUSSIA

||||||||||||||||||||||||||||||||||||||||||||||||||||||||||||||||||||

I n 1941 Joseph Stalin was the absolute and unchallenged dictator of Soviet Russia. He controlled the country with a fist of iron, a secret police that numbered in the hundreds of thousands, and a psychopathic willingness to murder tens of thousands of his own people on a whim. Beginning as a peasant with a marginal education, Stalin rose to power after the death of Lenin by using a combination of intimidation and execution. His temper was legendary, and anyone who incurred his wrath suffered horribly. No one was immune, not his oldest supporters, his family, or the most valuable scientist or general.

From 1936 to 1938, hundreds of party members, peasants, professionals, and most of the party's other leadership were executed or banished to Siberia. Anyone who might have a slight chance of being a future threat to his absolute power was quickly eliminated. This included any officer in the Red Army who showed initiative or was popular with his men. It was only after the fall of France in 1939 and with the German invasion threat looming that Stalin realized his purges may have gone too far. So he blamed and executed the head of his own secret police. Even after this, Stalin's paranoia ruled and the executions he personally ordered continued, if at a slower pace.

The point being that in Russia in 1941 one just did not disagree with Stalin. Nor did anyone act unless ordered to do so. Nor did any military leader even consider using some initiative if his unit's situation changed. This was particularly true for the surviving or replacement military commanders on any level. The slightest hint of disobeying an order from Stalin could be a death sentence.

On August 14, 1939, German Foreign Minister Joachim von Ribbentrop and the Soviet Foreign Minister Vyacheslav Mikhaylovich Molotov (yes, as in the Molotov cocktail) signed both a nonaggression pact and an economic understanding. This gave Stalin a sense of security; he felt that Germany needed Russia's resources and so it was in Hitler's interests to remain on good terms.

To the chancellor of the German Reich, Herr A. Hitler.

I thank you for your letter. I hope that the German-Soviet Nonaggression Pact will mark a decisive turn for the better in the political relations between our two countries.

J. Stalin

—QUOTED BY ALAN BULLOCK, *HITLER AND STALIN: PARALLEL LIVES* (NEW YORK: VINTAGE BOOKS, 1993)

By June 1941, Hitler's armies had overrun all of western Europe and most of the Balkans. Approximately 130 German divisions and thousands of aircraft were poised on the Russian border. In *Mein Kampf*, Hitler had openly stated that the future of the Aryan race was to conquer the lands of the subhuman Slavic races. He had been appointed and given absolute power in Germany to protect his people from the Communists in their own country. He had publicly berated Britain for resisting rather than joining him on a crusade against Communism.

The Russian intelligence agencies had for months found evidence that the German attack was coming. Stalin's top spy in Japan warned that Hitler had notified the Japanese of his intentions. That April, the British had even sent copies of some of the plans for Operation Barbarossa (the German invasion of Russia) to Russia. Still Stalin refused to believe that the Germans would attack. He considered it all to be a conspiracy by the allies to drag Russia into their war.

Stalin made it clear to his aides and commanders that he did not want to hear of this. He had convinced himself that Hitler would not attack. He would not change his opinion, and those who disagreed often suffered the fate of anyone who challenged Stalin. Historians have found dozens of warnings, copies of plans, copies of deciphered German diplomatic and military messages, and additional proof that was sent to Stalin or his intelligence chiefs. Stalin passed off all of the evidence as being a fabrication of the desperate British. He refused to allow the 3.1 million soldiers stationed on Russia's western border to pull back into defensive positions. There were defenses in depth at the old Polish border (the Stalin Line) and along the Berezina and Dniester Rivers. But Russian Chief of Staff General Georgy Zhukov was forbidden to even discuss the idea of pulling them back.

Telling Stalin he was wrong was not a route to promotion in the Soviet Army (except to cadaver). So those around the supreme leader of the Soviet Union cleaned up the intelligence reports before passing them to Stalin. For self-preservation they lost the reconnaissance photos that disagreed with what Joseph Stalin wanted to hear. Stalin was told what he wanted to hear. It did not matter that it was an inaccurate or totally incorrect worldview. It was Stalin's, and so everyone else and every document had to conform.

When Stalin's front line generals reported what they were suddenly facing across the border, his response was to advise those generals watching the Germans preparing to attack to avoid doing anything that would be a provocation. Even when German soldiers deserted and appeared at the Russian lines in support of Communism, Stalin ignored the warnings that German units were about to invade. Just a few minutes before the actual launch of Operation Barbarossa, trains full of Russian coal, steel, and foodstuffs continued to roll into Germany, many right past the poised Wehrmacht panzers, whose engines were running.

On June 22, 1941, Hitler launched Operation Barbarossa. The far more numerous Russian air force was destroyed at its air bases in the first few hours. Red Army units fought where they stood and were encircled. Half the Russian army was crushed in the first few weeks. Almost two million Russian soldiers died or were captured.

We know today that Stalin was simply unable to believe he had been so terribly wrong. When the enormity of the disaster became clear to the sole and absolute dictator of Russia, he mentally collapsed. Army commanders who had been taught that to act without instructions was a fatal error, got no orders. Troops that were being encircled got no permission to retreat. Stalin literally seemed to have disappeared for several days, doing nothing. Most records show he was somewhere in the lower levels of the Kremlin, but no one is sure. Once he emerged, the Soviet leader seemed disoriented and confused. The records of meetings with him in the first month after Barbarossa indicate that he had trouble focusing or accepting reports relating to the military disaster he had done nothing to prevent.

63

MISSED
OPPORTUNITY

Just Declare Victory

OCTOBER 1941, BERLIN

||||||||||||||||||||||||||||||||||||||||||||||||||||||||||||||||||||

The fall of 1941 was a heady time for Hitler. He had conquered France, and his armies were driving through Russia. The general staff was very concerned. They had seen the casualty figures, but the Führer had not. Since the launch of Operation Barbarossa, the two million men in the German and allied armies had captured or killed over three million Russian soldiers. That October, Army Group North was besieging Leningrad, Army Group South had occupied a massive area, and Army Group Center was preparing for a final drive on Moscow. It had forward elements within a hundred miles of the Soviet capital and main rail hub. Over half a million more prisoners were being squeezed into surrendering in a pocket centering on Kiev. From Berlin, the Red Army looked defeated. The Wehrmacht had destroyed more divisions than their pre-Barbarossa intelligence had indicated that the Soviets had. In September plans had already begun for reorganizing the German war machine to deal with Britain and the United States once Russia was finished off. (Fewer soldiers and more planes and ships.) The few neutral European nations that were left were bending to Hitler's will almost before he made any demands.

It was also a fact that the flanks of Army Group Center were unprotected. Most of the German divisions were fighting at half strength or less. Some of the "battalions" in Army Group Center contained only 250 men and were led by lieutenants. The vaunted panzer armies had lost more than half their tanks, and replacement vehicles were being held back by Hitler to create three new panzer divisions. Even ammunition was becoming a major concern as the German supply lines were stretched to their limits. Gasoline had become scarce, and guerrilla warfare was erupting in the occupied territories. The Wehrmacht was stretched and at its limit. Also the mud season was coming. Once the fall rains began, wheeled vehicles would be useless on Russia's dirt roads, and the panzers would be forced onto those same roads in order to move at all.

On the Russian side, there were only a dozen fresh divisions dug in before Moscow. Siberian forces were rushing eastward, and other units were converging on the city. Many of the government leaders had already evacuated beyond the Urals, and Stalin was considering joining them. Morale in the Red Army was at an all-time low. Only draconian measures prevented mass desertions and collapse. Entire armies were surrendering once trapped. Even highly ranked officers predicted a German victory within weeks. While most of the industrial equipment had been evacuated, the new Ural Mountain factories were just beginning to produce tanks and ammunition. The residents of Moscow were being herded by the Narodnyy Komissariat Vnutrennikh Del—Stalin's secret police, who are normally referred to as the more pronounceable NKVD—out of the city and forced to dig lines of defense. Some civilians were told they would be given a rifle and were expected to resist when the Germans broke through.

In London and Washington, military leaders predicted that Moscow would fall before the new year. Roosevelt sent Stalin a personal note promising three thousand trucks (which would not arrive until 1942), hoping to boost Russian morale. The Japanese, encouraged by Germany, were already far into their preparations for the surprise attack on Pearl Harbor and the Philippines.

It was against this background that Stalin sent out tentative feelers toward a peace offer. Russia would give up the Baltic nations and much of her eastern territories, including Ukraine. They would even begin to supply raw materials and oil to Germany again. What would remain would be a weakened Russia that would be much less of a threat in the future. Most of the Nazi resource problems would also be solved. Russia and Stalin would survive. Yet Hitler dismissed the offer. He saw total victory as being close and said so to anyone and everyone.

Army Group Center's attack on Moscow ground to a halt within sight of the Kremlin. With the end of the war so close, winterizing the German army had been given a low priority. Winterizing could be completed at their leisure after Moscow and Leningrad fell. Worse yet, because they continued to be on the attack, all three German army groups were exposed in forward positions suitable for offense, not defense. When the Russians gathered their strength for a winter offensive, the German armies were overextended, unable to support each other, and offering too many open flanks.

Germany was not the only nation that assumed an imminent Russian defeat. Assured by her ally that they would soon be victorious over Russia, Japan felt free to start their own war with America and the Allies. Had Russia fallen, then the United States and Britain would have been alone and facing the full force of the Nazis. The Japanese military government was emboldened to first grab French Indochina. When the United States reacted with sanctions, Japan launched surprise attacks all across the Pacific on December 7, 1941.

Moscow did not fall, and Leningrad held out through starvation and destruction. The weakened and overextended German army suffered greatly from both winter and the first Russian Winter Offensive. Adding to the bad news for Hitler was Franklin

Roosevelt's announcement that victory in Europe would be the first priority. The peace feelers from Stalin were an opportunity for Hitler to solidify his control of Europe. Never again would he have a chance for so advantageous an end to the war. But Hitler was so sure of a complete victory that he dismissed the chance to have won a great one. After all, at that point in the war, Germany had never failed to conquer any nation on the Continent. So Hitler did not really consider the virtual concession offered though neutrals by a panicked Stalin, and he lost the best chance the Third Reich had for a negotiated victory. Four years later, it was the Russians who were occupying Berlin.

64

||||||||||||||||||||||||||||||||||||||||||||||||||||||||||||||||

UNDERESTIMATED
THE OPPOSITION

Infamy

||||||||||||||||||||||||||||||||||||||||||||||||||||||||||||||||

There were many reasons why the Japanese Empire chose to start a war with the United States. At the core of it all was the reality that the Japanese islands are nearly destitute in mineral resources or oil. Everything needed for their growing industrial machine and society had to be imported. This put them at the mercy of the European colonial powers that controlled Indochina: exporters such as the United States and Russia, and their mineral-rich but less-advanced neighbors. For an ambitious and modernizing nation that saw itself as the standard bearer of all Asian peoples, this vulnerability was an intolerable situation.

Japan had been an ally of the United States, Britain, and France in World War I. But after the war, they were given short shrift when the German possessions were distributed. President Woodrow Wilson successfully opposed giving Japan any of the former German territories. America and Japan were the two Pacific powers competing both for political and commercial influence. At the 1921–1922 Washington Naval Conference, the one where the maximum fleet tonnages were set by treaty, Japan got a smaller than expected maximum. Again the United States was the cause. Furthermore, America then pressured Britain to end her long-time alliance with Japan, which alienated and insulted the Japanese government. Japan felt isolated and betrayed. Combined with the economic strain of the Great Depression, which did not spare Asia, this led to a radicalization of both the Japanese people and their military.

Taking advantage of a civil war in China that had begun in 1927, the Japanese army easily occupied Manchuria. The relatively backward nation was rich in minerals, land, and many of the resources Japan needed. There was no real justification for the occupation, and the Western nations all protested and condemned it. All ignored the fact that their own colonial empires had been obtained the same way. This further alienated Japan and increased its sense of isolation. After grabbing Manchuria, Japan, hoping to become self-sufficient in resources and control the markets of the Pacific Rim, then took advantage of the weakened China to occupy first the Chinese coastal cities and then large swaths of the Chinese countryside. They even went so far as to seek out the last Chinese emperor and return him to the throne as a puppet (he avoided execution and ended his days as a gardener). The Japanese view of conquest as an economic necessity was reflected by the name they gave their Pacific empire: The Greater Co-Prosperity Sphere.

For years the Western press printed stories, many true, about Japanese atrocities. This was the era of the Rape of Nanking, in which the Japanese army slaughtered and raped the citizens for days, killing tens of thousands of Chinese. After the surrender of France and after the Blitzkrieg, the Japanese invaded and quickly conquered French Indochina. At that point, the United States felt forced to react. It did so by striking at Japan's great vulnerability.

Japan had not yet had time to really develop the mineral resources of Manchuria or the oil in Java. It remained primarily dependent on importing most of its oil, scrap metal, and finished steel from the United States. As a result, when Dean Acheson, the secretary of state, announced sanctions that included a ban on the sale of oil and scrap metal to Japan, that nation not only was put in a desperate strategic situation but its economy began to collapse. Japanese military leaders, who were also in political control, were angered by what they felt was hypocritical and unfair treatment, primarily intended to keep them from having the same type of empire that the Europeans and the United States already had.

There was also another pressing reason Japan had to act. There was just enough oil in the Japanese reserves to allow their fleet eight months of full activity. It was a fleet that contained some of the most modern and powerful ships in the world and was a matter of great national pride. Because they were engaged in a war with China and occupying Indochina, they had to have the support of their fleet. The United States also reacted by greatly increasing financial and military aid to Chiang Kai-shek's China. (Remember the Flying Tigers, the American volunteers who flew for China against the Japanese before Pearl Harbor?)

Adding to the pressure on Japan, the United States froze all Japanese assets in America, which denied Japan the dollars needed to trade for oil or minerals on the world market. Doing nothing meant the failure of Japan's war in China and the end of its ambition of being the Britain of Asia.

Doing nothing meant the collapse of the Japanese war in China, their economy, and also the military-dominated government. War against America now seemed inevitable to the Japanese leadership. It is how the Japanese went about starting it that was perhaps the greatest among the many mistakes that lost them World War II. They were also encouraged by their ally Germany to start the war. In November 1941, the Nazis were approaching Moscow and saw their victory in Russia as imminent. Thus they were sure their only opponents would be Britain and the United States.

The attitude of the Japanese leadership toward the average

American had to have been a large part of the decision to attack Pearl Harbor. The United States in the 1930s was a land of extremes and excess. Prohibition had created an age in which speakeasies and flappers were the rage and bank robbers dominated the headlines. To the disciplined and highly organized Japanese, all Americans appeared irredeemably decadent. The United States' hesitation in getting involved in World War II in Europe reinforced the Japanese impression that Americans had no spine for war. War, then, seemed the best way to pressure the United States into recognizing Japan's right to create an empire.

The decision to go to war with the United States led to the question of how to best begin that war. Japanese myths often show how a weaker but honorable hero overcomes a powerful adversary by outthinking him. Surprise and deception were considered an honorable way to even the odds. The Japanese would emulate such a David and Goliath story and use their guile and own strengths to strike at the Americans so hard that Japan could force a quick and favorable treaty from the Americans. If the American people had been as soft, self-indulgent, and unpatriotic as the Japanese assumed, then the surprise attack on Pearl Harbor could well have broken their will. The loss of their battleships and carri-

---

RACIAL STEREOTYPES

Americans were themselves not immune to being blinded by racial prejudice. They were sure the Japanese, being little men with squinty, bad vision, would be no threat and would certainly make bad soldiers and pilots. American naval pilots, despite the experiences of the Flying Tigers, often felt that the Japanese were physically incapable of beating them. American racial arrogance helped make the surprise attacks on the Hawaiian Islands and the Philippines successful.

ers would have forced America to accept a diplomatic solution. But, of course, the Japanese viewed America as if it were a part of Japan. They never understood that in American individuality the rules of Japanese society did not apply. What would have been considered a weakness in the Japanese was the strength of the Americans.

In what must be considered one of the great misjudgments in history, it was decided by Japan that an attack crippling the American Pacific Fleet would be so traumatic that the United States would react by agreeing to a peace advantageous to Japan.

> *Yesterday, December 7, 1941—a date which will live in infamy—the United States of America was suddenly and deliberately attacked by naval and air forces of the Empire of Japan.*
>
> President Franklin Roosevelt, asking Congress for a declaration
> of war, December 8, 1941

|||||||||||||||||||||||||||||||||||||||||||||||||||||||||||||||||||||||||||||

65

UNFINISHED JOB

Tora Tora Tora Too Little

DECEMBER 7, 1941, HAWAII

|||||||||||||||||||||||||||||||||||||||||||||||||||||||||||||||||||||||||||||

The seas were rough, and dawn came late in the winter sky on December 7, so it was after 6:00 AM when the last of the 183 planes (forty-nine high-altitude bombers, fifty-one dive-bombers, forty torpedo planes, and forty-three fighters) were airborne. The crews of the six aircraft carriers began preparation to launch another wave of planes within an hour. The Japanese planes turned toward Pearl Harbor guided by the signal of a local music station.

At two minutes past seven, two privates, manning one of six radar stations on the island of Oahu, saw a large number of jagged lines, each indicating an aircraft. It was in the early days of the technology and there was little more information than that about the fifty-plus aircraft approaching the island. The privates forwarded their observation to a central information center, who assumed the radar had picked up on an expected flight of B-17 bombers.

Fifteen minutes after being seen on radar, the first wave of

Japanese aircraft approached Pearl Harbor. The attack commander, Mitsuo Fuchida, saw rows of parked ships, including every battleship America had in the Pacific. He did not see the two aircraft carriers he hoped would be there. Fuchida ordered his radio operator to send out a code. It was "To ra, To ra, To ra," which meant "Attack, surprise achieved." In Japanese *tora* means "tiger," which is how the message was interpreted by some of the attacking pilots.

It was a Sunday, and despite warnings from Washington, the American fleet was still in a peacetime stance. Most of the sailors were ashore or asleep. The first bombs fell at five minutes before 8:00. Torpedoes followed a few minutes later. It was seen from the Ford Island headquarters, and the message went out: "Air raid on Pearl Harbor X This is not drill."

In the next minutes, squadrons of bombers and torpedo planes attacked the double and triple lines of unmoving ships that were the U.S. Navy Pacific Fleet. After bombs rained onto Battleship Row from the high-level bombers, the dive-bombers screamed in, releasing heavy-armor-piercing bombs that smashed through the decks and sides of their targets and exploded inside. The Japanese torpedo planes were at first a concern as they had to use specially adapted torpedoes due to the shallow depth of the harbor. Torpedoes then needed seventy-five feet to splash then run in, but Pearl Harbor was only forty-five feet deep. But wooden modifications worked as planned, and at 8:10 a bomb penetrated the deck of the *Arizona*, setting off its entire store of gun powder, approximately a million pounds. The blast tore apart the insides of the ship. Soon the quiet harbor was filled with smoke and flame. Eight American battleships were sunk or seriously damaged.

Other squadrons of dive-bombers attacked the American air bases. Concerned about sabotage, the army had lined up all their planes in their runways and this made them easy targets. After dropping fragmentation bombs, the Japanese fighters and dive-bombers made strafing runs. Each pass allowed the attackers to damage or destroy several of the lined-up planes. They were perfect targets. Within minutes, more than three hundred planes were destroyed.

Half an hour after the first wave had left, the second flight of Japanese aircraft struck. The fifty-four high-altitude bombers, seventy-eight dive-bombers, and thirty-five escorting fighters did not have the element of surprise and were met with intense anti-aircraft fire. A few American planes were also in the air. This wave still effectively struck more ships, sinking the battleship *Pennsylvania*, the cruiser *Raleigh*, and three destroyers. Eighteen ships, including all of the Pacific fleet's battleships, had now been either sunk or incapacitated. Almost every other warship in the harbor had some damage. At the same time, other Japanese bombers hit the naval dry docks but only lightly damaged them. The Japanese lost twenty-nine aircraft from the second wave.

When the aircraft of the second wave returned to the carriers, they reported to Vice Admiral Chuichi Nagumo. Their report was that the dry docks had not been sufficiently damaged and the oil and fuel tanks, ammunition, and warehouses full of ship's stores remained intact. The submarine base had been hardly touched at all. These all had to be dealt with before Pearl Harbor could be considered neutralized as an effective naval port. Neutralizing Hawaii would force the U.S. Navy in the Pacific to base itself more than a thousand miles eastward on the California coast.

Because the Japanese ships needed to remain hidden from the remaining American land-based planes and aircraft from the three missing carriers, the Japanese maintained radio silence. The decision fell to Vice Admiral Nagumo to make. He could have finished off the base, but at a higher cost while alerting defenses. There was also the risk of losing the only carrier fleet Japan had if they were discovered during the attack. He was said to have considered launching a third wave, as his junior officers encouraged or politely demanded. But Nagumo was operating under orders that read that once the American fleet was crippled, the safety of the thirty-three ships under his command, including most of Japan's aircraft carriers, was the highest priority.

The Japanese strike force had already lost over a hundred aircraft. This was nearly a third of their total air strength. With the location of the American carriers unknown, the intent of Nagumo's orders was clear. He led Japan's only carrier fleet. The ships, planes, and experienced pilots were irreplaceable. Considering the stiff antiaircraft fire and fighter resistance met by the second wave, there was no question that any third attack would be costly. The vice admiral ordered a withdrawal, and no third wave was launched.

Nagumo's cautious decision was based on a lack of intelligence. He had no choice. Yes, the American carriers were rushing back. But they were nowhere near Hawaii and would not be within effective range that day. Two had been on a mission to shuttle aircraft to other islands, and a third carrier was on its way to San Francisco. His decision left the dry docks and repair facilities intact. Work began almost immediately repairing the ships that had been damaged or sunk. Because the fuel and supplies were untouched, Pearl Harbor continued to be able to act as a principal naval and air base for the Pacific fleet. Had a third wave been as effective as the first two, the base would have been crippled for months or years. The limited shipping and need to convoy more oil, parts, and other replacements would have meant months of shuttling on the limited number of ships available in the Pacific. Without a functional base or way to refuel, what remained of the Pacific fleet would have been forced to retreat to San Diego and San Francisco. Hawaii might even have been vulnerable to invasion. The battlefields of the Coral Sea and Midway Island would have been beyond the effective range of west coast–based American ships. Those tide-turning victories might not have happened. Had Nagumo ordered that third strike, the war in the Pacific would have been far different.

66

||||||||||||||||||||||||||||||||||||||||||||||||||||||||||||||||||||||||||||||||

BLIND ADHERENCE
TO ORDERS

Just Obeying Orders

||||||||||||||||||||||||||||||||||||||||||||||||||||||||||||||||||||||||||||||||

I can run wild for six months . . . after that, I have no
expectation of success.

—ADMIRAL YAMAMOTO, IMPERIAL JAPANESE NAVY

soroku Yamamoto was correct; for the first six months of World
War II in the Pacific, the Imperial Japanese Navy (IJN) won victory after victory. The closest they came to an air-to-air battle
defeat was the Battle of the Coral Sea, and there they sunk one of
the four American aircraft carriers, the *Lexington*, and badly damaged another, the *Yorktown*, at the cost of only a small escort carrier. The military controlled the Japanese government, and it
gained prestige and popular support with each victory. Then the
Americans did something that had very little military effect but
that forced a massive reaction from the Imperial Japanese Navy.
"Keeping face" was an important part of the Japanese culture, and
the prestige of the navy suffered when General Jimmy Doolittle's
bombers struck several Japanese cities. This was a navy problem
because the bombers were launched from the carrier *Hornet*. So

the IJN had failed to protect the homeland. In reaction, a plan was devised to gain revenge for Doolittle's raid and destroy the three remaining U.S. aircraft carriers.

The U.S. Navy lost eight battleships and three light cruisers in the December 7 surprise attack on Pearl Harbor. This meant that for the next six months the navy had no modern battleships in the Pacific and very few cruisers. The IJN could field ten battleships and thirty-eight cruisers. The U.S. Navy also had just two launch-capable fleet aircraft carriers against six Japanese fleet carriers and an additional six smaller carriers. With such a preponderance of strength, Admiral Yamamoto, who had planned the Pearl Harbor attack, decided he had to attack somewhere that the Americans could not afford to lose. The U.S. Pacific Fleet would risk a battle only if forced. The ideal choice was to invade the two Midway Islands. The Midways, Eastern and Sand, were the only American bases west of Hawaii. If lost to the Japanese, they could serve as a base from which to launch an invasion of the Hawaiian Islands. If based on Midway, the IJN would be closer to Honolulu than would American reinforcements based in San Diego or San Francisco.

Because of a decryption breakthrough, the U.S. Navy was aware that Midway was the target and when the invasion would occur. Unfortunately, the navy was down to just two fleet air-

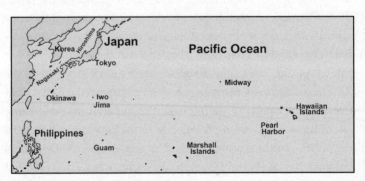

The Pacific Ocean and Midway Islands

craft carriers. But with a bit of effort and ingenuity, the crippled *Yorktown* carrier, which should have taken two months to repair, was functional and sailing toward Midway within two days. Because the United States knew when and where the Japanese were going to attack, if not the route they would sail on, the three U.S. carriers were in place northeast of Midway before the Japanese submarine screening line, intended to warn of their approach, was in place.

So thinking the American fleet was still in Pearl Harbor, the Kido Butai, the IJN First Carrier Fleet, approached Midway. In it were four of Japan's six large carriers. The other two were off on what was a diversionary effort in the Aleutian Islands. Because Japan's messages were being read, it was a useless diversion. Commanding that carrier fleet was Admiral Chuichi Nagumo. He had commanded these ships since before Pearl Harbor. At best Nagumo was described, even by his fellow officers, as stolid and dependable. His greatest strength was a willingness to obey the orders of the brilliant Yamamoto. But trying to obey orders is what cost the Japanese all four of their carriers and permanently changed the tide of the naval war in the Pacific.

The Kido Butai led the attack. It was made up of four carriers and more cruisers than were in the U.S. Pacific Fleet. Because its job was both to destroy the American carriers when they appeared and to neutralize Midway's defenses, its planes were the first to enter combat. Nagumo's orders were clear. The primary objective was to engage and destroy the two remaining American air carriers. Because they had to be drawn out by the attack on the Midway Islands, his second priority was to have his air groups first soften the well-defended islands.

Following his orders, the Kido Butai prepared a little more than half of its attack aircraft and fighter escorts for an assault on Midway. This meant they were armed with fragmentation bombs designed for use on ground targets. As per his orders and priorities, once the Midway attack was launched, Admiral Nagumo armed the rest of his aircraft with torpedoes and armor-penetrating bombs. This prepared them for any unexpected appearance of the American carriers. The air attack on Midway was effective, but it did not put the runway there out of action or destroy vital gasoline tanks and defensive positions. Because the American carriers were thought to be no closer than Hawaii, when the Japanese commander got the radio message that a second air attack on Midway was needed, he ordered the armament on the planes still on the carriers be changed to land attack bombs.

The change out on the aircraft on Nagumo's four fleet carriers was almost complete when a scout plane reported sighting an American carrier. It was the *Yorktown*. The presence must have been a surprise and shock. If Nagumo launched the land attack his aircraft were armed for, he would have to wait for the returning aircraft from the first attack to be refueled and rearmed before going after the American ship. But going after the American carriers was the primary reason for the entire operation. For some time Nagumo hesitated, much to the consternation of his officers. Then he decided to obey Yamamoto's orders. The carriers were priority one, and he would make them so. Nagumo ordered the armaments on his on-deck aircraft to be changed a second time, back to torpedoes and armor-piercing bombs. The process would take under an hour.

It was a close thing. The change back to naval ordnance was almost complete when three flights of American torpedo planes attacked. The Kido Butai had already been attacked earlier by planes from Midway and not taken a single hit. As the patrolling zeroes tore into the hapless American torpedo planes, their luck held. Not a single torpedo struck. Two American attacks had not cost them more than a few planes. But the torpedo planes' attack did delay the launch of the second-wave aircraft. While the Japanese zeroes were pursuing and shooting down the last of the U.S. torpedo planes, three flights of U.S. dive-bombers struck three of the four carriers. Their bombs easily penetrated the wooden flight decks of the Kido Butai and exploded among the armed and fueled planes just below. Within minutes, three of the Japanese fleet carriers were burning out of control.

Had Nagumo launched his second land attack, the American bombs would have been damaging but not fatal. They would have hurt the carriers, but there would not have been the secondary damage from their own fueled and bomb-armed aircraft exploding. But rather than take a chance, Nagumo had obeyed his orders, and that changed the course of the war in the Pacific.

Later that day, planes from the remaining Japanese aircraft carrier, the *Hiryu*, crippled the *Yorktown*. They later returned and finalized that often-wounded American ship's fate. However, because the *Yorktown*'s damage-repair crews had put out all of the fires from that day's first attack, the carrier was moving again. So the Japanese were under the impression that when they finally sunk the beleaguered *Hornet*, they had gotten both the remaining American carriers. At almost the exact same time that the Japanese planes were attacking the *Yorktown* aircraft, the *Hiryu* was sunk by the planes flying off the *Hornet* and *Enterprise*. With no place to land, every remaining aircraft, and pilot, of the Kido Butai was lost. With no air support, Yamamoto was forced to call off the invasion of Midway.

Midway was never again threatened. The Imperial Japanese Navy never recovered from the losses at Midway. The initiative in the Pacific theater changed, and the Americans determined the course of the war from then on. Soon the massive industrial machine that was America in the 1940s was producing a fleet carrier every month. The Pacific naval battles after Midway Island were about defending what Japan held, not expanding their empire. Almost six months after Pearl Harbor, Nagumo obeyed his orders to the letter and lost Japan's First Carrier Fleet.

67

FATAL LOSS OF CONFIDENCE

Conceding Defeat

1942, SINGAPORE

||||||||||||||||||||||||||||||||||||||||||||||||||||||||||||||||||||||||||||||

The loss of Singapore can be attributed to overconfidence followed by the collapse of confidence. There is no question that the Japanese army that carried out the operation was both experienced and ruthless. There is also no question that sixty-five thousand Japanese soldiers outfought and outmaneuvered almost a hundred thousand British. But the fault for the worst British defeat of World War II has to be attributed to arrogance and poor tactics, followed by the collapse of confidence. It did not have to happen.

Singapore was the lynchpin of the British presence in Asia. The city, base, air base, and port were on an island at the tip of the Malay Peninsula. Singapore was the location of Britain's largest naval base and largest garrison in the Far East. It was considered by the British leadership to be impregnable. The entire base had been updated and reinforced in 1938. The massive naval guns would doom any enemy ship, and its garrison was, well, British. In addition, two of the Royal Navy's most powerful ships were based there, the battleship *Prince of Wales* and the battle cruiser

Repulse. There was no question in the minds of the men stationed there that they would have little trouble defeating the Japanese. If you had pointed out to the English officers how effective the Japanese were against the Chinese, they would have explained that they'd had success simply because that conflict included second-rate soldiers fighting second-rate opponents. It would be far different against real, British soldiers. Racial arrogance was very much a part of what led to the defeat. They were so confident that one young officer worried, "I do hope we are not getting too strong in Malaya, because if so the Japanese may never attempt a landing." He did not need to worry.

One key mistake the British made was one of the most common. It was based on the enemy doing what was expected of it. They prepared their defenses assuming the Japanese would attack Singapore from the water. Because of this, the massive naval guns were all positioned to fire only out to sea. They proved useless.

Lieutenant General Tomoyuki Yamashita's Japanese Twenty-Fifth Army landed on an undefended shoreline on the Malay Peninsula on December 8, the day after Pearl Harbor. They quickly captured the Kota Bharu Airport. From there they were able to launch a series of air raids that destroyed a majority of the British aircraft on the ground. Even this did not stir the British from their complacent confidence. The general consensus was that it would just be a bother to "shove the little men off."

The Japanese were experienced jungle fighters who knew that the British would win a set-piece battle. Their strategy was to move as quickly as possible and outmaneuver any defensive positions. The entire campaign was to be carried out with the calculated cruelty the Japanese soldiers were trained to practice. Among their standing orders was to execute all prisoners immediately. A pamphlet giving the order was passed out and in part read, "When you encounter the enemy after landing, think of yourself as an avenger coming face to face at last with his father's murderer. Here is a man whose death will lighten your heart."

The British, burdened by wheeled vehicles and artillery, were basically forced to use the sparse road network on the Malay Peninsula. The Japanese virtually abandoned their own guns and used commandeered bicycles to transport both themselves and supplies. Every time the English set up a defensive position, the Japanese simply went around it through the "impassable" jungle.

On December 10, 1941, in an attempt to disrupt the landings of both the *Prince of Wales* and the *Repulse*, the Japanese rushed north up the Malayan coast. With its planes destroyed, the Royal Air Force (RAF) could not offer the two ships any air cover. The result was wave after wave of Japanese torpedo bombers coming just above the water uncontested. Both ships were sunk and their crews lost. Winston Churchill wrote about being notified of the loss: "I put the telephone down. I was thankful to be alone. In all the war I never received a more direct shock." Morale both in England and in Singapore plunged. Overconfidence was replaced by near panic. After being badly defeated in the Battle of Jitra over the next two days, the British army, under Lord Arthur Percival, was in full retreat. By the end of January, the last of the defenders had crossed over the Johore Strait that separated Malaya from Singapore.

The British prepared their defenses and waited. On February 8, the Japanese attacked across the strait. The attacking army contained twenty-seven thousand soldiers facing ninety thousand defenders, including reinforcements that were still unloading even as the battle ended. Percival had spread his men along the entire coast of Singapore, a distance of about seventy miles. In defending everything, he was spread too thin. Nor did he employ a strategic reserve. The Australian Twenty-Seventh Brigade was able to punish the Japanese as they crossed the strait, holding them to a small beachhead. But Brigadier Duncan Maxwell became concerned when he could not contact the Australian Twenty-Second Brigade on his left flank. He ordered a withdrawal from the shoreline. The Japanese quickly exploited his error and hurried to land armored units. There was not a single British tank and few antitank guns in Singapore. The British and colonial forces resisted, but the Japanese beachhead spread until they captured the warehouses that contained most of Percival's ammunition and supplies. Fighting desperately, the British held their lines and most of Singapore. They were under constant air attack and running low on ammunition of all types and fresh water. By the morning of the 15th, the British situation was desperate. They considered a push to regain their supplies, but they ran out of antiaircraft ammunition. Air attacks hindered any assembly, and that afternoon, Percival sent a messenger to discuss the terms of surrender.

During the entire campaign, the British suffered 7,500 dead and 10,000 wounded. In addition, 120,000 men surrendered in Singapore to a third that number of attackers. Given the Japanese attitude toward prisoners, Percival did his men little service in surrendering. Most died in captivity, all were kept in horrible conditions. Eight thousand of those prisoners were virtually worked to death to construct the Burma-Thailand railroad, including the bridge over the River Kwai.

68

STUBBORN PRIDE

Festung Stalingrad

SEPTEMBER 1942–FEBRUARY 1943, RUSSIA

There is a myth that Hitler ordered the taking of Stalingrad because of its name. While he had to be pleased at the thought of upsetting Joseph Stalin by occupying the city named for him, there were a number of valid military reasons for taking the city. The name probably added to Stalin's insistence that the city be held at all costs, but again Russia could not afford the strategic loss. Stalin was so determined to hold the city that the residents of Stalingrad were prevented from leaving the city. Even after Friedrich Paulus's Sixth Army and Hermann Hoth's Fourth Panzer Army assaulted the city in August of 1942, no one was allowed to flee across the Volga River. The reason given for this by Joseph Stalin was that the defenders would fight better if they were protecting civilians. Tens of thousands of women and children were sacrificed to preserve Russian morale. The population was also put to work building defenses and bunkers.

Stalingrad sat on the Volga River and was the center of both road and rail networks. Taking the city would prevent most Russian reinforcements from reaching the Caucasus, which was Army Group South's real goal. While the battle for the city went on, the second half of Army Group South continued to drive toward Baku. The Caucasus contained the oil fields that supplied the Soviet army and could support the German war effort. The Volga was also the main route for grains and other foodstuffs traveling north from the Soviet Union's warmer growing regions. Control of the Volga and the transport networks that all met in Stalingrad would have severed an important part of the Soviet Union. The loss would have crippled what remained of the country within months. The Russians also understood Stalingrad's strategic value as shown by the effort they put into holding on to the city despite massive losses. Stalin sent his best general, Marshal Georgy Zhukov, the man who had saved Moscow, to organize the city's defenses and counteroffensives that followed. Zhukov's political officer was Commissar Nikita Khrushchev, who in 1956 became prime minister of the Soviet Union.

Hitler knew if he controlled Stalingrad, he could cut off the Volga completely. The city would also have provided a secure flank for Army Group South. At this point they were advancing against light resistance. A secure flank would free them to push to Baku and the oil fields. When the battle for the city did end in the defeat of the Sixth Army, the advancing army forced a rapid retreat by all German forces south of the city. The defense of Stalingrad saved Russia's main source of oil.

There was another reason for Hitler to attack the largest city in southern Russia. America had entered the war. Russia had failed to slow the Nazis with their first winter offensive, but even as the Germans advanced again, the momentum was changing. If Russia fell, then the United States and Britain would stand alone. Such a prospect might well force them to accept a truce that accepted Nazi control of all of Russia. But to separate the Allies, a major victory was needed.

Stalingrad offered such a victory. There Hitler could show that the Russian dictator could not even defend his namesake city deep inside Russia. It was the only place Hitler could find a win spectacular enough to intimidate or discourage Russia's allies. There just was nowhere else. A starving Leningrad still held out and promised to continue to hold. Moscow was by then out of reach. Anything less than a dramatic victory would not be enough. Stalingrad was one of the few opportunities Hitler had to ensure German supremacy on the Eastern Front and solve the problem of its oil shortage. There was even a chance that Stalin would again offer a truce if he lost the strategic city. But if the attack was justified, what followed was a disaster. Today the German defeat at this city, situated over a thousand miles from Moscow and fourteen hundred miles from Berlin, is considered the turning point of World War II in Europe. Hitler's great mistake was not in attacking Stalingrad. It was doing so with too weak a force and then sacrificing a quarter of a million soldiers' lives trying to hold it.

After crossing the open steppes by late July, Army Group South approached Stalingrad. Hitler's habit of issuing orders had managed to delay the battle a week when he first detached the Fourth Panzer from Hoth and sent it south to reinforce the push toward Baku. This overloaded roads and created a several-thousand-vehicle traffic jam. Then when that jam was finally sorted out, Hitler ordered the Fourth Panzer to turn around and rejoin Paulus's Sixth Army as it began assaulting Stalingrad. This meant that the strength of Army Group South was split into two armies that were too far apart to support each other.

The attack on Stalingrad began with a fierce aerial bombardment at the end of July 1942. It smashed many of Stalingrad's defenses and temporarily stopped all traffic on the Volga. The air battle also shattered the Soviet air force in the area. Workers were organized into untrained militia. Men and women were handed weapons and herded toward the Germans. One factory continued to produce tanks, which were then manned by untrained workers. They fueled and armed the new vehicles and drove the few miles to the front lines with the tanks they had just made, still unpainted and without even gun sights. The slaughter of Russians was immense, but their resistance also took a toll on the Germans.

The Luftwaffe bombing continued until most of Stalingrad consisted of rubble and burned-out buildings. The burning piles of rubble were often two stories high. As the Sixth Army and Fourth Panzer penetrated into the city, the fighting was not just house to house but often floor to floor or room to room. It was not unusual for one floor to be held by the Germans and the floor above or below by the Russians. The fighting expanded to the sewers below the city, where men fought hand to hand in the stinking darkness.

The Soviets shuttled new troops and ammunition across the Volga every night. The life expectancy of a Russian soldier entering this grinder was at most twenty-four hours. A Russian officer was expected to survive about three days. There was no choice but to attack. The penalty for failing to move toward the Nazis was being shot by the NKVD, the Soviet's fanatic secret police, who stood behind the Russian units armed with automatic weapons. To avoid the effective German artillery and Stukas, the Russians tried to stay as close as they could to the German lines. They called this hugging the Nazis. The Sixth Army had to go room by room and building by building with little help from their superior technology. Each night Russians would infiltrate back into buildings cleared earlier. Snipers were ever present for both sides. The Russians' defense of the strongpoints was particularly intense, with some key positions changing hands several times. German losses were high, with more dead than wounded.

Russian artillery on the far side of the Volga pounded the Nazis' rear positions. By day the Nazis controlled the air, and at night the recovered Russian air units bombed the German-occupied parts of the city, until by November, 90 percent of the city was in ruins. But still the Germans pushed the Russians back until they were limited to holding a thousand-yard-deep strip on the west bank of the Volga. After the Luftwaffe's Stukas flew more than twelve hundred bombing missions and three months after they first attacked, German units broke through to the Volga River. A few weeks later, as winter began, the Russians held only separated and surrounded strongpoints near the river.

The entire Sixth Army and Fourth Panzer had been sucked into Stalingrad. The river lines on each side of the city were held by much weaker Italian and Romanian infantry divisions. On November 19, nearly a half a million Russian soldiers and hundreds of tanks swept over the German allies' units holding the banks of the Don River north of Stalingrad. They pushed south, and even German reinforcements could only slow the massive Russian advance. The Germans, and what remained of their allies, were barely able to keep the route to Stalingrad open. The lower Don, below Stalingrad, was protected by only one poorly equipped Romanian Corps and a single motorized German division. Then on December 12, another large Russian force pushed past those few defenders and began to encircle Stalingrad from the south.

The Russians mounted two more attacks against the mostly Italian and Romanian units defending the lines into Stalingrad. Each pushed back the divisions on either side of Stalingrad farther, until they finally met. Within another month most of the Sixth Army had been cut off and surrounded. Over a quarter of a million of the Wehrmacht's best soldiers were still in Stalingrad. But the Sixth Army was in good condition and had enough gasoline for its vehicles, including the remaining tanks. The Russians were spread thin since they had to build defenses facing both the city and the German forces to their west. There was, for a few weeks, no question that Paulus's Sixth Army could break out. But when he requested permission to do so it was denied.

> *Surrender is forbidden. 6 Army will hold their positions to the last man and the last round and by their heroic endurance will make an unforgettable contribution towards the establishment of a defensive front and the salvation of the Western world.*
>
> Adolf Hitler, January 24, 1943

General Paulus had been appointed because of his loyalty to Adolf Hitler. He obeyed. Now the Germans were under siege inside Stalingrad with the Russians pressing them inward. An army of over 250,000 men needed a lot of food and ammunition. Hermann Göring assured Hitler that his Luftwaffe could supply the trapped army, but in reality he was able to fly in barely a fifth of their needs. Priority had to be given to ammunition, and soon food was scarce. Over the next months, 250 Junkers were shot down trying to keep the Sixth Army supplied. But as the area held by the Germans was compressed, it became harder to land or, later, even to drop supplies. Pilots reported that the soldiers inside the city were often too weak to unload what food was flown in. Bitterly cold weather soon added a new level of hell to the battle for Stalingrad.

Eighteen days after Stalingrad was encircled, an attempt to break through to the city was launched by General Erich von Manstein's Army of the Don. An attempt was made to relieve the city, but the panzers were stopped twenty-nine miles short. When the Soviets launched another major offensive on December 16, this pushed the Wehrmacht even farther away from Stalingrad, and all hope of escape or relief was lost. By January 23, the last Nazi-controlled airfields inside Stalingrad had been lost. Attempts were made to drop supplies into the remaining pockets of resistance, but it was just a trickle. Twice the Russians contacted Paulus and offered to allow what remained of the Sixth Army to surrender. The lack of food, fuel, medicine, and even wood for heating had already made many of the Sixth Army's remaining troops ineffective. Twice more, Paulus contacted Adolf Hitler. Both times Hitler repeated his order to fight on to the last bullet.

Hitler continued to order Paulus to fight on, even as the situation became more hopeless. House-to-house fighting had continued and casualties had been high. Men too weak or too frostbitten to fire their weapons put up little resistance. Hitler promoted Paulus to field marshal and then reminded him that no German field marshal had ever surrendered. But with his army starving, running out of ammunition, and trapped in pockets around the city, the German commander had no choice. The remnants of his army would be overrun within days. Neither side was taking many prisoners. His helpless soldiers would be slaughtered. On February 2, 1943, Field Marshal Friedrich von Paulus surrendered. Stalingrad did become a morale and propaganda coup, but for Stalin. The myth of Nazi invincibility was shattered, and the sagging morale of the Soviet army greatly improved.

Of the 300,000 German soldiers trapped in Stalingrad, 42,000 had been wounded and evacuated by air. Of the quarter million men trapped when the city was encircled, only 91,000 remained when Paulus surrendered; 150,000 were dead. Virtually none of the survivors was still capable of combat. Of those 91,000, only 6,000 would ever return to Germany, some several years later. Most were kept as slave laborers, and many died from overwork and poor food. Within a year, Nazi Germany was desperately short of soldiers. The Nazis were arming old men and sixteen-year-old boys and using this Volkstrum in their front lines. A quarter of a million experienced soldiers could have slowed the Russian advance or stopped the allies in Normandy. But those soldiers were gone, doomed by Hitler's orders. The equipment and weapons lost at Stalingrad were one quarter of the equipment used by the entire Wehrmacht. Adolf Hitler's splitting of Army Group South ensured that neither objective was achieved, and his order to stay in Stalingrad doomed an entire army. They were mistakes that cost the Wehrmacht more than it could afford.

HIS OWN WORST ENEMY

Ten More War-Losing Decisions by Hitler

1939–1945, EUROPE

There is an unlikely and apocryphal quote attributed to Winston Churchill. He was approached by some commandoes who wanted to go assassinate the Führer. They had a plan all worked out, but the prime minister forbade it. "Hitler is one of our best assets. Do not kill him. Someone competent might take over." It is unlikely this actually happened, but it could have. There is no question that Adolf Hitler did some things right, particularly in the 1930s. He also made a number of incredible mistakes that time after time damaged the German war effort or even lost the war. Beyond the five mistakes already discussed Hitler made other bad choices that are worth noting. If Churchill did not say something like that, he should have.

69: Weapons Research

In 1940 after the fall of France, Hitler and his generals were sure that the war was all but won. So they decided that there was no more need for high-cost, crash weapons programs. With only

England left, there would be no need for any rush in developing new fighters, bombers, tanks, antitank weapons, or even jets. So most programs were either slowed down or stopped. Two years later, the German army was fighting with many of the same weapons it used to invade Poland. Only then was research given the priority it should have had all along. Of course, once research became important, wonder weapons rather than incremental improvements were what Hitler demanded. And most certainly he got some: the V1 and V2, the Me 262, and the King Tiger tank. But they were not enough.

70: Wartime Economy

The day after Pearl Harbor, President Roosevelt ordered the United States to go to a wartime economy. The production of autos and other consumer goods was stopped, and the production of weapons began. This was not the pattern for Germany. At the start of 1943, a large number of German factories were still producing such consumer goods as furniture, wallpaper, toys, and stylish clothes. Albert Speer was not ordered to fully convert the German economy to support the war until 1943.

71: Women

One of the greatest problems facing Nazi Germany was staffing its factories with so many men in uniform. The solution they primarily used was slave labor made up of prisoners of war. This opened the door to sabotage and was by no means a reliable workforce. Hundreds of thousands of Russian and other minority prisoners were literally worked to death. One group that was never asked to work in the factories was German women. Hitler was adamantly opposed to women working in anything more physical than a clerical job. In the Allied nations, women filled in at almost every position in factories and on farms, and were even shuttling bombers. Even with the severe manpower shortages in the last years of World War II, there was no Bertha the Riveter in Germany.

72: The *Bismarck* and Other Wastes

The Royal Navy in 1939 had fifteen battleships, seven small aircraft carriers, fifteen heavy cruisers, and forty-one light cruisers. The U.S. Navy had fifteen battleships, five aircraft carriers, eighteen heavy cruisers, and numerous other ships, though they were divided between the two coasts. France had five battleships, one aircraft carrier, and thirteen cruisers.

Germany had all of four battleships, three pocket battleships, two heavy cruisers, and six light cruisers. Looking at the numbers raises the question as to why Hitler insisted that Germany spend immense wealth in the 1930s building up a surface navy that could not even challenge Britain alone. Admiral Karl Dönitz's calculations were that if he had 300 submarines in the Atlantic, he could effectively stop all trade with Britain within months. He nearly did so with 120 vessels. So if the same resources had been spent producing three hundred more U-boats, the battle for the Atlantic would have been a German victory, and Britain would have been starved into submission. But the U-boats were not prestigious. The beautiful, but useless *Bismarck*, *Scharnhorst*, and *Gneisenau* were most impressive in peacetime. Hitler's most modern and spectacular pocket battleship, the *Bismarck*, was sunk on its first combat cruise.

73: The Me 262

It is unlikely that Hitler's order to change the Me 262 fighter/interceptor into a tactical bomber delayed the production of the first real combat jet more than a few months. It was eventually basically ignored. What Hitler did do was not understand or emphasize the jet's development until it became clear the Allied bombing program was crippling Nazi Germany. Hitler's arbitrary decisions about the jets are an incredible example of his lack of understanding of weapons systems and the limitations of the armies he controlled. By the time there were enough Me 262s to perhaps put a dent in the American daylight bombing campaign, there was neither enough fuel nor enough qualified pilots to make use of them. The most common plane used by the Luftwaffe in 1945 was an improved version of the same aircraft that flew in the Battle of Britain, the Me 109.

74: Declaring War on the United States

The Nazis had encouraged Japan to attack America. This was especially true in the fall of 1941 when they were sweeping across Russia and that war too seemed to be nearly won. Hitler spoke of how after defeating Stalin and the Soviets, he had to prepare to deal with the British Empire and America. The United States had been overtly supporting Britain since the fall of France. So when the Japanese struck so successfully at Pearl Harbor, he was enthused. If they could distract the Americans, Britain had no chance. To support his allies, a few days after Pearl Harbor Hitler announced a German declaration of war against the United States. The United States had declared war on Japan, but Congress had resisted President Franklin Roosevelt's urging to include Germany. But when Germany declared war, Americans soon saw the Nazis as being part of the same conspiracy as the Japanese. It must have come as a shock to the Nazis when Roosevelt not only asked for and got a return declaration but announced that America's first priority would be defeating Germany and freeing Europe.

75: Splitting Decision

Too many times the success of the German armies was hampered by orders directly from Adolf Hitler that divided their efforts between multiple objectives or changed their objectives in the middle of an operation. One example is the splitting away of panzers from Army Group North just as it was ready to crush Leningrad. The city was left surrounded, but it was given time to build what proved to be impregnable defenses. The armor was sent to support the attack on Moscow but had no effect. Hitler also ordered panzers away from the push on Moscow, a possible war winner, to help the stalled Army Group South. As it turned out, the tanks didn't help, and the drive on Moscow stalled within sight of the Kremlin. Another example is the splitting of Army Group South into two parts. One continued to drive toward the vital oil fields near Baku. The lack of oil later crippled the German war machine. The other half of Army Group South turned east and attacked Stalingrad. Either would have been a suitable objective, but because Hitler tried to do both, neither was achieved. When the Russian counterattack surrounded and then recaptured Stalingrad, the rest of Army Group South was forced to retreat or be cut off.

76: Faked Out

The Allies made a major effort to convince all of the Germans that the real D-Day landing in Europe would be at Pas-de-Calais. There were a lot of reasons this would have been a good choice. Pas-de-Calais's coastline is the closest to England. You can see England across the Channel. There is an excellent port, Calais. Any invading army would need a good port to handle the massive tons of supplies and ammunition required by a modern army. The Allies did everything to give the impression that the main landing would be there. They planted false papers on bodies; they created a radio network that sent messages about nonexistent divisions to a fake headquarters and then tied up George Patton as its figurehead. And the ploy worked. But it also worked because of Hitler's blatant distrust of his military leaders and their judgment. There were two panzer divisions in France close enough to have counterattacked the beaches on the second day. This was the OKW Reserve and intended for just such a use. They were close enough to perhaps throw the Allied landing back into the sea. But rather than give them to the general who was on the scene, Field Marshal Gerd von Rundstedt, Hitler had insisted they not be deployed until he agreed. It was 7:30 in the morning. Hitler was asleep, and because he tended to work at night, he would not awaken on his own for hours. The German dictator had such a temper when awakened that no one dared disturb him. And so the Twelfth SS and Panzer Lehr waited for orders while tens of thousands of men poured into France over the D-Day beaches. Disobeying a direct order from Hitler would get even a field marshal shot by the Gestapo. It was not until 4:00 PM that the panzers got the order to attack the beaches. By then the sky had cleared and the Allied air forces were smashing anything that moved. Almost as soon as they could start, both divisions had to hide in forests near the roads and wait for dark. What would have been a fast run on the cloudy morning became a nightmare wait. It was not until the next morning that they finally attacked. By then they were too late and the beachhead was too well established for them to push it in or even contain it.

77: Kursk

The Battle of Kursk salient was to be a case of the German army drawing in and destroying the best of the Soviet army. The trouble was that both sides knew that was where the German attack would come. Then Hitler delayed the start for weeks while new tanks were delivered. This meant that by the time the Germans struck, the Soviets had filled the salient with line after line of defenses, hundreds of antitank guns, millions of mines, and multiple tank armies of their own. Within days, the Nazi formations had been fought to a halt and forced to retreat with severe losses. Germany never regained the initiative.

78: The Battle of the Bulge

There were several problems with Hitler's plan for attacking the Allies in December 1944. First among these was that the armored units he gathered were at the expense of the collapsing defense on the Eastern Front. The hundreds of tanks and tens of thousands of fresh soldiers might well have had a chance at stopping, or at least slowing significantly, the Russians. The Russian armies were themselves both facing manpower shortages and continuing to outrun their supply lines. They were strained. Badly outnumbered and short on everything, the German commanders were still making the Soviets pay heavily for each advance. With reinforcements, the weary Russian units and their supporting elements might well have been forced to halt. But there was really no chance of such a success in the west. Hitler attacked there because he felt that if the British and Americans were pushed, they might sign a separate peace agreement. This was unlikely because even with a sweeping Nazi victory any losses would have been easily made up within weeks. But then there was no real chance for success in the Battle of the Bulge. There simply was not enough fuel left for all of those new panzers to drive to their final objectives without resistance. Certainly not enough to fight their way across the Meuse, much less to the Channel coast. It was a sign of how far he had degenerated that Hitler gambled all of his reinforcements on an attack whose viability, much less success, depended on capturing large amounts of the other side's fuel. He sacrificed the Eastern Front to mount an attack on the Americans and British that could not succeed.

You have to wonder what the world today would be like if the Third Reich had been led by a sane and competent leader . . .

III

GIVING IT ALL AWAY
FOR NOTHING

Yalta

1945, CRIMEA

IIIIIIIIIIIIIIIIIIIIIIIIIIIIIIIIIIIIIIIIIIIIIIIIIIIIIIIIIIIIIIIIIIIIIIIIIII

At the Yalta Conference, Franklin Delano Roosevelt made concessions that cost freedom to tens of millions of people he did not represent. To understand why this happened you have to look at the world situation in February 1945. The Nazis were on the ropes but not yet out. The Battle of the Bulge had ended, and Russian forces were pressing into Germany. In the Pacific, things were much further from settled. The British were still recapturing Burma, the Japanese armies in China were holding, and General Douglas MacArthur was still recovering the Philippine Islands. Japanese resistance on the islands, taken by the U.S. Pacific Fleet, had clearly shown just how costly the final assault on Japan itself would be.

Complicating all this was that Roosevelt's health was failing. He would die just two months later. There was also something new to any negotiation, the perception that there would be only two superpowers after the war, the Americans and the Soviets. This relegated the most savvy of the two Allied leaders attending, Winston Churchill, to a secondary role.

Perhaps the most important factor in Roosevelt's failure at Yalta was what each leader desired to accomplish. When they met, all three national leaders were looking ahead to after the war in Europe. Dominating Roosevelt's concerns was the cost of defeating Japan. The Japanese were hard-pressed but nowhere near defeated. They had almost two million soldiers, mostly in China, all of whom were imbued with the desire to fight to the death. The civilians on the Japanese mainland were being told that if the Americans landed, they were to attack with pikes and spears. Women and children were drilling with the primitive weapons. Up to a million soldiers were also poised to defend the home islands. The projected casualties for an American conquest of Japan was half a million men. Franklin Roosevelt was convinced that the United States had to have Russian help to mitigate this cost. He also wanted, in a similar way to Wilson and the League of Nations, to get Russian participation in the United Nations.

Winston Churchill was more concerned about the spread of Communism but was also thinking about the restoration of lost British colonies. Unfortunately with the European war less a concern, Roosevelt took the lead and Churchill had only limited input in the final agreement.

Joseph Stalin was concerned with the world after the war. He wanted Communism to spread as far as possible. He also wanted to make sure that all the nations on the European border of the Soviet Union were controlled by him. Having been surprised once by a German attack, he insisted on building a buffer zone around the Soviet Union. He would not even discuss the future of Poland, the traditional route of attacks into Russia. Finally, Stalin was anxious to occupy as much of Germany as he could and to be assured of control of Berlin once it fell.

Roosevelt needed Stalin's help against Japan, and Churchill had little influence on the decision. Stalin wanted, well, everything he could grab and his armies could occupy. Even the location of the conference showed how the Communist leader had the upper hand. Roosevelt suggested a neutral island in the Mediter-

HERE IS WHAT WAS AGREED TO AT YALTA AND WHAT IT REALLY COST

Russia agreed to join in attacking Japan. What really happened was that Russia grabbed Mongolia from the Japanese, then Manchuria, and then North Korea. None of those invasions was of any real assistance to the American effort. Then before there was to be an actual invasion of Japan, and with a belated reassurance that the emperor would not be harmed, the Japanese surrendered.

Russia agreed to join the United Nations but only after getting a new clause in the charter that gave them a permanent membership and a veto in the Security Council. Effectively the Russians would join only if they could be guaranteed the UN could never do anything they disapproved of. They were boycotting the sessions when the Korean War started, so no veto was possible. That was a mistake the Soviets never made again. We see the result of Roosevelt's concession today in the total inability of the UN to take any significant action against Russian interests anywhere, and their obstruction in such places as Syria. Stalin was forced to agree to a division of Berlin into three sectors, but when the British and Americans asked that there be a sector for France, he insisted it be taken out of their sectors only.

ranean. Stalin insisted on and got Yalta, which is in the Crimea, a part of the Soviet Union.

To get the Russians to join in an invasion of Japan that he did not turn out to need, Roosevelt effectively invited Stalin to invade Mongolia and Manchuria. Over Churchill's objections, he simply accepted Stalin's word that he would allow free elections in all the Red Army–occupied nations of Europe. Needless to say, no free elections ever happened. All the American president did was give Stalin a free hand to take whatever he wanted, and what he wanted was the wealth of those occupied nations and a buffer zone. This doomed millions of Romanians, Hungarian, Poles, East Germans, and others to seventy years of Soviet domination and exploitation.

Only once the power of the organization was emasculated did the American president get everyone to join the United Nations. The effectiveness of that body in keeping the peace is shown by the many wars, genocides, rebellions, and the extended cold war that have been fought since it was founded.

Bluntly put, the normally savvy politician Franklin Delano Roosevelt conceded everything and gained little at Yalta. He was simply beaten and outmaneuvered by Joseph Stalin.

80

||||||||||||||||||||||||||||||||||||||||||||||||||||||||||||||||

HALF-BAKED NATIONAL SOLUTIONS

Great Leap Forward

||||||||||||||||||||||||||||||||||||||||||||||||||||||||||||||||

Depending on whom you ask, Mao Zedong was either a murderous tyrant or a brilliant visionary. Many in China toe the party line that Mao was a national hero, citing his efforts to provide free health care, enhance rural education, and improve the status of women. Yet there is no good answer to the Western critique of Mao as a violent dictator with a flawed economic vision. Mao sought to energize Chinese agriculture and industry with the Great Leap Forward, the second of two five-year plans meant to modernize China's economy. The leap was anywhere but forward, as Mao's policies crippled the economy and resulted in a devastating famine. The Great Chinese Famine was perhaps the worst humanitarian disaster in history and starkly revealed the flaws of Maoism. Mao's legacy cannot be separated from the millions who died due to his ineptitude and brutality.

In 1958, China was struggling to keep up with the industrial economies of the West. Mao sought to rectify this situation via rapid industrialization. The first prong of his plan was to jack up steel production in China. Mao unrealistically projected that China would surpass the United Kingdom as a steel producer within fifteen years. He set a lofty goal of doubling steel output within the year. Yet Mao did not want to pay for modern engineers or the requisite equipment, instead relying on backyard furnaces that simply melted whatever was at hand. Because workers were untrained and used scrap metal as input, the output was nearly useless, low-quality pig iron. The program was quietly abandoned in late 1959 when Mao realized that he was paying wages without any economic benefit. Iron production grew the first few years of the program, but then sharply declined in 1961. The entire effort was a huge investment with little return, and the result was that the Chinese economy experienced negative growth from 1958 to 1961. Ironically, this period of the Great Leap Forward included the only years from 1953 to 1983 in which that occurred.

If the misguided plans of the Great Leap Forward hampered industrial growth, they were even more devastating on agriculture, the largest part of the Chinese economy. Throughout the 1950s, peasants were encouraged to live in agricultural collectives made up of several dozen households. As part of the forced relocation, 30 to 40 percent of all rural individual houses were destroyed or turned into fertilizer. This was the greatest destruction of real estate in human history. In these new communes, Mao mandated the use of agricultural techniques advocated by Soviet pseudo-scientist Trofim Lysenko. Lysenko believed that it was better to overcrowd especially fertile land than to distribute crops over moderately productive land. One technique was close cropping, in which seeds of the same type were densely sown in the mistaken belief that plants did not compete with members of their own species. The fallacy of this had been known by farmers for centuries, but it was not up for discussion. You did it the Maoist way or suffered. This stunted plant growth and undermined productivity. Another bad policy was deep plowing, which was conducted because Mao thought the most fertile soil was several feet below the surface. In shallow regions, this churned up rocks and sand, burying the topsoil and diminishing yields.

The impact of these faulty policies was magnified by a series of environmental disasters. In 1958, a swarm of locusts devoured crops. The locust population was normally kept down by predators like the sparrow, but Mao had ordered virtually all of the sparrows killed in his shortsighted Four Pests Campaign. In 1959, the Yellow River flooded fields and destroyed crops. Droughts plagued 1960, with 60 percent of China's agricultural land receiving no rain at all. Yet even when crops had a good yield, they were often left to rot uncollected in the fields. This was because Mao had diverted so many agricultural workers into steel production. With a diminished workforce, grain production also suffered dramatically.

The result was widespread famine. Yet for some time party leaders were unaware of the extent of the danger. This was a product of the Maoist bureaucracy, where failure could be a life-or-death affair. Local authorities passed on false reports of record harvests to their superiors, who in turn exaggerated numbers to the next official up the chain. Central planners distributed grain based on these inflated numbers. The result was that an inordinate amount of grain was given to urban dwellers and shipped off as exports, while rural farmers starved. China exported grain as a means of reducing the debt to the Soviets. To save face, Chinese leaders also refused offers of aid from countries like Japan. Top officials often ignored reports of starvation and withheld grain in public granaries. Rather than admit their mistakes officials accused the peasants of hiding grain and farmers were often tortured or murdered. Those party officials who criticized the policy, like Marshal Peng Dehuai, were labeled "bourgeois" and purged.

Due to starvation, suicides, overwork, and government violence, at least fifteen million people died during the Great Leap Forward. This is a conservative estimate put forth by the Chinese government at the time. It is more likely that about thirty million died, and some demographers believe the number might be closer to forty-five million. In one harrowing description of the starvation, party official Yu Dehong stated: "I went to one village and saw 100 corpses. . . . No one paid attention to them. People said that dogs were eating the bodies. Not true, I said. The dogs had long ago been eaten by the people." At least 2.5 million of the deaths were at the government's hands. Peasants accused of failing to meet grain quotas were often tortured and killed. Some of the more brutal punishments included being clubbed, buried alive, forced to eat feces, mutilated, or sent to labor camps.

The crisis politically weakened Mao, and he was forced to step down as president. He retained his status as chairman of the Communist Party and used this position to reclaim power during the Cultural Revolution. Because those who criticized Mao were often brutally punished, reform was almost impossible. Senior statesman Liu Shaoqi described the disaster as "30% fault of nature, 70% human error." Shaoqi's candid criticism of Mao came back to bite him when Mao returned fully to power. Shaoqi was labeled a capitalist traitor in 1969 and tortured to death. It was this smothering of criticism that made Mao so susceptible to failure. Mao was a brilliant man with little regard for life, and his often unrealistic or misguided but always ambitious plans for China suffered because he crushed dissident opinions. Perhaps that is the mistake that caused all the others, and millions of deaths, to happen.

81

CHOOSE YOUR
FRIENDS MORE
CAREFULLY

Dwight Eisenhower's
Misguided Friendship

1953, IRAN

||||||||||||||||||||||||||||||||||||||||||||||||||||||||||||||||||||||||||

A s revolution spread across the Middle East during the 2011 Arab Spring, many political commentators trembled at the possibility of emergent theocracies. After all, the 1979 Iranian Revolution, while ostensibly democratic, produced an Islamic dictatorship that would become a headache for the West that has lasted to this day. The centrality of the Iran issue to modern political discourse is evidenced by things such as the Republican primary presidential debates of 2012, in which each candidate jockeyed to prove that he was the toughest on Iran. Only Congressman Ron Paul deviated from this trend, explaining that the Middle East hated the United States only for its imperial policies. While Paul's views might seem unusual at times, he is right that the problems of today are best understood by looking to the past. Had the United States not propped up a corrupt, dictatorial shah in Iran for decades, it might have a democratic ally rather than a theocratic enemy in the world's most volatile region.

Mohammad Reza Pahlavi, the shah of Iran, succeeded his father in 1941. His father had remained neutral during World War II, and in response Britain and the USSR replaced him with Reza, who was more accommodating. The shah allowed Iran to become a major supply conduit during the war. It became known as the Persian Corridor. Reza issued blanket amnesty to his father's political enemies and resolved to conduct policy in a more enlightened, refined fashion than his predecessor. Indeed, the shah would earn admiration among many Western observers during his reign for his liberal policies. A moderate Muslim, the shah went on to implement the White Revolution, a series of reforms meant to modernize the economy and secularize politics. The shah also recognized Israel as a legitimate state and extended suffrage to women. A pro-West politician, he was viewed as a stabilizing force by Americans.

Yet the shah had a mean antidemocratic streak. This should have been reason to condemn him, but the United States was more concerned with keeping anti-Communist leaders in power. In 1951, Dr. Mohammad Mosaddegh was democratically elected as prime minister of Iran. Mosaddegh sought to reform the country democratically and socially. He supported unemployment compensation, health benefits for workers, reductions in forced labor, and, significantly, nationalization of the country's oil reserves. This latter position was a concern for Britain, which relied on the British Anglo-Iranian Oil Company for much of its energy needs. When in July of 1952 the shah denied Mosaddegh his constitutional right to name a minister of war and chief of staff, Mosaddegh resigned. The new prime minister sought to resolve the oil dispute, but his tenure was cut short by widespread protests on Mosaddegh's behalf. The shah, frightened by the unrest, reappointed Mosaddegh and granted him the powers he sought.

Mosaddegh used his newfound leverage to further limit the monarchy's powers and implement reforms on behalf of Iran's peasants. When Mosaddegh cut off diplomatic relations with Britain, the West grew anxious. President Dwight D. Eisenhower and outgoing Prime Minister Winston Churchill believed that Mosaddegh, despite his criticism of Iran's Communist Tudeh Party, was slowly steering the country toward socialism. Eisenhower authorized the CIA to foment a rebellion on the shah's behalf. In Operation Ajax, the CIA incited riots, spread propaganda, and financed opposition groups. Though the shah was nervous about opposing his prime minister, the United States bullied him into dismissing Mosaddegh. The military arrested Mosaddegh and the new prime minister orchestrated new oil deals that heavily favored the United States and Britain. Mosaddegh was convicted of treason and kept under house arrest until his death in 1967.

Over the next few decades, opposition to the shah, who was justifiably viewed as a Western puppet, grew. The shah's ambitious Westernization programs were viewed with suspicion. Beginning in 1963, opposition coalesced behind the leadership of Shia cleric Ayatollah Ruhollah Khomeini. In response to the White Revolution, Khomeini called the shah a "wretched miserable man" bent on the "destruction of Islam in Iran." His continued agitation over Iran's relationship with Israel caused the shah to send the cleric into exile. Though Khomeini was gone, his ideas continued to fester. Fundamentalist Islamists were joined in opposing the shah by constitutionalist liberals, Marxist groups, and leftist ayatollahs.

In the 1970s, the shah tried his very hardest to alienate his subjects. For the 2,500th anniversary of the Persian Empire, the Shah spent $100 million in a lavish celebration. He erected a 160-acre tent city, in sharp contrast to the impoverished villages nearby. This opulent display reinforced the growing income gap between the richest and poorest, by which the shah and his allies reaped the lion's share of the country's oil revenue. The shah also suppressed political dissent by banning opposition parties and imposing membership dues on formerly apolitical Iranians. Opponents were dealt with by the shah's secret police, the SAVAK. Ironically, the thrust of the opposition came from young students who had benefited from the shah's educational reforms.

While the United States disapproved of the shah's authoritarian measures, they tempered their criticism. Just six months before the shah would flee Iran, the CIA concluded that the country "is not in a revolutionary or even a pre-revolutionary situation" and that the shah would enjoy unchallenged rule for the next decade. This was a hopelessly naive perspective. Protests were steadily expanding; while tens of thousands marched against the shah in the summer of 1978, the number had swelled to over six million by December. With 10 percent of the country marching, this was one of the largest protests in history. The shah's heavy-handed responses, including the implementation of martial law and the massacre of protesters that September, inflamed the opposition. The shah sensed the futility of his strategy and abruptly shifted course, appointing moderate Shapour Bakhtiar as prime minister. Bakhtiar dissolved SAVAK, freed political prisoners, promised free elections, and invited Khomeini to return to Iran to create a Vatican-like Islamist state. Khomeini rejected Bakhtiar for capitulating to the shah and seized control of the country. He appointed a new prime minister and became the undisputed leader of Iran. The new state was an Islamic theocracy. A dictatorship had been replaced by a dictatorship, but this new regime was hostile to Western interests.

The policy makers of today have inherited this mess. Iran is controlled by radical Islamists who view the United States as the "Great Satan." Former U.S. Secretary of State Madeleine Albright had this to say about the 1953 coup: "The Eisenhower Administration believed its actions were justified for strategic reasons; but the coup was clearly a setback for Iran's political development. And it is easy to see now why many Iranians continue to resent this intervention by America in their internal affairs." Indeed, Eisenhower and successive presidents were foolish to support the shah. He was a petty, dictatorial man who frustrated Iran's path to democracy. Had Eisenhower simply played nice with Mosaddegh, the Middle East of today would be more stable, more democratic, and more favorable to Western interests.

82

|||||||||||||||||||||||||||||||||||||||||||||||||||||||||||||||||||||||||||||||

SUPPORTING THE
WRONG LEADERS

Hearts and Minds

1954–1972, UNITED STATES AND
VIETNAM

|||||||||||||||||||||||||||||||||||||||||||||||||||||||||||||||||||||||||||||||

During the Vietnam War, a phrase began popping up in President Lyndon Johnson's speeches: "hearts and minds." It became almost hackneyed, as Johnson sought to emphasize winning a human campaign rather than a military one. The strategy relied on the inherent appeal of American values: capitalism, democracy, and industry. Yet American values could not stand up to the powerful force of American hypocrisy. Johnson lost public support at home and abroad by bolstering corrupt dictators rather than fostering democracy. Johnson was not the sole culprit. Presidents Kennedy and Eisenhower did it before him, and Nixon continued after him. The U.S. strategy throughout much of the cold war involved supporting anti-Communist autocrats rather than risk a democratically elected Socialist. In Vietnam, this tactic backfired, as it united the Vietnamese and American citizens against the war effort.

It began with a Vietnamese general named Ngo Dinh Diem. Diem was ruthlessly anti-Communist and devoutly Catholic. He was very popular within the Eisenhower administration and because of this was selected by Vietnam's hereditary emperor, Bao Dai, to serve as prime minister of South Vietnam. The U.S. Navy helped Catholics migrate from North Vietnam to the south, providing Diem with a loyal support base. Diem was initially very weak, and the CIA protected him from potential coups. In 1955, Diem consolidated power by scheduling a referendum to determine whether to become a republic or to restore the monarchy. Diem's brother Ngo Dinh Nhu helped organize the elections. The results were rigged, and Diem recorded 98.2 percent of the vote, receiving over 600,000 votes in Saigon, where only 450,000 voters were registered. Diem declared himself president and thwarted a measure to reunify with the Communist north, having the gall to suggest that the Communists would cheat in the elections. When in 1959 the United States pressured Diem to hold legislative elections, he arrested a prominent critic and cracked down on attempts at assembly.

Beyond his electoral dishonesty, Diem was just plain cruel and ruthless. He brutally suppressed Communists and other political dissidents, killing around fifty thousand and imprisoning another seventy-five throughout his tenure. With the endorsement of U.S. advisers, he implemented the Strategic Hamlet Program. This program attempted to separate peasants from Communist insurgents by establishing fortified villages where peasants would be confined. Peasants resented being forcibly relocated into these spaces. Corrupt officials pocketed virtually all of the money that was supposed to compensate the peasants, kicking some back to Diem. Moreover, the Vietcong had little difficulty infiltrating and sabotaging the communities. By the end of 1963, only about 20 percent of the strategic hamlets were still controlled by the South Vietnamese.

What truly energized opposition to Diem was his treatment of the Buddhist majority. Diem's policies demonstrated clear favoritism toward Catholics. Buddhist protesters were killed, and the murders were blamed on the Vietcong. No one fell for the ruse, and opposition toward Diem mounted. Buddhists began to publicly self-immolate. The pictures of these monks, stoically sitting in Vietnam's streets as the fire consumed them, stirred the hearts of the American public. Diem became vilified at home and abroad. Eventually, the CIA conveyed to Diem's rivals that they would not intervene in the event of a coup. Diem was deposed by General Duong Van Minh. Diem refused exile and tried to escape but was assassinated.

The next few years were tumultuous. Minh inspired little confidence, as he was a lethargic man who preferred playing tennis to running a country. He halted the Strategic Hamlet Program and lifted Diem-era censorship. Yet he also destabilized the country by arresting large numbers of former Diem officials and by failing to repel Vietcong attacks. He lasted only three months before being overthrown by Nguyen Khanh.

The Americans were surprised by the coup but endorsed Khanh, hoping he could stabilize South Vietnam. He proved just as corrupt as his predecessors. Khanh disbanded the vaguely democratic Council of Notables, which had served as a forum for dissent. He appointed officials based on loyalty rather than competence. He was advised heavily by U.S. Ambassador Henry Cabot Lodge Jr. The two agreed that democracy had little place in South Vietnam and that a police state was necessary to win the war. Khanh drafted a new constitution which granted him emergency powers and hamstrung his rivals, but this was met with protests and riots. Maxwell Taylor, who had replaced Lodge as the ambassador, urged Khanh to ignore their demands. Yet Khanh, fearing reprisal, began offering a steady stream of concessions to the Buddhists. He also fought incessantly with rival generals, causing him to disband the High National Council. This irked Taylor, who angrily chastised him: "We Americans are tired of coups[;] . . . you have made a real mess. We cannot carry you forever if you do things like this." Khanh began defying Taylor. When it was revealed that Khanh planned to broker a deal with the Communists, Taylor conveyed to Khanh's rivals that the United States was "in no way propping up General Khanh or backing him in any fashion." Khanh was forced out in a bloodless coup in 1965.

Khanh was replaced by Nguyen Van Thieu, who was described in a CIA report as "intelligent" and "highly ambitious." Under Thieu, the cyclical coups ended. Unfortunately Thieu was also Diem part deux. After the devastation of the Tet Offensive, he declared martial law and used it as an excuse to arrest or exile many supporters of his chief political rival, Vice President Nguyen Cao Ky. The South Vietnamese began calling him "the little dictator." He ran for reelection in 1971. His political opponents anticipated a fraudulent election, and thus no one ran against him. Under Thieu, the war effort gradually deteriorated. American aid stopped flowing, as the American public disliked supporting such an obviously corrupt dictator at a high cost in casualties and money. The Nixon administration downsized the American participation and eventually withdrew American troops, leaving Thieu exposed. The war was lost, and Thieu was forced to resign. Before entering exile, he lamented, "You Americans with your 500,000 soldiers in Vietnam! You were not defeated . . . you ran away!"

Indeed, the Americans had run away. Then again, look at the list of the men who had ruled Vietnam. The American public could no longer in good conscience support these anti-Democratic leaders. These were men who were either put in power or supported by the United States and the CIA. By supporting these vile men, the U.S. government doomed its position on the moral high ground. More significant, the corruption and brutality of Diem, Thieu, and Khanh turned Vietnamese opinion against both puppet and puppeteer. Johnson had hoped to win the hearts and minds of the public, but he supported authoritarian yes-men. The American war effort could have been successful if it had stayed true to core American values.

83

THE HIGH COST OF
SAVING FACE

The Catholic Church Sex
Abuse Scandal

1960–2012, THE VATICAN

John Geoghan learned the hard way what happens to those who prey on young children. The former Catholic priest had been defrocked and imprisoned for sexually abusing over 130 children during his thirty-year career. He was brutally murdered in his cell by fellow inmate Joseph Druce on August 23, 2003. Further investigation revealed that Geoghan's debauchery was merely the tip of a clandestine, vile iceberg. The prosecution of Geoghan and four other priests was extensively covered by the *Boston Globe*. Soon thereafter, abuse victims across the United States and in countries like Ireland and Canada were emboldened to come forward with their stories. With each revelation, the extent of the abuse—and the cover-up, with evidence implicating both popes of the twenty-first century—further tainted the Roman Catholic Church. For decades, the Catholic Church sought and failed to resolve abuse cases internally. The church's paramount objective was to avoid exposure and maintain its reputation. Ironically, its efforts to stymie public knowledge of the abuse eventually resulted in far worse scandal.

With the exception of a few notable cases, the issue of priests sexually abusing children remained largely out of the public eye until the mid-1990s. Priests were most deviant during the 1960s and 1970s, but dioceses were, by and large, able to avoid public scrutiny. The church would often settle with the accusers without ever alerting the authorities. It was standard practice to give the church leeway in handling affairs internally. Oftentimes, the Catholic Church would seek to solve the issue via prayer or counseling. Many bishops believed that pedophilia was a sin that could be expunged from the soul through spiritual reflection. Rather than stripping the man of his priesthood (a process referred to as *defrocking*), the church often shuffled offenders to new parishes. The church frequently failed to prevent such priests from again coming into contact with children, resulting in repeat offenses. Even in such instances, it was rare for the priest to be exposed for his crimes as it was the priority for many dioceses to avoid scandal, not protect children.

A few cases in the 1980s brought public attention to sexual abuse by Catholic clerics, but after the cases were settled, coverage faded. A series of incidents in Ireland in the 1990s made little headway because prosecuting priests in the heavily Catholic nation proved difficult. While a few books were published on the subject in the mid-1990s, the issue did not truly seize public attention until the early 2000s. In 2002, the *Boston Globe* rigorously covered the prosecutions of Geoghan and his fellows. For exposing the world to the abuse and the cover-up, the *Boston Globe* received the Pulitzer Prize. That coverage gave courage to victims of sexual abuse all around the United States. Shortly thereafter the church was inundated with allegations of pedophilia. An investigation of Bernard Francis Cardinal Law, archbishop of Boston, showed that an active effort had been made at the highest levels to conceal child molestation. Cardinal Law refused to reveal the identities of many accused priests and was only ordered to resign after sixty-five Boston parishes were forced to close down. Even after his resignation, he eluded true punishment, as he retained his cardinal status and became archpriest of the Basilica di Santa Maria Maggiore in Rome.

The church's response to the scandal was mixed. At the diocesan level, many accused priests were defrocked and bishops who participated in the cover-up were forced to resign. Dioceses were told to close churches and schools in response to the financial pressure of settling with the victims. U.S. dioceses have paid nearly $3 billion in settlements since 1950 and paid $615 million in 2007 alone. Knowing this, parishioners reacted by contributing less. The U.S. Conference of Catholic Bishops commissioned the John Jay College of Criminal Justice to publish a report on the extent of the problem.

The John Jay Report demonstrated that the Catholic Church was overly willing to forgive abusers, failed to grasp the seriousness of the problem, and used faulty treatment methods in dealing with repeat offenders. The report stated that there were 10,667 reported victims between 1950 and 2002, mostly male, 3,000 of them accounted for by 149 particularly lascivious priests. The Irish government published the Ferns Report in 2005 as well as the Ryan and Murphy Reports in 2009. These documents detailed the endemic sexual molestation in church-run schools and orphanages. It revealed the extent of the cover-up by the archdiocese of Dublin, and chastised state authorities for not equally applying the law to the church.

Amid all these responses, the Vatican initially remained silent. The pope was heavily criticized for his apparent indifference to the plight of the abused children, though evidence suggests that many members of the Roman Curia were appalled by the revelations. Eventually the Vatican responded, requiring background checks for all church employees and establishing procedures for handling abuse. Pope John Paul II stated in 2001 that sexual abuse was considered a grave sin, or *delictum gravius*. He would later state that "there is no place in the priesthood and religious life for those who would harm the young." Yet John Paul II was criticized, especially after his death, for his continued inaction in dealing with child molesters within the church. In one particularly high-profile case, the beloved pope intervened to protect his friend Mexican priest Marcial Maciel Degollado from punishment. Degollado had abused seminarians in the late 1990s. As head of the Congregation for the Doctrine of the Faith, Cardinal Ratzinger (who would eventually become Pope Benedict XVI) sought to punish Degollado, but was frustrated by the high-ranking Cardinal Angelo Sodano. When Ratzinger became pope, he stated his intention to remove the "filth" that permeated through the church. Benedict forced Degollado from active ministry and ordered him to spend the rest of his days in prayer.

Though Benedict cracked down on men like Degollado, he himself was suspected of covering up abuse earlier in his career. The case involved Peter Hullermann, who was a German Catholic priest who abused several boys during the 1970s and 1980s. When he was accused of "indecent advances" toward children in his parish in 1977, Hullermann did not deny the allegations. But rather than being punished, he was transferred to the archdiocese of Munich, which was headed by Archbishop Ratzinger. Ratzinger's diocese did not notify civil authorities of the indecency allegations. It then approved psychiatric treatment for Hullermann. Hullermann's psychiatrist stipulated that Hullermann give up alcohol, be supervised at all times, and not work with children. These conditions were not met, and Hullermann was reassigned to pastoral care work by Vicar General Gerhard Gruber in 1980. Hullermann was investigated by police in 1985 for sexually abusing minors and distributing pornography. He was found guilty, fined, and finally relieved of his duties. When the story about the molestations broke in 2010, Gruber assumed sole responsibility for Hullermann's reassignment. While it was revealed Gruber wrote a memo on the subject that was supposed to end up in Ratzinger's hands, there is no definitive proof of whether the future pope ever read the memo. However, private letters by Gruber suggest that the archdiocese begged him to assume the blame in an apparent attempt to preserve Benedict's image.

The Roman Catholic Church is still reeling from the scandal. Many cases remain unsettled and priests unpunished. The beatification of the late Pope John Paul II was marred by his inaction during the scandal. Prominent atheists like Christopher Hitchens and Richard Dawkins called for Benedict to be repudiated for his role in the cover-up, saying he deserved to be tried for "crimes against humanity." Catholics became less trustful of the church. In response to the 2010 Hullermann story, Germans' trust in the pope dropped to a paltry 39 percent. Many former believers became disillusioned with Catholicism and left the church.

It was not that Catholic priests were more predatory than their counterparts in other denominations. They weren't. It was the flagrant disregard for justice that infuriated believers and nonbelievers alike. Perhaps the priests and their superiors thought they were above the law of man. Maybe they thought they would be judged by God and that their belief would save them. In covering up the scandals to save its reputation, the Catholic hierarchy made things immeasurably worse. Regardless of concern for its prestige, the church should have cracked down on child molestation from the beginning. The church sought to avoid a PR problem by obscuring crimes from the public. Because of this misguided effort, the Roman Catholic Church is now facing its greatest challenge since the Protestant Reformation.

84

||||||||||||||||||||||||||||||||||||||||||||||||||||||||||||||||||||||

SEXUAL STUPIDITY

A Very British Scandal

1960s, ENGLAND

||||||||||||||||||||||||||||||||||||||||||||||||||||||||||||||||||||||

I n Billy Joel's famous single, "We Didn't Start the Fire," Joel chronicles some of the most important events of the first forty years of his life. In the stanza devoted to 1963, sandwiched between references to Malcolm X and the assassination of John F. Kennedy, Joel commented on the infamous Profumo Affair with the line "British politician sex." The brief, sordid affair between British Secretary of War John Profumo and call girl Christine Keeler became a national controversy due to Keeler's previous relationships with Soviet officials. The affair, and Profumo's lies to Parliament in an attempt to conceal it, proved politically damaging for the conservatives in Britain. The Tories lost control of Parliament for the first time in over a decade. Thus was ushered in a political revolution to accompany the cultural revolution of the early 1960s.

Britain in the early 1960s was a changing place. Prime Minister Harold Macmillan, called "Supermac" for his pragmatism and wit, enjoyed a comfortable majority over the fractured Labour Party. But discontent brewed on the horizon, as modest economic progress was wracked by chronic inflation and rocky labor relations. A hundred-member Conservative majority in the House of Commons had dwindled substantially by 1962. The famously unflappable Macmillan panicked and abruptly fired seven senior ministers in what would be called "the night of long knives." The Conservative Party was in disarray, while the Labour Party was reinventing itself under new leadership. The Labour Party's ascent was slow, but appeared inevitable, as young voters were becoming increasingly disillusioned with the old guard. The Profumo Affair catalyzed liberal activism and dealt the knockout punch to a deflating Conservative Party.

It was yet early in the 1960s, before the free-love, pro-drugs cultural revolution. The cold war dominated public thought, and there was a pervasive fear of Communist infiltration. In 1961, George Blake was given a record forty-two-year sentence for espionage, though he would later escape. The failed Bay of Pigs episode, along with Soviet accomplishments like sending Yuri Gagarin into space, created a growing impression that the United States was outmatched. When the Cuban Missile Crisis brought the world to the edge of nuclear conflict, anxieties about the USSR reached an all-time high. Thus when it was revealed that British Secretary of War John Profumo had spent a few weeks consorting with the former lover of Soviet naval attaché Yevgeni Ivanov, the affair became a public scandal. There was an unspoken concern wondering if the call girl was acting on her own or as a tool of her former lover.

Profumo first met Keeler at a house party hosted by prominent Conservative politician Viscount William Astor. Also present were his wife, Valerie Profumo, and Stephen Ward, an osteopath and socialite who had pursued an on-and-off relationship with Keeler for some time. Profumo was taken with Keeler, and for the next few weeks they had a passionate affair. The episode could have eluded public attention were it not for the tumult of Keeler's love life. In late 1962, a former lover of Keeler's, Johnny Edgecombe, attempted to forcibly enter Ward's flat by firing several shots into the door's lock. This caused the media to investigate Keeler, at which point they learned about her relationships with both Profumo and Ivanov. Sex scandals are bad for the government, but ones where the other lover was a Communist topped the news.

In March of 1963, Profumo committed a foolish error. Labour MP George Wigg, claiming to be concerned about the national security implications of the affair, discussed rumors of the relationship openly in Parliament. While Profumo threatened to press libel and slander charges against anyone who repeated such allegations outside the house, Wigg was protected from such reprisal by parliamentary privilege. Profumo, rather than owning up to his mistake, lied to Parliament, saying that there was "no impropriety whatsoever" between him and Keeler. Just ten weeks later, under mounting scrutiny, Profumo decided to confess. For misleading the house, Profumo resigned in disgrace.

The scandal didn't go away, at least not immediately. Ward was prosecuted for "immoral earnings" (a euphemism for being a pimp) and subsequently committed suicide. After a few months of investigation, Lord Alfred Denning issued a report detailing his findings. Though it was later alleged that Ivanov and Ward asked Keeler to quiz Profumo on American nuclear policy, there has never been substantiated evidence to suggest that Keeler wrenched any sensitive information from the secretary. The public gobbled the report up, though many were disappointed by the lack of juicy details. Shortly thereafter Macmillan, beset by ailing health and undermined by the entire affair, resigned as prime minister. The Tories faced a leadership crisis and narrowly lost to the Labour Party in the subsequent elections. A power shift had occurred, and Profumo's infidelity had ushered it in.

The intrigue surrounding the scandal has endured. A Danish film called *The Keeler Affair* was released in 1963, and in 1989 a movie called *Scandal* temporarily renewed interest in the subject. Keeler's autobiography, called *The Truth at Last*, was published in 2001 and made a number of unsubstantiated claims about Soviet infiltration of the British intelligence agency MI5. Profumo himself never spoke of the subject again, but he vindicated himself in the eyes of many for his extensive volunteer work over the ensuing decades. His wife forgave him and even said that the adversity strengthened their bond. He was honored by Queen Elizabeth II with the designation CBE (Commander of the Most Excellent Order of the British Empire, one step below knighthood) and attended Prime Minister Margaret Thatcher's seventieth birthday in 1995. He died of a stroke in 2006. Despite the scandal, he is remembered in a positive light for his subsequent contributions to society.

Yet the impact of the affair should not be discounted. The Labour Party had a majority in the Commons of a mere four seats. Had the Profumo Affair never occurred and Macmillan not resigned, it is unlikely the leftists could have wrested control from the Conservatives. Just as important, the Profumo incident left a lasting impact on the British psyche. It was a pivotal event for Britain, both politically and culturally, and a symbolic reflection of changing attitudes. As such, Profumo's mistake ended up becoming one of the most important political events in Britain of the latter half of the twentieth century.

85

DON'T RUN A WAR FROM YOUR OVAL OFFICE

LBJ Escalates the Vietnam War

1964–1968, UNITED STATES AND VIETNAM

I n the 1964 presidential election, Lyndon B. Johnson had the audacity to present himself as a foreign-policy dove opposed to escalation in Vietnam. Contrasting himself with opponent Barry Goldwater, Johnson assured voters that "We are not about to send American boys nine or ten thousand miles away from home to do what Asian boys ought to be doing for themselves." He feared getting "tied down to a land war in Asia," lamenting that 190 Americans had died there already but suggesting that a thousand times that many might be lost "in the first month if we escalated that war." He was successfully reelected, in large part due to his portrayal of Goldwater as an extremist. Yet such promises were wholly disingenuous. Johnson, ignoring the advice of wiser men, had no intention of fulfilling his pledge of peace. He soon expended thousands of lives and billions of dollars in a war with little strategic value. Its lack of real importance was shown by the simple fact that the United States–based government lost and elsewhere in the world little changed. Johnson supposedly feared getting tied down in Asia, but it was he who fastened the knot.

Johnson's predecessor, John F. Kennedy, was far more clear-headed on the Vietnam issue. Like Dwight Eisenhower before him and Johnson after him, Kennedy subscribed to the domino theory, which argued that if one country succumbed to Communism, its neighbors would too. His advisers were divided on the issue. One man, General Douglas MacArthur, was particularly persuasive. MacArthur was a World War II hero and had commanded UN forces in the Korean War before being relieved by President Harry Truman. In a 1961 meeting with Kennedy, MacArthur warned the president that he could deploy millions of troops in Asia and still be outnumbered. He pointed out that Vietnam had little strategic value and criticized the military advice Kennedy was receiving from the Pentagon. MacArthur's advice was echoed by France's president, Charles de Gaulle, a former general who had witnessed firsthand the quagmire that was Vietnam, as France had occupied Indochina for decades.

Kennedy remained publically committed to the war effort, sending military advisers to South Vietnam and supporting the ill-fated Strategic Hamlet Program. He also secretly supported a coup against South Vietnam's incompetent president, Ngo Dinh Diem. Yet he became increasingly uncomfortable with the war effort, and revealed to leading dove Senator Mike Mansfield that he was planning a withdrawal. Kennedy wanted to bide his time, delaying the inevitable controversy until after he was reelected. Kennedy surmised that if he withdrew before the election, there would be conservative reprisal. Kennedy remarked to aide Kenneth O'Donnell after meeting with Mansfield, "In 1965, I'll become one of the most unpopular Presidents in history. I'll be damned everywhere as a Communist appeaser. But I don't care. If I tried to pull out completely now from Vietnam, we could have another Joe McCarthy red scare on our hands, but I can do it after I'm reelected. So we had better make damned sure I am reelected."

Tragically, Kennedy never got the chance. He was assassinated in 1963, and Johnson was thrust into the presidency. MacArthur, who had planted the seed of doubt in Kennedy years earlier, tried to impart the same warning to Johnson. Johnson failed to heed the general's advice, and MacArthur died before witnessing just how right he was.

President Lyndon Johnson changed his tune in mid-1964, when a couple of incidents spurred public support for the war. The first, occurring on August 2, involved a sea battle in the Gulf of Tonkin where the USS *Maddox* skirmished with North Vietnamese torpedo boats. Four North Vietnamese soldiers were killed, but the United States incurred no casualties. Two days later, the U.S. National Security Agency (NSA) claimed a second skirmish, though the weather was bad and it was likely the radar images were electronic illusions rather than actual torpedo attacks. An NSA document was declassified in 2005, clarifying that the second incident never actually occurred. Johnson was aware of this, privately commenting, "For all I know, our Navy was shooting at whales out there." Yet he used the "confrontations" to convince Congress to pass the sweeping Gulf of Tonkin Resolution, which granted the president far-reaching authority to conduct military operations in Southeast Asia without requiring a formal declaration of war by Congress.

Buoyed by the resolution, President Johnson did the opposite of what he had promised and massively escalated the conflict. He authorized Operation Rolling Thunder, a three-year bombing campaign intended to break the Communists' morale. Lieutenant Colonel John Paul Vann had this to say about such a strategy: "This is a political war and it calls for discrimination in killing. The best weapon for killing would be a knife . . . the worst is an airplane." Operation Rolling Thunder merely turned Vietnamese public opinion against the United States. Johnson supplemented the bombing by putting boots on the ground. Kennedy had believed that the war must be won by the South Vietnamese, but Johnson departed from that view. He steadily committed more and more troops, though they failed to make much headway.

In 1968, the North Vietnamese launched a large-scale surprise attack on over a hundred cities. This was called the Tet Offensive, and though the Communists suffered great losses, its very existence was viewed as an indicator of the failure of the American military. The offensive contradicted Johnson's claims that victory was at hand and caused public opinion of the war to sour. By then, Johnson was so unpopular that he decided not to run for reelection. Richard Nixon, successfully portraying himself as the anti-war candidate, succeeded Johnson as president. Though Nixon did not immediately withdraw and earned his own protests and criticism for bombing Laos and Cambodia, he eventually did end the war. However, he ended it in a way that included the complete collapse of the government allied to the Americans.

Lyndon Johnson's problem was that he was more concerned about the appearance of victory than he was about sensible military policy. He actively managed media coverage, emphasizing stories that portrayed progress while downplaying events that revealed the deteriorating situation in Vietnam. Though Johnson claimed the war was about resisting unjust aggression, the Pentagon Papers, a secret history of the war transcribed by Secretary of Defense Robert McNamara and released in 1971, told a different story. The papers claimed that 70 percent of the reason Johnson persisted in the war effort was to "avoid a humiliating defeat." Yet it was his stubborn refusal to leave Vietnam that truly damaged the U.S. government's credibility, both at home and abroad. Johnson should have done what Kennedy did and listened to the wise counsel of General MacArthur and others. Johnson's military decisions were based on his political needs. His mistake was paid for with the blood of fifty thousand Americans and tens of thousands of Vietnamese, and left a scar on the soul of the nation he had been elected to lead.

86

IDEOLOGY OVER REALITY

The Cure for the Cure

1966–1976, CHINA

When accused of leading China away from Communism, General Secretary Deng Xiaoping famously replied, "I don't care if it's a white cat or a black cat. It's a good cat as long as it catches mice." Deng was trying to say that he cared little whether his programs were considered capitalist or Communist so long as they were successful in modernizing the Chinese economy. For the ideological Mao Zedong, this was dangerous thinking. Mao was threatened by Deng and his ally Chairman Liu Shaoqi. The chairman had lost control of much of the Chinese government and he had to regain it. To do this Mao launched the Cultural Revolution, a brutal campaign aimed at squashing his political rivals and asserting "Maoist" thought.

The Great Leap Forward was supposed to make China one of the leading manufacturing and industrial nations in the world. But the effort was hampered by political concerns, a lack of knowledge, patience, and shortcuts such as the notorious backyard steel furnaces. After the dismal failure of the Great Leap Forward, Mao was politically weakened. He yielded control of state affairs to Liu Shaoqi, an early critic of Mao's five-year plan. Mao became a figurehead and withdrew to study Marxist thought. Liu, along with Deng, sought to reform China's faltering economy using free-market principles. Working with fellow moderate Premier Zhou Enlai, the men disbanded the ineffectual People's Communes and imported grain to alleviate the famine. Mao began to worry that China was going down the same path as the Soviet Union. Mao had harshly criticized Soviet Premier Nikita Khrushchev as a Marxist "revisionist" for reversing many of Joseph Stalin's policies. He feared that Deng and Liu were "capitalist roaders," or men intent on setting China on the road to capitalism.

In 1966, under Mao's direction, the Chinese Politburo declared the advent of a "Great Cultural Revolution." Mao had recently dismissed several prominent officials, including the mayor of Beijing and the chief of staff of the People's Liberation Army, for being anti-Mao. The declaration alleged that bourgeois influences had infiltrated the highest ranks of the party, intending to seize power and oppress the proletariat. Mao mobilized the country's youth to form a mass movement called the Red Guards, a paramilitary organization intent on purging Mao's rivals. The Red Guards denounced counterrevolutionaries and pursued a violent campaign against intellectuals, revisionists, and theists. Propaganda was widely distributed, including the popular book *Quotations from Chairman Mao*. Mao was intent on creating a cult of personality that rivaled that of men like Stalin and Benito Mussolini.

With Mao's return to power, his rivals were immediately purged. Liu was sent to a detention camp, tortured, publically humiliated, and expelled from the party. Once considered to be Mao's successor, Liu died in the hands of the Red Guards, who denied him medical treatment for diabetes and pneumonia. Deng fared better. He was forced to retire and sent to work in a rural factory, but four years later Zhou convinced Mao to bring Deng back into politics. In the meantime, Deng's family had been targeted by the Red Guards. His son was tortured and thrown off a four-story building. He survived as a paraplegic. Zhou had survived the purges by aligning himself with Mao, though like Deng, some of his family members had not. After having been diagnosed with cancer, Zhou regarded Deng as his successor. Deng became vice premier and began handling daily affairs. He used this opportunity to again restructure the economy, this time by streamlining the railway system and ramping up steel production. The Red Guards forced hundreds of thousands of the best-educated and most-productive young men and women in China onto work farms or worse.

The Cultural Revolution was declared to be over in 1969, though in practice it continued until Mao's death in 1976. During this span, Mao continued to expunge his enemies. His chosen successor, Lin Biao, was implicated in an attempted coup and was forced to flee the country. His plane crashed en route to the Soviet Union in 1971, leaving the question of Mao's successor unsettled. The Gang of Four, rigid Maoists led by Mao's wife, Jiang Qing, sought to fill the void. They spearheaded a campaign to portray Zhou and Deng as "rightist" and dangerous. When Zhou died in 1976, Deng delivered his eulogy. Mao refused to attend the funeral, and the Gang of Four set out to impose restrictions on public mourning of the premier. This turned public opinion against the gang, resulting in a violent protest in Tiananmen Square. The gang blamed Deng as the mastermind behind the riots. They convinced Mao to again purge Deng, elevating Hua Guofeng to premier instead.

The Gang of Four's rule was short-lived. Mao died later that year, and Hua arrested the four. Hua originally pursued a Maoist economic model, but at Deng's urging, he soon began to modernize the economy. Deng became the de facto leader of China. He used this position to liberalize China in what was called the Beijing Spring. Many, like Liu, were rehabilitated and posthumously reintegrated into the Communist Party. Deng declared Mao a national hero, saying, "His accomplishments must be considered before his mistakes," and commenting that he was "seven parts good, three parts bad." The country, finally stable, was able to politically and economically move forward from Mao's nightmarish regime.

In a narrow sense, Mao's Cultural Revolution was not a failure. After all, he achieved his goal of retaining power and implementing his vision of Marxist thought. Yet it also had dire ramifications. Hundreds of thousands were killed or tortured at the hands of the Red Guards. Reforms that would have energized China's economy were derailed for being too capitalist. The government spent enormous sums of money financing the Red Guards, who in turn undermined the economy by destroying property and art. The education system ground to a halt, as students were encouraged to participate in revolution rather than study. This had a long-term effect on literacy throughout the country. Virtually all engineers, scientists, and professionals were purged, causing a 14 percent decline in industrial production in 1967. Economic activity picked up a bit under Zhou's guiding hand during the early 1970s. Yet his efforts were rolled back by the inept Gang of Four, who oversaw a period of no growth.

Mao was not without accomplishments during this period. China improved its health system, launched its first satellite, and advanced its nuclear technology during this time. Yet such things could have occurred without the Cultural Revolution. The political instability of revolution and the anti-capitalist impulses of the Maoists undermined industry and agriculture alike. The Maoists cared more about the color of the cat than his ability to catch mice. Under Deng's leadership, China was set on a path to a robust market economy. Mao may be regarded as China's greatest hero, but it is Deng who deserves that honor. As he fixed his country, Deng put it more wisely than Mao ever had when he said: "Reform is China's second revolution."

Mao successfully retained power and attained a demigod-like

status in the eyes of the Chinese public, but his Cultural Revolution stymied economic growth and deprived China of many of its most able leaders. Where Deng was pragmatic, Mao was viscerally ideological. The latter's actions destroyed the economy and set back China's modernization by decades.

87

MORE VERY BRITISH SEX

The Lambton Affair

I n the years following the Profumo Affair, sexually deviant British ministers were playing a dangerous game. One would think that Profumo's indiscretions, which ended his career and shamed his party, would have deterred politicians from treading the same prostitute-riddled path. The cold war still raged, and thus both the British public and its intelligence agencies were quite paranoid about ministerial pillow talk with shady call girls. This didn't stop Antony Lambton, a leading Conservative with a kinky hobby. A decade after Profumo's sordid affair scandalized the nation, Lambton was caught bedding a dominatrix named Norma Levy. While the repercussions of the Lambton scandal do not compare to some of the other sex scandals discussed in this book, the story is equally intriguing.

Lambton was a curious fellow. He was born into a fabulously wealthy and storied family. The second son of the fifth Earl of Durham, he became the viscount when his older brother died. From 1951 to 1973, he served as a member of Parliament representing Berwick-upon-Tweed. During that time he gained a reputation as a capable, energetic MP for the Conservative Party. He even privately advocated that Profumo resign before the news of his affair became public, though he was not heeded. When the Labour Party gained control, he became a fierce critic of the majority and demonstrated his skills as a formidable debater. When the Tories returned to power in 1970, he was appointed parliamentary undersecretary for the Royal Air Force. That same year his father died, and Lambton succeeded to the earldom but disclaimed it so that he could remain a government minister, although he subsequently insisted on being addressed as Lord Lambton, as befit an earl. This became quite controversial, as the fact that he had renounced his peerage meant he no longer bore the title. The House of Commons Standards and Privileges Committee also denied him the title, but he persisted in using it.

Meanwhile, Levy was becoming one of the most popular prostitutes in England. The Irish call girl was born Honora Mary Russell and was educated by nuns. Her parents hoped that she would pursue such a life of prayer, but she had other plans. She moved to London, changed her name to Norma (just one of many names she would go by throughout her life), and started working as an escort at a club called Churchill's. She acquired a number of wealthy clients. It seemed the more prominent the customer, the more kinky his preferences. For instance, oil mogul Jean Paul Getty would have her don a white robe and lie in an open coffin, pretending to be a corpse while he looked on clad only in his underwear. Levy wrote down each client and his various turn-ons in her black book, a journal containing high-profile names like the Shah of Iran and the Duke of Devonshire.

Few of her clients were more famous than Lord Lambton. She began seeing Lambton at the end of 1971. She had sex with only Lambton a few times; more often than not, they merely smoked cannabis and conversed. In one incident, he had her watch while he had sex with a young male prostitute. He paid her with personal checks, a startlingly indiscreet move for a man of his prominence. She met him about a dozen times, a period during which, according to a later interview in the *Mail*, "he always treated me very well and was very likeable."

Three months before meeting Lambton, Levy married a man named Colin "Buster" Levy. He was supposedly a minicab driver, but in later years Levy scoffed at such a notion, citing his wealth and frequent traveling. Levy believes today that her former husband was involved with British security services, which encouraged him to pursue the relationship to keep an eye on her powerful clients. For this reason or perhaps merely to make a quick buck, Buster sought to capitalize on his wife's involvement with the renowned MP. In the room where Lambton and Levy had sex, he placed a hidden camera in a wardrobe facing her bed and embedded a listening device in the nose of her giant teddy bear. Later, evidence surfaced suggesting the MI6, the British equivalent of the CIA, was involved in a ruse to expose Lambton. It worked. The scandal broke when a picture of Lambton, in bed with Levy and another prostitute, surfaced. Lambton resigned from office and Levy fled the country.

Initially, Lambton claimed that he used "whores for sex" because "people sometimes like variety. It's as simple as that." Yet in an interview with the MI5, British counterintelligence, Lambton attributed his infidelity to the fight over the aristocratic title. He claimed that being denied the designation "lord" made him "frantic," turning to hobbies like gardening and sex with prostitutes. He separated from his wife and retreated with a new mistress to a château, where he remained for the rest of his life. Lambton was cleared of wrongdoing by the MI5, which concluded that his indiscretions posed no security risk. It was a hurdle that needed to be cleared after the Profumo Affair. Shortly thereafter, fellow politician Lord George Jellicoe similarly resigned for using a prostitute. Though it was rumored that a third prominent minister was using an escort service, his name was never revealed. Three decades later, Levy revealed the man to be one of Britain's most respected elder statesmen, though the newspaper that interviewed her remained silent on his identity.

Levy herself spent the next few decades traveling between Europe and North America. Her marriage with Colin Levy was terminated after he attempted to run her over with a Mercedes. She remarried three times, once merely to acquire a green card, once to an alcoholic rancher, and once to a retired military man with rumored connections to the Mafia. She was deported from the United States five separate times for running prostitute rings. On one occasion, she escaped deportation by asking to visit the restroom in JFK airport and fleeing the building through a back entrance. She never really escaped her immoral lifestyle, running a prostitute ring for debt-ridden Princeton students and becoming deeply dependent on hard drugs. Shortly before his death in 2006 Lambton claimed, "Norma's dead, I'm certain of that." Yet Norma Levy, who was rumored to have contracted AIDS, in fact outlasted Lambton. She lives, as of this writing, in Canada, struggling with her past and attempting to pursue a normal life.

The Lambton Affair did not have far-reaching political consequences. It was quite a scandal for Prime Minister Edward Heath's government, but he was already being challenged by the rising Margaret Thatcher. Yet the scandal is notable for its delicious debauchery. The British public had never acquired the sordid details of the Profumo Affair. The Lambton Affair satiated this hunger. The scandal, revealed via James Bond–style subterfuge, was, above all things, an entertaining diversion. It marked an era with shifting attitudes on sex and politics and where sex scandals became the regular fare for sensationalist British newspapers and magazines.

‖‖

88

TAKING AN UNNEEDED RISK

Watergate

1972, WASHINGTON, D.C.

‖‖

President Richard Nixon, beset by allegations of misconduct, once declared, "I am not a crook." He was trying to avoid a scandal that threatened to ruin his presidency. When taped White House conversations revealed that he was deeply involved in the Watergate break-in, Nixon was forced to resign in disgrace. It turned out Nixon *was* a crook, but if he had been a bit better of a crook he might have avoided the controversy altogether. Nixon could have destroyed the incriminating tapes before they were publically revealed. Had he done so, the Watergate scandal might have become only a footnote in the history books. Instead, it permanently ingrained itself in the American imagination, pervading popular culture and destroying public trust in all politicians. Not only hurting those in office but likely lowering the quality of those who have since chosen to run for office.

When the Watergate Office Complex was robbed on July 17, 1972, no one thought much of it. A security guard noticed that someone was taping the doors and called the police. Five men were arrested for conspiracy and burglary. At first it seemed a petty crime, not a political hit job. But the burglars had funds that could be traced to the Committee to Re-Elect the President, a pro-Nixon fund-raising organization dubbed "CREEP" by the Democrats. The story became hot news overnight. The *Washington Post* led the charge, using contacts like the mysterious "Deep Throat" to reveal a cover-up with ties to the White House. (Incidentally, Deep Throat is now known to have been assistant FBI director Mark Felt.)

This prompted an investigation by the Senate. The hearings were widely covered and viewed by a majority of Americans. Upon learning that Oval Office conversations were recorded, special counsel Archibald Cox subpoenaed the tapes. Nixon refused on the grounds that doing so would compromise national security. President Nixon was the attorney general's and the special counsel's boss. He ordered Cox to withdraw the subpoena, but Cox refused. When Attorney General Elliot Richardson refused to ax Cox, Nixon replaced him with someone who would. The newly appointed Robert Bork reluctantly dismissed Cox and appointed Leon Jaworski, who resumed the investigation. The press cried foul and dubbed the event the "Saturday Night Massacre."

Jaworski pressed on, eventually convincing Nixon to release transcripts of the tapes with sensitive national security information omitted. Nixon apparently believed that the investigators wouldn't notice the twenty-minute gap in one of the tapes. The Supreme Court ordered full access to the tape and the House Judiciary Committee recommended impeachment proceedings against the president. The whole tape was released, revealing a conversation between Nixon and aide H. R. Haldeman detailing a plan to cover up the burglary and provide hush money to the conspirators. Rather than endure the disgrace of impeachment, Nixon resigned. Vice President Gerald Ford succeeded to the presidency and then promptly pardoned his former boss, a move that infuriated the public.

The impact of Watergate is undeniable. Ever since, the media has delightedly affixed the *-gate* designation to any public scandal, ranging from "Nipplegate" (during Janet Jackson's ill-fated Super Bowl performance) or "Fajitagate" (when police officers assaulted two civilians over a bag of fajitas). Combined with the government deception surrounding Vietnam, it fractured the relationship between elected officials and their constituents. It also had political repercussions for the Republicans, as Ford's association with Nixon allowed one of the last century's more dubious presidents, Democrat Jimmy Carter, to win in 1976. Nixon himself lost the opportunity to build on some of the impressive accomplishments of his first term, including widespread desegregation and a withdrawal from Vietnam. Nixon was clearly a brilliant man, despite his lack of scruples. Given his ability, it's curious that he so blundered in covering his tracks. Why didn't he destroy the tapes before the public ever heard of them? They were his personal property until subpoenaed. Better yet, with a double-digit lead in the polls, why bother having anyone break into the Democratic Committee offices at all?

For a long time, it was assumed that Nixon chose not to destroy the tapes due to some blend of arrogance and caution. He believed that as the president he was accorded an executive privilege that protected him from the scrutiny that might accompany lesser men. In his memoirs, he wrote that destroying the tapes would "create an indelible impression of guilt." In a later interview, Nixon revealed that at the time he had not believed the tapes to contain any damning evidence. He recalled having asked Haldeman to destroy the tapes before any outsider had ever heard of them, though Haldeman has since stated that the order was unclear. Richard Nixon even admitted that if they had been destroyed, he doubted he would have had to endure the "agony of resignation."

Two decades after the incident, newly transcribed tapes revealed more to the story. These tapes partially corroborated Nixon's account of the events, suggesting that he indeed ordered the tapes to be destroyed. His first instinct was the correct one, and had he followed it then, his presidency would likely have survived.

Nixon backtracked, thinking that he could creatively use the tapes to show that he had never ordered the break-in. In a March discussion with White House counsel John Dean, Nixon had said that he could acquire $1 million in hush money. He met with Dean a month later, saying with a laugh, "You know, that mention I made to you about a million dollars. . . . I was just joking, of course, when I said that." Nixon intended to keep *that* tape, believing his supreme acting skills would eliminate any doubt on the issue. Yet in subsequent months Nixon, notoriously bad with technology, frequently slipped up in his conversations with his aides. At one point, as Haldeman protested, "Don't say that," Nixon bragged about how he could pardon any of his lackeys, so long as he had a fall guy.

Nixon was too confident in his ability to manipulate. The tapes were wrenched from him, and he was forced to resign in shame. He later attributed it to "bad advice from well-intentioned lawyers." Nixon never admitted guilt, but he did confess that he mishandled the situation. Nixon was slain by his ego, and the result was a scandal to trump all scandals. In July of 1973, one of Nixon's assistants, Alexander Butterfield, was being asked about whether a recording system existed. He sighed and replied, "I was hoping you fellows wouldn't ask me that." Had Nixon the sense to disable the system and destroy the tapes beforehand, history wouldn't have shifted at the words of a small-time secretary.

||||||||||||||||||||||||||||||||||||||||||||||||||||||||||||||||||

89

THE MEANS WAS
THE END

The Iran-Contra Affair

1986, WASHINGTON, D.C.

||||||||||||||||||||||||||||||||||||||||||||||||||||||||||||||||||

There is no faster way to make a new enemy than to besmirch the name of Ronald Reagan in front of a staunch conservative. Okay, so let's try. Reagan was called the Teflon President in his day for the way he deflected criticism. Today, Reagan is the ideological giant of the Republican Party. The fortieth president is remembered fondly for his business-friendly tax policy and tough stance on Communism. Yet critics remember a man at times out of touch with his own administration. There is perhaps no greater example of this than the Iran-Contra Affair. The episode was an international embarrassment in which President Reagan demonstrated a grievous lack of judgment. While there is controversy to this day surrounding the extent of Reagan's involvement in the affair, there is little doubt that the president should have better reined in his subordinates.

The Contras were a militant anti-Communist group in Nicaragua. The Sandinista National Liberation Front, a Socialist political party, had assumed control of Nicaragua after the 1979

Nicaraguan Revolution. Reagan was quite fond of the Contras, calling them the "moral equivalent of our Founding Fathers." The United States enthusiastically supported the rebel movement until Democrats in Congress passed the Boland Amendment in 1982. The amendment outlawed U.S. assistance to the Contras for the purpose of overthrowing the Nicaraguan government. This was done partly to bring the United States in line with international law. It was mostly intended to sever connections with the Contras, however, because the group was involved with drug trafficking in the United States and was also well-known for its violent behavior, including rape, torture, and kidnapping. Yet Reagan did not want to see his beloved Contras defeated, and he admonished National Security Advisor Robert McFarlane, "I want you to do whatever you have to do to help these people keep body and soul together."

Meanwhile, the United States sought to improve relations with Iran. Ever since the Iranian Revolution of 1979, which ousted the unpopular but pro-West Shah, relations between the two countries had been tense. The Iranian Hostage Crisis at the tail end of the Carter administration caused President-Elect Reagan to declare that the United States should not pay "ransom for people who have been kidnapped by barbarians." While those fifty-two hostages were released twenty minutes after Reagan's inauguration, Reagan himself faced a similar crisis when seven hostages were seized by Hezbollah terrorists. McFarlane approached Reagan with a proposition. If the United States sold arms to a "moderate" faction of Iranians, they would leverage their connections to secure the release of American hostages. Later, the Walsh Iran/Contra Report would demonstrate that there was no moderate faction and instead the arms went directly to Iran. Yet Reagan felt he had a duty to rescue the hostages and convinced himself that he was dealing with moderate middle men rather than those he had once referred to as barbarians. Reagan approved the transaction. Through Israel, the United States sold over fifteen hundred antitank and antiaircraft missiles to Iran. While three hostages were released, three more Americans were simply captured to replace them. The deal had done little more than deliver weapons to an anti-West nation at war with its neighbor, Iraq.

McFarlane resigned in late 1985 and was replaced by Admiral John Poindexter. Poindexter authorized Lieutenant Colonel Oliver North to divert funds acquired from the arms deals to Contra rebels. Of the $30 million received in the deal, $18 million was covertly diverted to the Contras as a means of circumventing the Boland Amendment. The arrangement was exposed in November of 1986 after an airlift of guns was downed over Nicaragua. The Iranian government confirmed the story that same month. North was fired, and Poindexter resigned, but not before North destroyed a number of documents germane to the case. Any evidence of Reagan's involvement was eradicated.

Reagan immediately created a panel led by Senator John Tower to investigate the matter. The Tower Commission revealed little evidence that Reagan actively knew of the deal but criticized the president for failing to control the National Security Council staff. In 1987, Reagan spoke directly to the American people on the subject. He declared, "As angry as I may be about activities undertaken without my knowledge, I am still accountable for those activities. . . . [A] few months ago I told the American people I did not trade arms for hostages. My heart and my best intentions still tell me that's true, but the facts and the evidence tell me it is not." North later wrote that there was little doubt Reagan knew about the deal and speculated that the president was "enthusiastically" in favor of the transaction. The American public was quite skeptical of Reagan, as only 14 percent believed the president. This caused a precipitous drop in Reagan's approval ratings, from 67 to 46 percent, though, as usual, Reagan rebounded from the controversy.

North, Poindexter, and McFarlane all eventually faced indictments for their role in the cover-up. North escaped conviction on a technicality, whereas other involved parties received a pardon from Reagan's successor, President George H. W. Bush. Yet, while the impact of the affair domestically was in the end rather small, the damage to U.S. credibility was not. Nicaragua sued the United States before the International Court of Justice and won, but the United States used its position on the UN Security Council to block any enforcement of the verdict. The United States demonstrated that it would accede to the demands of hostage takers, a dangerous precedent. It also reinforced perceptions of the United States as a meddlesome, imperial nation more concerned with fighting Communism than with protecting human rights. Finally, we cannot forget the weapons for the current leaders of Iran, who have not been very grateful. And while Reagan's reputation as a great conservative persists, the Iran-Contra Affair will forever leave a stain on his legacy.

||||||||||||||||||||||||||||||||||||||||||||||||||||||||||||||||||||||||

90

HAD EVERYTHING
TO LOSE AND DID

Gary Hart and Donna Rice

1987, WASHINGTON, D.C.

||||||||||||||||||||||||||||||||||||||||||||||||||||||||||||||||||||||||

When Richard Nixon is offering you condolences, you know you're in trouble. Such was the case for former Colorado Senator Gary Hart in 1987. Hart, the former front-runner in the race for the Democratic nomination for president, had just withdrawn his candidacy due to mounting controversy over an extramarital affair with a twenty-nine-year-old model. The former enemies (Hart had managed George McGovern's unsuccessful bid against Nixon in 1972) commiserated over the media, which had been particularly harsh on each of them. Nixon commended Hart for handling "a very difficult situation uncommonly well." Hart's mistake was not in his handling of the situation. Rather, Hart was careless in his infidelity, exposing himself to media scrutiny without perceiving the potential ramifications of his behavior. Hart delivered the nomination to Michael Dukakis on a silver platter. Dukakis would go on to get pulverized in the general election. Hart might have been able to contend with George H. W. Bush in the election. Instead, the sex scandal ruined his political career.

After McGovern's defeat, Hart successfully ran to represent Colorado in the U. S. Senate in 1974. A decade later, Hart made his first attempt at running for president. In a long, drawn-out battle, he lost the Democratic nomination to Walter Mondale. Hart made a few gaffes during his candidacy, such as squandering a lead in New Jersey after mocking the state. He was also criticized for his insubstantial positions on a number of issues. During a debate, Mondale famously quipped, "Where's the beef?" about Hart's policies, quoting a popular Wendy's advertisement. Mondale was crushed by Ronald Reagan in the 1984 election. Hart let his Senate term expire with eyes on a presidential bid in 1988. When the time came, Hart was widely regarded as the favorite to win the Democratic nomination.

Hart declared his candidacy in April 1987. A month later, he came under fire when rumors surfaced that he was having an extramarital affair. In the weeks leading up to the controversy, Hart met a young model named Donna Rice. According to Rice's friend Lynn Armandt, their first meetings were harmless. Hart invited Rice on a cruise to Bimini. Rice convinced Armandt to tag along. The three joined Hart's friend, lawyer and lobbyist William Broadhurst, on the cruise. Armandt claimed that Rice was no homewrecker, but she was instead a naive, doe-eyed young woman who fell in love with the older Hart. Rice later confided in Armandt that she and Hart slept together during the cruise. What struck Armandt was Hart's carelessness about the whole situation. "I thought he almost wanted to be caught," she later remarked. "He's a very smart man, but he was doing stupid things like being blatant with Donna." Yet she also sympathized some with Hart, saying that she did not think he was in love with Rice but that he found her "refreshing" and "apolitical," a rarity for men in his position.

A few weeks passed, and Hart remained in contact with Rice. The four reunited, though Armandt later said that she was uncomfortable and wanted to wash her hands of the whole situation. Rice stayed in Hart's townhouse, and Armandt in a guest room of

Broadhurst's home. Just two days earlier, in response to claims that he was a womanizer, Hart had issued this bold challenge: "Follow me around. I don't care. I'm serious. If anybody wants to put a tail on me, go ahead. They'll be very bored." The dare proved a grave miscalculation. Two *Miami Herald* reporters had staked out his home and snapped pictures of Rice leaving that morning. Hart argued that the media was too quick to pass judgment, pointing out that they failed to watch both entrances of his home and claiming that she had entered that same day via another door. The story was tenuous, and the American public knew it. Hart's support dropped precipitously from 32 to 17 percent, putting him ten points behind Dukakis in the impending New Hampshire primary.

Hart may yet have survived the controversy, but a few days later the media acquired an incriminating picture taken of the two during the Bimini cruise. The photo showed a beaming Rice sitting on Hart's lap. The *National Enquirer* published the photo that June. Though a majority of Americans believed the media was treating Hart unfairly and that infidelity did not impact a president's ability to govern, Hart's candidacy was over. Hart dropped out of the race, sharply criticizing the media's sensationalist coverage that he believed diverted attention from real, pressing issues. He renewed his candidacy in December, declaring, "Let's let the people decide!" Yet the scandal and his response had destroyed his support base, and he attained a paltry 4 percent in the New Hampshire primary.

Hart never returned to politics. He flirted with the idea of a presidential candidacy in 2004, but ended up endorsing John Kerry instead. The scandal is important because it terminated the career of a rising political star. If Hart had secured the Democratic nomination, he might have been able to mount a challenge to Bush in the 1988 election. If he had defeated Bush, the next decade would have looked quite different, as Hart would have pursued radically different policies on the economy and on matters such as the Gulf War; moreover, we might have been deprived of the national fanfare surrounding the Monica Lewinsky scandal, as Bill Clinton would surely not have sought the nomination with an incumbent Democratic president. Ultimately, Hart was sunk more by his carelessness than the actual affair. By throwing caution to the wind, he sacrificed his chances at the most powerful office in the world.

91

PASSIVELY
AGGRESSIVE, ER,
PASSIVE

Michael Dukakis Doesn't Fight Back

1988, UNITED STATES

He was too good to be president. In September of 1988, in an attempt to defend against claims that he was soft on national security, presidential candidate Michael Dukakis decided to conduct an ill-fated photo shoot with an M1 Abrams tank. The effect was less than ideal. The Democrat looked anything but tough with his goofy grin and oversize helmet, and many voters saw it as a visual representation of Dukakis's inability to protect them. Yet as unfortunate as this PR mishap was, it was not what truly damned his campaign. What hurt Dukakis most was his unwillingness to retaliate as the Bush campaign hammered him with negative ads. Bush successfully painted Dukakis as weak on crime, but Dukakis failed to take Bush to task for unrealistic promises like his "No New Taxes" pledge. Dukakis squandered a significant lead in the summer of 1988 and ended up losing the election in a landslide. Had he run a better campaign, the Bush family might have slipped into obscurity.

Dukakis made his first mistake before ever running for president. If you are a governor running for a higher office, the obvious claim you make is that you are a skilled administrator. But that means your time as governor will be carefully scrutinized, and even one policy mistake can haunt you. In 1972, Massachusetts had put a policy in place that gave weekend furloughs to prisoners. The program permitted inmates to temporarily leave prison and encouraged them to meet with family and friends. Proponents argued that this helped reintegrate criminals into society and pointed to lower recidivism rates among participants. The Massachusetts Supreme Court ruled that under the language of the law, prisoners with a "life without parole" sentence were eligible for the program. The Massachusetts legislature moved to tweak the language of the policy to exclude first-degree murderers, but in 1976 Dukakis vetoed even that measure.

It was a senseless move. There was little point in resocializing a person who would never return to society. What incentive did a person with a life sentence have to adhere to the honor code? The only chance of ever being free was to escape, and the furlough program made it trivially easy to do so. One man, Willie Horton, was imprisoned for robbing and murdering a seventeen-year-old gas station employee. He participated in the program and took advantage of his weekend break. Horton slipped away to Maryland, where he beat and knifed a man before brutally raping the victim's fiancée twice. The couple survived, but they were severely traumatized. Horton stole their car before being captured by the police. A Maryland judge refused to return the man to Massachusetts, saying he was "not prepared to take the chance that Mr. Horton might again be furloughed or otherwise released. This man should never draw a breath of fresh air again."

During the election, this issue came to haunt Dukakis. The Bush campaign ran a "Weekend Passes" ad, which showed a mug shot of Horton and criticized Dukakis's record on crime. This was followed by the "Revolving Door" ad, which showed a line of convicts casually entering and exiting a prison via a revolving door. This ad was particularly effective at swaying the public because polls demonstrated it created a firm contrast in voter opinion on each candidate's toughness on crime. Dukakis called the Horton incident a statistical aberration, but his words merely made him seem robotic and passionless.

This perception of Dukakis was deepened by his views on capital punishment. The Democrat was on record as being against the death penalty. In an October debate between Bush and Dukakis, moderator Bernard Shaw asked him if he would hypothetically favor the death penalty for a man who raped and murdered his wife. Dukakis responded by blandly outlining the statistical ineffectiveness of capital punishment. Dukakis apologized to his campaign manager for the answer, saying that he had misheard the question. The damage was done. Dukakis's poll numbers dropped from 49 to 42 percent that night, as voters were appalled by his dispassionate debating on such an emotional topic.

Dukakis's own attacks on Bush fell flat. An ad against the Bush-Quayle ticket depicted Dan Quayle as incompetent and inexperienced, warning "Quayle: Just a heartbeat away." Rumors were spread by both sides. Dukakis fired his deputy field director for spreading rumors that Bush was having an affair, and members of the Bush campaign similarly insinuated that Dukakis suffered from mental illness and that his wife had burned an American flag to protest the Vietnam War. Yet Bush's most effective attacks were in painting Dukakis as an elitist liberal, an impression fostered by Dukakis proudly declaring that he was card-carrying member of the ACLU. It became impossible for Dukakis to shake that perception.

When the election rolled around, George Bush crushed his opponent. Dukakis won a handful of states, but Bush secured a whopping 426 electoral votes. Unlike Walter Mondale four years earlier, Dukakis had a decent chance at the presidency. Yet he squandered a large summer lead by failing to connect with voters. He repeatedly gave Bush opportunities to strike without ever mounting a coherent attack plan of his own. Had he been elected, he no doubt would have pursued very different policies in the

Gulf War and on the economy. Yet the impact, as Dukakis to this day laments, extended far beyond Bush I's term. Dukakis, a harsh critic of George W. Bush's administration, still feels he must apologize to the American people. "If I had beaten the old man," he griped in 2008, "we never would have heard of the kid, and we wouldn't be in this mess."

92

||||||||||||||||||||||||||||||||||||||||||||||||||||||||||||||||

OVERREACTION

Tiananmen Square

1989, CHINA

||||||||||||||||||||||||||||||||||||||||||||||||||||||||||||||||

I f you run a Google search on "Tiananmen Square" from a computer located in the United States, you will be inundated with one image in particular. You will see a nondescript man holding shopping bags, standing in front of a procession of tanks that could easily crush him beneath their treads. It is one of the most famous images of the twentieth century. Yet if you run a Google search on "Tiananmen Square" from a computer located in China, where the picture was taken in 1989, you will instead be exposed to sunny-faced pictures of tourists and nationalistic photos of government rallies. Thanks to the Chinese government's censorship, few in China recognize the iconic photo. In a century characterized by totalitarian governments and human rights abuses, the valor of the "Tank Man" became an inspirational symbol for all oppressed peoples. Socialist hard-liners in China sought to stymie economic reforms, but in doing so, they energized democratic movements across the globe.

In the several weeks leading up to the massacre, students occupied Tiananmen Square in an attempt to force reform. At first, there was little condemnation from the party elite. These students were mostly the sons and daughters of wealthy, influential Chinese families, and the Politburo did not want to alienate these citizens. Yet gradually, the students were joined by disillusioned workers. For a nation that was born through the sweat and blood of discontented peasants, this was an alarming development. The credibility of the Chinese Communist Party (CPC) rested on defending the proletariat from the "bourgeois elite." The protesters were viewed as dangerous rebels. When Soviet leader Mikhail Gorbachev visited in an attempt to normalize relations between the two great Communist states, the ceremony honoring his arrival was held at the airport rather than in Tiananmen. This was an embarrassing episode for the Chinese government. Government officials who had expressed willingness to compromise with the protesters were removed from office. Premier Li Peng led this crusade, purging former Premier Zhao Ziyang. Zhao wanted to make concessions to placate the students, but Li viewed them as a threat. Li's draconian policies would only stoke the protests and earned China worldwide condemnation.

The protests had been going on throughout May. They were largely peaceful, using hunger strikes and the media to convey their message. They sought economic reforms and criticized the rampant corruption of the Chinese government. While the protesters were not ostensibly against the Communist Party, members of the Politburo claimed that the protesters sought to oust Communism and replace it with bourgeois liberalism. They further argued that the protests were incited by nefarious Westerners intent on overthrowing the CPC. After declaring martial law on May 20, the government deployed the People's Liberation Army to Beijing. Tens of thousands of demonstrators gathered around tanks and jeeps, impeding their movement. Protesters lectured soldiers, stating that they were supposed to be defenders of the people. They sought to warm the soldiers' hearts, bringing them food and water and having their children call the troops tender names like "Uncle Soldier." Many of the soldiers were touched by the display. The CPC withdrew its forces after a few days. This was a deep humiliation for the Politburo. It resolved not to let this happen again.

In the early days of June, the protest was picking up steam. A new hunger strike was called and thousands flocked to the square. On June 2, the party formally moved to clear the square of protesters. Chinese officials preferred to clear the demonstrators out peacefully, but they authorized the use of force if necessary. In response, protesters erected barricades throughout the city to impede the army's progress. In the early hours of June 3, the violence began. Protesters threw rocks and Molotov cocktails at advancing troops. In response, the soldiers fired on the protesters and raked nearby apartment buildings with gunfire, killing peaceful onlookers. They continued through the streets of Beijing, decimating resistance. Upon reaching the square, they offered amnesty to protesters if they left peacefully. The students held a vote before departing to avoid further violence. By the early morning of June 4, the square was cleared. Estimates of the death toll ranged from several hundred (official government estimates) to several thousand. At least seven thousand soldiers and citizens were wounded.

The army blockaded the square and prevented entry to all civilians. A group of protesters, workers, and concerned parents tried to secure entry into the square the morning of June 5, but were repulsed with gunfire. Soldiers fired on retreating civilians, leaving dozens dead in the streets. Later that day, the resistance had scattered. As tanks drove along Eternal Peace Street en route to Tiananmen, only one man was bold enough to continue resisting. He stood in front of the procession of tanks, blocking their progress. The tank tried to circumvent the man, but he boldly leaped in its path. The driver of the tank turned off the engine. The man climbed on the tank, had a brief conversation with the driver, and then clambered off. When the tank again started moving, he continued to impede its path. A few moments later, a group of unidentified men came and ushered the Tank Man away. The whole scene was captured by Western journalists cloistered in a building overlooking the affair. They smuggled the picture out of the country, whereupon it became plastered on the front page of newspapers worldwide.

No one knows what happened to Tank Man. Some speculate that he was seized by government officials and subsequently executed, whereas others maintain that he still lives somewhere in China. Either way, his brave act served as an inspiration for others. The Communist world was already beset by protests throughout its many member states. The Tank Man's bravery further inspired dissidents throughout Eastern Europe and contributed to the collapse of the Soviet Union. The United States and the European Union imposed an arms embargo on China because of this brutal crackdown on its citizens. Within China, hard-liners like Li Peng initially took the dispersion of the rebels in the square as a victory. Yet eventually reformists won out, and China accepted economic modernization and even free enterprise. While political liberty is still suspect in China, the country's de facto embrace of capitalism after Tiananmen has allowed its mammoth economy to flourish. For his effect on the world, the "Unknown Rebel" was featured in *Time* magazine's 100 Most Important People of the Century. Despite his anonymity, Tank Man changed the world and the handling of the protesters doomed China's hard-liners.

The heavy-handed reaction to the Tiananmen Square movement forced an even more heavy-handed cover-up that continues to embarrass and be feared by the Chinese Communist leadership. On the 2012 anniversary, there was a heavy security presence all over and around the square. Those few protesters who dared to appear and remind the world of the Communists' crackdown were quickly dealt with. To this day, the Chinese Internet filter purges out all references to the 1989 events that took place in Tiananmen Square.

|||||||||||||||||||||||||||||||||||||||||||||||||||||||||||||||||||||||||

93

DIDN'T FINISH
THE JOB

Leaving Saddam in Power

1990, IRAQ

|||||||||||||||||||||||||||||||||||||||||||||||||||||||||||||||||||||||||

When asked twenty years later about his handling of the Gulf War, former President George H. W. Bush called it a "moral" war and gave himself an A minus because "there are certain things I could have done better." If we were to judge Bush's handling of the war based solely on Operation Desert Storm itself, the grade is perhaps accurate. American-led coalition troops had no problem repulsing Iraqi invaders out of Kuwait. Yet the grade is far too generous, for Bush erred egregiously at the war's end by encouraging rebellion but offering no material support to oust Iraqi dictator Saddam Hussein. Hussein continued his brutal reign until President George W. Bush invaded Iraq in 2003. Had the elder Bush moved against Hussein, he could have prevented America's costly eight-year invasion under his son. Through his inaction, Bush condemned Iraqis to another decade of oppression under the genocidal Hussein.

George H. W. Bush's first mistakes preceded the war. Iraq was gearing up to invade Kuwait, but the Bush administration believed Hussein's rhetoric to be mere saber rattling. Hussein attempted to bully Kuwait into yielding a number of valuable oil fields near the Iraq-Kuwait border. Hussein also wanted Kuwait to forgive a sizable debt Iraq incurred during the Iraq-Iran war of the 1980s, which Hussein argued had been a valiant Iraqi defense of the Arab world against Persian aggression. Kuwait refused, causing Hussein to deploy a hundred thousand troops to the border. U.S. Ambassador April Glaspie met with Hussein, who candidly admitted that war was likely. Glaspie assured Hussein that the United States viewed the conflict as an Arab one in which America had no interest.

Iraqi troops invaded Kuwait on August 2, 1990, and within a few hours they controlled the country. It did not take long for the United States to form a coalition against Hussein. The United Nations, led by British Prime Minister Margaret Thatcher, demanded that Hussein withdraw his troops by January 15, 1991. The media reported harrowing tales of violence against Kuwaitis, giving momentum to calls for an intervention. When Hussein did not withdraw his forces by the deadline, Operation Desert Storm began. It was a remarkably one-sided affair. In the first phase, American planes bombed strategic locations, including weapons facilities, communication centers, and Hussein's palace, though he had already fled to a safe residential area. In mid-February, the ground assault began when Iraq's army remained in Kuwait, setting oil wells afire. The ground assault forced the Iraqi army out of Kuwait. Iraqi troops surrendered in droves, and tank skirmishes ended with lopsided results. The coalition suffered a mere 379 deaths, half of them due to friendly fire or accidents. On February 26, a mere two days after U.S. General Norman Schwarzkopf proceeded with full force, official Baghdad radio outlets announced that Iraq would comply with UN demands.

It was here that the elder Bush made his mistake. Years later, Bush made it clear that the primary American objective was to "kick this guy out of Kuwait" and that ousting Hussein from Iraq "didn't enter my mind." At the time, Bush's message was far more ambiguous, and he was quoted as saying, "The Iraqi people should put [Hussein] aside and that would facilitate the resolution of all these problems that exist, and would certainly facilitate the acceptance of Iraq back into the family of peace-loving nations." Bush's message was broadcast around Iraq. The U.S. Air Force also dropped leaflets around the country exhorting Iraqis to rise up against Hussein. Oppressed Shiites and Kurds took the message to heart and rose up in revolt. This movement was called the Intifada, and given Iraq's depleted military resources, it had a legitimate chance at success.

Unfortunately for the rebels, Bush had apparently changed his mind about the desirability of revolution. The American military had received sharp criticism for the "Highway of Death," where the military unnecessarily bombed a retreating Iraqi convoy. Bush wanted to wash his hands of the war. He had preferred any coup be an internal military affair, replacing one strongman with another friendlier to U.S. interests. Despite all its support for democracy, the United States was not particularly keen on facilitating a potentially destabilizing democratization process in Iraq. When rebels asked for assistance, U.S. troops were ordered to ignore their pleas. Rebels did not ask that the troops fight alongside them. Instead, they asked for medical treatment and ammunition. The U.S. military refused to help and even destroyed a cache of weapons rather than give it to the rebels. Moreover, the United States carelessly authorized the Iraqi army to use helicopter gun ships on its side of the cease-fire line. This thoughtless concession allowed the army to slaughter insurgents from above. The Iraqi army brutally put down the rebellion, using illegal chemical weapons; its troops raped women and summarily executed Shiites in the streets. The United States did nothing. At home, Bush exultantly declared victory.

The United States was well-equipped to topple Hussein's brutal regime. If it had truly been a "moral" war, as George H. W. Bush put it, then the president would not have stood complacent as the rebellion he incited was torn to shreds. Perhaps Bush did not want America to become mired in Iraq. If so, he should have imparted this wisdom to his son. By not holding Hussein accountable for his crimes, Bush legitimized them. Hussein was free to continue his oppressive policies without fear of reprisal. Bush could have taken care of business and spared his son a costly, controversial war. Because he hesitated, a million Iraqis have died, either at Hussein's hands or during the turmoil of Operation Iraqi Freedom.

III

PROMISE TOO MUCH

Read My Lips

1992, UNITED STATES

IIIIIIIIIIIIIIIIIIIIIIIIIIIIIIIIIIIIIIIIIIIIIIIIIIIIIIIIIIIIIIIIIIIII

t was a campaign promise. Depending on whom you ask, George H. W. Bush erred by either making it or breaking it. Political campaigns are traditionally chock full of grandiose promises and unrealistic claims. Bush made one of history's bolder promises upon receiving the Republican nomination for president in 1988. Seeking to allay the concerns of fiscal conservatives, Bush affirmed his commitment to Reagnomics by vowing "Read my lips: no new taxes." As a candidate, it was a brilliant move. Bush earned a comfortable victory over Democrat Michael Dukakis, who at the time the promise was made led Bush in the polls. Yet as president, when faced with a reeling economy and staggering deficits, Bush found it difficult to keep his word. He ultimately decided to raise taxes, a decision that was lambasted by Democrats and Republicans alike. It was a significant factor in the 1992 elections, as Bill Clinton used the broken promise as evidence of Bush's untrustworthiness.

During the 1980s, President Ronald Reagan considered taxes undesirable but at times a necessary evil. As his vice president,

Bush espoused a similar stance. As Reagan's term expired, Bush competed with other Republicans, including Bob Dole and Pat Buchanan, for the Republican nomination. Conservative activist Grover Norquist promulgated a no-new-taxes pledge and encouraged Republican candidates to sign it. Bush refused at first but tentatively signed it in 1987. Though he finished third in the Iowa caucus, he overcame Dole in the New Hampshire primary by painting his opponent as a tax raiser. With superior organization and fund-raising plus being blessed by Reagan's endorsement, George H. W. Bush handily secured the nomination.

Leading up to the Republican National Convention, Bush sought to cement his stance as an opponent of taxation. His speechwriters included a line promising not to raise any new taxes. Though Bush's economic adviser Richard Darman opposed the phrase, calling it "stupid and dangerous," the advice of others won out. Bush vowed that though "Congress will push me to raise taxes," he would respond "Read my lips: no new taxes." The phrase caught on after the speech and became a significant factor in a nasty election. Amid venomous exchanges between the two campaigns, the no-new-taxes pledge buoyed Bush to a decisive victory.

Upon entering office, Bush realized the difficulty of adhering to such a blanket policy. Bush had figured that the growth of the late 1980s would continue. Unfortunately for him, he was instead faced with a recession. Moreover, the high military spending and low taxes of the Reagan administration had left him with ballooning deficits. Democrats were in control of Congress and were unwilling to make cuts to expensive entitlement programs like Medicare or Social Security. When formulating the budget for the 1990 fiscal year, Bush unsuccessfully proposed deep spending cuts without any new taxes. Democrats thwarted the attempt and forced Bush to compromise. This set a pattern that continues today, with Congress forcing unsustainable deficits rather than service cuts. Bush and the Democrats agreed to a budget package that increased the marginal tax rate and phased out exemptions for high-income taxpayers. Bush also increased spending in some areas. Many of those spending increases were social programs dealing with the recession, such as a bill providing extended benefits for the unemployed. In response, a *New York Post* headline read: "Read my lips: I lied."

Republicans were furious. Minority whip Newt Gingrich was particularly incensed and led Republican opposition to tax hikes. Republican National Committee co-chair Ed Rollins encouraged Republicans in Congress to distance themselves from the president. Bush's approval ratings plummeted, paving the way for Democrat gains during the 1990 midterm elections. Bush's ratings recovered some for his handling of the Gulf War, but no one had forgotten his broken promise by the time the 1992 elections rolled around.

It is rare for an incumbent president to face a real challenge within his party for the nomination, but such was the case for Bush. Buchanan, who criticized Bush for breaking his pledge, earned support from hardcore Republicans for his staunch social conservatism and commitment to lower taxes. He excoriated Bush for cutting "a seedy backroom budget deal with the big spenders on Capitol Hill." Though Buchanan was unsuccessful in winning the nomination, he did secure a stunning 40 percent of the vote in the New Hampshire primary. Though many Americans believed higher taxes might have been necessary, they thought Bush failed to explain his policy shift and felt betrayed over his broken promise. Bush apologized for the tax hike, saying, "I did it, and I regret it and I regret it." Buchanan eventually endorsed Bush, but the campaign proved a distraction and provided ammunition for Bush's Democratic detractors.

During the general election, Democratic candidate Bill Clinton aggressively used television ads to highlight Bush's empty promises. Voters came to question Bush's integrity. Moderates also became disillusioned with Bush, who was forced to adopt a more conservative platform to defeat Buchanan for the nomination. Clinton painted Bush as out of touch with the middle class and inept at handling the economy. When Clinton won, voters, who in exit polls cited Bush's broken tax pledge as their most important issue, elected Clinton by a two-to-one margin. Later, men like Rush Limbaugh believed Bush would have won easily were it not for the reneged promise; others, like White House press secretary Marlin Fitzwater, called it the "single biggest mistake of the administration." Conservatives tend to believe the reversal was the problem, whereas liberals think Bush erred in making such an unwieldy promise.

It's difficult to decide which one was truly the mistake. Bush surely was setting himself up for disaster when he made the promise. On the other hand, he might never have been elected for his first term otherwise. In principle, there was nothing wrong with Bush's willingness to compromise. Yet his compromises allowed his opponents to depict him as fickle and dishonest. Had he stuck to his guns, Clinton might never have become president and the 1990s would have been radically altered. Gingrich, made a hero for his criticisms of Bush, might never have been able to lead the Republican Revolution of 1994. Absent that, it's questionable whether Speaker Gingrich would have been able to mount a serious presidential campaign in 2012. Bush's claim took about twenty seconds, but the impact has lasted over twenty years. Budding politicians would do well to avoid his trap. To promise to do something and fail, like Clinton did with health-care reform, may look bad, but it doesn't look dishonest. To promise not to do something and go back on that pledge, as Bush did, is a myopic tactic with long-term consequences.

95

EVERYONE LOSES

The Major League
Baseball Strike

1994, UNITED STATES

At some point in the post-Y2K era, most major sports in the United States have experienced a work stoppage. In 2011, both the National Football League and National Basketball Association experienced a lockout. The National Hockey League lockout occurred from 2004 to 2005. Yet Major League Baseball (MLB) is noticeably absent from this list. The reason is simple: The last time MLB went on strike, it never recovered. The baseball strike of 1994–1995 is widely regarded as the worst in American history. It forever altered the fans' perception of the owners and players. The strike occurred when owners and players warred over revenue. The irony is that their greed so damaged the sport that MLB lost money for the next decade.

The strike began when owners pushed for new measures to benefit smaller-market teams. Those measures included a scheme to share local broadcast revenue between teams. The contentious issue, however, was a measure to enact a salary cap that would prevent teams from spending more than a specified total on their players' salaries. While owners claimed that average player salary would steadily increase in the new agreement, players were skeptical. Their skepticism was well-founded, as the owners intended to decrease the players' share of the revenue from 56 to 50 percent. MLB Players Association leader Donald Fehr rejected the owners' offer on July 18, 1994. He stated later that the players felt "pushed into" striking. The players walked off the job on August 12. Negotiations over the next month proved fruitless. The association offered a counterproposal on September 8, but the owners rejected it, arguing that they would be unable to cover costs. The next day acting commissioner Bud Selig canceled the rest of the season, including the World Series.

Preceding the lockout, the 1994 season had no shortage of compelling stories. The Montreal Expos were having their best season ever, posting a league-leading 74–40 record, despite having the second-lowest payroll among the teams. After an ensuing decade of mediocrity, the Expos were shipped to the States to become the Washington Nationals. Another compelling story was that of Matt Williams, who was on pace to match Roger Maris's single-season home run record of sixty-one. Tony Gwynn, who was batting .394 at the time, missed out on a chance to become the first player ever to bat over .400 in a season. Seattle Mariners star Ken Griffey Jr. lamented, "We picked a bad season to have a good year."

In 1995, the government got involved. Five bills were introduced in Congress to end the strike. President Bill Clinton ordered bargaining to resume and find an agreement by February 6, to no avail. With the season about to start, many teams began using replacement players so that they could still have regular season games. Others refused to field the players, either out of solidarity for players on strike or because they felt it would aggravate the labor dispute. Future Supreme Court justice Sonia Sotomayor issued an injunction in late March preventing the owners from using replacement players and blocking their attempts at unilaterally implementing a collective bargaining agreement without player input. The strike finally ended in early April, just days before the season was scheduled to begin. Sports media heralded Sotomayor as a hero who had delivered a "wicked fastball" to the baseball owners.

When play resumed, the fans made their displeasure clear. Attendance plummeted by 20 percent and didn't return to prestrike levels until the mid-2000s. This resulted in hundreds of millions of dollars in lost revenue annually. Due to lost ad revenue and squandered broadcasting deals, canceling the 1994 World Series alone accounted for a loss of $180 million. The World Series averaged a robust 22.3 rating in the decade preceding the strike, but that figure dropped to a 15.3 average in the ensuing decade.

Those who did attend the opening games of the 1995 season demonstrated their anger. One fan paid a plane to fly over Riverfront Stadium in Cincinnati with a banner reading "Owners & Players: To hell with all of you!" A game in Pittsburgh almost ended in a forfeit when fans delayed action for nearly twenty minutes by throwing various objects onto the field. In other games, fans bore signs and T-shirts accusing players and owners alike of greed. America's favorite pastime had been forever colored by the strike. It was regarded as an unforgivable act of war on baseball fans. Not until the home-run chase between Mark McGwire and Sammy Sosa in 1998 was there renewed interest in Major League Baseball. Unfortunately today, even that storied contest is tainted, by the steroids scandal.

MLB has regained its popularity, but it has been replaced as America's favorite sport by professional football. Such a transition might have occurred regardless of the strike, but the strike of 1994–1995 no doubt helped usher in football's reign. When the NFL went on strike in 2011, the issues were resolved without missing a single game. While baseball has experienced labor stability since the 1994 lockout, baseball fans have not forgotten. In a sport where it famously takes three strikes to get out, it only took MLB one strike before it was out of favor, out of revenue, and out of the hearts of the American public.

96

|||||||||||||||||||||||||||||||||||||||||||||||||||||||||||||||||||||||||||

MADE THE WRONG
DIFFERENCE

Nader

1996, UNITED STATES

|||||||||||||||||||||||||||||||||||||||||||||||||||||||||||||||||||||||||||

When Republican candidate George W. Bush narrowly defeated former Vice President Al Gore in the 2000 election, Democrats were furious. Democrats accused Republicans of voter fraud in key swing states. They also criticized the Supreme Court for frustrating efforts to recount ballots in Florida, a battleground state whose winner would decide the presidency. The Democrats' blame-game scapegoated no one more than Ralph Nader, and for once, the complaints of the politicians were accurate. Nader, a lifetime activist with strong liberal views, ran as a third-party candidate for the Green Party. By siphoning votes that likely would have gone to Gore, Nader almost certainly was the difference maker in the election. By spoiling the election, Nader undoubtedly changed history, as Gore would have behaved very differently in office than Bush.

Nader had been a national figure for over thirty years. He earned fame as a young man for his book *Unsafe at Any Speed*, which criticized American automobiles as unsafe. His actions helped facilitate passage of the 1966 National Traffic and Motor

Vehicle Safety Act, which mandated cars possess safety features like seat belts and stronger windshields. Nader would go on to publish a number of books criticizing government corruption and ineptitude with the help of young activists dubbed "Nader's Raiders." He became a prominent figure in the environmental movement as a leading critic of nuclear energy and water pollution. He declined a bid for president in 1972, but ran as a write-in candidate in 1992 and on the Green Party ticket in 1996.

Nader knew that he would never become president. Third-party candidates in the United States lack the organization, funding, and exposure of major-party candidates. Third-party candidates also suffer from the United States' winner-take-all electoral system. This system dates back to the first years after the revolution and reflects the American landed aristocracy's distrust of the masses. Rather than have the president elected by the popular vote, the electoral system has citizens vote for electors who actually choose the president. The electors are assumed to be wiser and more knowledgeable than the ordinary voters. This was the thought by the Founding Fathers because it was likely the electors would be the same men who created the system, the rich land owners.

In the Electoral College, the candidate with the most votes wins all the electors for that state regardless of how slim the difference. In other countries, a proportional system allows smaller parties to receive representation according to the number of votes they receive. This means that extremists, both conservative and liberal, can achieve modest success even if they come nowhere close to winning a majority. In the American electoral system, winning a state with 50.1 percent of the vote earns the candidate 100 percent of the electoral votes. There have been calls to change the system, accurately saying it makes some votes more important than others. The electoral system also causes candidates to unduly focus on swing states like Florida as opposed to firmly Democratic states like California or firmly Republican states like Texas.

Though Ralph Nader had no chance of winning the election,

his campaign was not pointless. Nader wanted to receive at least 5 percent of the total votes, as doing so would qualify his Green Party for federally distributed public funding in the next election. Nader failed to reach this benchmark with only 2.74 percent of the vote, but his modest success did force states like Delaware and Maryland to put the Green Party candidate on the ballot in the next election (he was on the ballot in only forty-four states in the 2000 election). Thus Nader did what was best for his party, the Green Party. He viewed establishment Democrats and Republicans as two sides of the same evil coin, and thus had no compunctions about potentially diverting votes away from Gore, whose positions were often the same as his own.

As the election results came in, it was apparent that Gore could seal a victory if he won either New Hampshire or Florida. Both states went down to the wire, with New Hampshire being decided by 7,000 votes, and Florida decided by a mere 537 votes. Nader received 97,000 votes in Florida and 22,000 votes in New Hampshire. Democrats pointed out that Nader's supporters, composed mostly of left-leaning environmentalists, would likely have voted for Gore if Nader hadn't been on the ballot. Nader disputed the notion that he played spoiler, arguing that according to polls "25% of my voters would have voted for Bush, 38% would have voted for Gore and the rest would not have voted for all." Instead, Nader pointed to the Supreme Court decision to halt Florida's recount, Gore's loss in his home state of Tennessee, and disloyal Democrats who voted for Bush as the real culprits in Gore's defeat.

For liberals, the excuses fell on deaf ears. Nader was harshly criticized by environmentalists like Sierra Club president Carl Pope, who in an open letter to Nader charged that he recklessly broke his word by campaigning in swing states. It is indeed unclear why Nader chose to campaign in states like Florida, which could affect the national outcome, when he could easily have campaigned in uncontested states like California or New York where voters could have chosen him without fear of giving Bush the election. Nader's strategy was counterproductive, as it helped

Bush get elected when Gore's policies were far more in line with the Green Party platform. Nader also incurred personal costs for the controversy. Public Citizen, an activist organization founded by Nader in 1971, had accomplished much under his direction, but that heritage was lost. It immediately suffered for its affiliation with the candidate. Even now when asked about Nader, Public Citizen downplays their relationship. Nader's legacy became his role as spoiler rather than his impressive record as an activist.

Nader was not to repeat his role in 2004. Still the incumbent George W. Bush defeated Democratic candidate John Kerry without needing Nader's help. In 2008 Nader ran again as an independent. In both elections Nader failed to break 0.6 percent of the popular vote. Yet for all his irrelevance in these elections, Nader will always be remembered for helping George Bush get elected in 2000. Had Gore been elected, he likely would have pursued aggressive policies to curb global warming and other environmental hazards. He likely would never have invaded Iraq and would have shaped the post-9/11 world in a dramatically different fashion. He would have acted much more in the way that Ralph Nader, and those who voted for the third-party candidate, wanted. Nader should have been pragmatic rather than idealistic. He chose to campaign hard in the wrong states. In doing so, he helped elect a candidate who disagreed with him on just about everything.

DEPENDS ON THE DEFINITION OF *TRAGIC FLAW*

Monica Lewinsky and the Blue Dress

1995–1997, WASHINGTON, D.C.

||||||||||||||||||||||||||||||||||||||||||||||||||||||||||||||||||||||

I f you conduct a Google search on the term "Lewinsky jokes," you'll get over 463,000 results. If you search for "Bill Clinton jokes," you'll get another 806,000. Most are lewd, many are crude, and a disturbing amount involve the former president in the nude. Clinton was a shrewd politician who oversaw an economic boom and worked tirelessly to promote peace in the Balkans and the Middle East. He could have gone down in history as a champion of the Democratic Party. Instead, Clinton is more commonly remembered for his philandering and deception. The Monica Lewinsky scandal left an unsightly blemish on the Clinton presidency. The controversy mitigated Clinton's political effectiveness at the tail end of his tenure and compromised his ability to support Vice President Al Gore in the 2000 election. Clinton's infidelity damaged his party politically and tarnished his personal legacy. It is likely that there has been no other example of oral sex with such far-reaching consequences.

Clinton's problems began with a woman named Paula Jones, although he was already under fire for a series of other ethics violations, including the Whitewater controversy, the FBI files controversy, and the travel office controversy. Though Clinton was eventually exonerated in each of these cases, they served to give the impression of Clinton as unethical. The Jones incident reinforced this impression. Jones alleged that in 1991 Clinton, who was governor of Arkansas at the time, attempted to solicit her for sexual favors. She claimed he invited her to his hotel room and exposed his genitals to her. Clinton attempted and failed to postpone the case until after his presidency, arguing that a sitting president could not be sued. During the proceedings, the prosecution sought to demonstrate that this was not an isolated incident and that Clinton habitually pursued extramarital relationships. All this was further complicated by his being married to the most politically active First Lady in decades, Hillary Clinton. It was just as the many past affairs were being exposed that the twentieth century's most famous "other woman" came to the public's attention.

Monica Lewinsky was a young intern at the White House. Between November 1995 and March 1997, Lewinsky and Clinton had nine sexual encounters. Many people observed that Clinton and Lewinsky spent a large amount of time together and suspected an affair. Then Lewinsky was called to testify in the Paula Jones case in January of 1998. There she submitted an affidavit denying any sort of relationship with the president. On November 13, Clinton settled with Jones for $850,000, but he refused to apologize. Clinton's attorney maintained that Jones's allegations were baseless, but that the president settled to eliminate a distraction.

Unfortunately for Clinton, the Jones case had become the least of his worries. Shortly after Lewinsky issued an affidavit denying their relationship, she requested that her friend Linda Tripp perjure herself to conceal the affair. Lewinsky and Tripp had become close during their time together at the White House. Lewinsky confided in Tripp about her relationship with the president. Unbeknown to Lewinsky, Tripp began secretly recording their conversations. When Lewinsky commented that Clinton had ejaculated on her blue dress during one of their encounters, Tripp convinced Lewinsky not to dry-clean the garment. When Lewinsky requested that Tripp lie under oath, Tripp delivered the tapes to independent counsel Kenneth Starr. Starr was at the time investigating Clinton's role in the earlier list of ethics controversies. When the story was released, the media frenzy surrounding the event caused Lewinsky to withdraw to her mother's residence at, of all places, the Watergate complex.

In the ensuing months, Clinton was extremely deliberate and careful with his words. On January 26, he stated under oath that he "did not have sexual relations with that woman, Miss Lewinsky." Clinton also said that "there is not a sexual relationship, an improper sexual relationship or any other kind of improper relationship." During this time, the First Lady, Hillary Clinton, stood by her husband, claiming that the allegations were part of a "vast right-wing conspiracy" to undermine the president. For months, Lewinsky refused to testify. In July, Lewinsky received legal immunity in exchange for her testimony before a grand jury. She surrendered the semen-stained dress and admitted to the sexual relationship. Her final words on the matter were this: "I hate Linda Tripp."

Starr concluded that Clinton had perjured himself and obstructed justice. Clinton countered that he had not, arguing that his statements were technically not lies. The definition of "sexual relations" offered in the Jones case excluded receiving oral sex. Clinton said that though he had indeed pursued an indecent relationship with Lewinsky, he had never performed sex acts on her. Concerning his statement about there being no inappropriate relationship with Lewinsky, Clinton famously stated "that depends on what the meaning of the word 'is' is." Since at the time of his statement Clinton was no longer involved with Lewinsky, the president argued that he had been using the present tense and hence was not lying. Clinton had certainly intended his testimony to mislead, but technically he hadn't lied.

The 1998 midterm elections narrowed the Republican majority in Congress. During the lame-duck session, Republicans attempted to impeach Clinton for perjury and obstruction of justice. It was a brazenly political move, as Republicans sought to leverage an unfortunate personal situation to their political advantage. The hypocrisy was made even clearer because prominent Republicans like House Speaker Newt Gingrich had engaged in extramarital affairs of their own. Nonetheless, the House successfully impeached Clinton in December of 1998. (*Impeached* is not convicted, just sort of indicted.) Clinton was more fortunate in the Senate, where a two-thirds majority was required. Democrats and a few moderate Republicans united to torpedo the impeachment proceedings, with the charge of perjury being defeated 55-45 and the obstruction charges falling short at 50-50. Even so Clinton was fined, and his Arkansas law license suspended, but his presidency survived.

For the rest of his term, Clinton was politically weakened by the scandal. Americans viewed him as immoral and elevated the importance of ethics in the 2000 election. Gore tried to distance himself from Clinton during his campaign. Had the scandal never erupted, Clinton would have delivered a powerful endorsement in a tight election. Political scientists later suggested that Gore's refusal to associate with Clinton undermined him in key swing states. A Gore presidency would have looked very different from a Bush presidency, and thus Clinton's sexual escapades had far-reaching consequences. Though Clinton's popularity eventually rebounded, he will always be remembered for his indiscretions. He was not the first man in power to have a mistress, and he won't be the last. But he was an early victim of a new technological age where his sexual escapades were aired to the entire world. For that reason, Lewinsky jokes aren't going away any time soon.

98

A FAILURE TO
COMMUNICATE

Another Brick in the Wall

A terrorist bomb damages an American warship in Yemen. A mysterious meeting with a one-legged man takes place in Malaysia. A Middle Eastern man with no flight experience tries to learn to fly a 747 jumbo jet at a flight school in Minnesota. Two foreign men travel to the United States by a devious route. A boy in Yemen is hired to watch a truck and boat trailer, but the owners never return. Taken separately, these bits of information are meaningless, but when linked together, the pieces are a puzzle leading to the worst terrorist attack on U.S. soil. Yet government agents within the FBI, CIA, and National Security Agency separately had all of the necessary information to link these pieces together. What happened? Nothing. The agents ran into a wall.

The first blocks in the wall were laid just after World War II. Before and during the war, the FBI, under J. Edgar Hoover, was tasked with investigating domestic espionage, sabotage, or subversion in addition to their regular duties. After the war, fearing that too much power in the control of one agency could lead down the path Germany had just walked, the intelligence tasks were formally split. The Central Intelligence Agency was created from the Office of Strategic Services to handle all foreign intelligence, while the FBI would handle domestic intelligence, along with all law enforcement responsibilities. By itself, this seemed to be a fairly safe division of labor, but it began a culture of separatism and turf wars. Other intelligence agencies (in the military and within existing agencies), as they developed, were also given specific areas and tasks.

Under Hoover, the FBI's covert action program focused not just on domestic organizations and domestic dissidents but also on numerous political figures, especially those disliked or distrusted by Hoover. The FBI regularly used illegal wiretaps and surveillance to accomplish their goals. Hoover had files on a number of Washington figures and was willing to use them if those individuals opposed him. The amount of real power this gave Hoover was immense and inappropriate for an appointed official. With J. Edgar dead, the Watergate investigations brought some of these activities to light, resulting in the dissolution of the FBI's Domestic Intelligence Division and reforms "designed to build a wall between federal law enforcement and the nation's intelligence community." The attorney general was given authority over domestic intelligence-gathering activities. It was up to the attorney general to protect individual rights and prevent any abuse. While traditional *criminal* search warrants or electronic surveillance required probable cause and a judge's approval, this allowed the attorney general to authorize searches and surveillance of foreign powers and their agents without any court review or approval. This was the case until 1978, when Congress passed the Foreign Intelligence Surveillance Act (FISA). FISA did not require a traditional court order or warrant but instead created a new court to review all requests for intelligence-related searches and surveillance. A new department, the Office of Intelligence Policy and Review (OIPR), was created as gatekeeper to approve and present all requests to the FISA courts. Any agents or agencies who wanted to search or spy on a foreign national had to go through OIPR to have the request approved to present it to the FISA court.

Congress, and the Justice Department, interpreted the new law to mean that searches would be approved only if the "primary purpose" was to obtain foreign *intelligence* information. They could not be used to build a criminal case (though criminal cases might follow) or to spy on domestic targets. The interpretation meant that criminal prosecutors could be briefed on FISA information but not direct or control its collection. With FISA, the next brick fell in place in the information wall.

In 1995, OIPR believed there was still too much informational crossover between the intelligence community and the criminal prosecutors, crossover that might allow a judge to throw out critical cases. Richard Scruggs, then head of OIPR, proposed a "Chinese wall" to divide everyone working on intelligence from those working on criminal investigations. Because the FBI handled both intelligence gathering and criminal investigations, this meant a wall limiting the sharing of information between agents working for the same agency or even on the same squad. On July 19, 1995, Attorney General Janet Reno issued an official set of procedures for contact between the FBI and the Criminal Division, creating the new restriction on sharing information.

No one really read these complicated and extensive procedures, including the people responsible for enforcing them. The FBI decided that the FISA law, with Reno's rules and procedures, meant that anyone doing a criminal investigation could not get pertinent intelligence information—or even talk to anyone—from the intelligence division. The intelligence division also decided that, if they couldn't share information with the criminal division, they certainly couldn't share with anyone outside their agency either. The CIA decided that it meant that *all* their intelligence was sacred and not to be shared outside their agency, which probably suited some competitive bureaucrats entirely. The actual rules as written precluded only prosecutors, not criminal investigators, from communicating with the intelligence community. Yet all the agencies used the law as an excuse to avoid sharing information. FBI managers warned their agents that sharing information outside the intelligence division would be a career-ending offense, even if they shared with investigators on the same squad. The OIPR, in control of all FISA requests, encouraged this interpretation, believing that a more conservative approach would make it easier to get FISA warrants and be able to use the information later for successful prosecutions. The wall became high and wide and blocked almost all cross-communication.

After the first World Trade Center bombing, Mary Jo White, U.S. attorney for the Southern District of New York, realized there was a serious flaw with the rules as they were being interpreted. She sent Reno a memorandum suggesting that terrorism should be addressed as a criminal matter rather than an intelligence matter to avoid all those dangerous walls.

Attorney General Reno, apparently realizing that her attempt to protect the FISA process had built serious unintended blockades, drafted a memo clarifying the rules and insisting that timely information sharing was not only allowed but absolutely required. It was only "uncoordinated and unnecessary" communications that were not allowed.

Reno's memorandum, however, was never issued. The FBI continued to believe that they had to have OIPR's approval, which was difficult to get, to share intelligence information with the Criminal Division. The OIPR did nothing to correct or discourage this interpretation.

In 1999, during the height of the millennium terror alert, the FISA court received a huge number of FISA applications. However, there were also a large number of related criminal cases, including an outstanding indictment against one Osama Bin Laden. In response, OIPR and the FISA court decided that the rules against information sharing needed to be tightened even more. As a result, while the Justice Department attempted to lower the information wall, OIPR and the FISA court were equally determined to build it even higher. The FISA court went so far as to order that certain Bin Laden–related FISA information could not be shared with anyone in the Criminal Division or with FBI agents working on any related criminal matter, without the court's permission. In fact, no one in the FBI or Department of Justice was even allowed to *see* any FISA material without signing a form acknowledging the restrictions. The attorney general's office, now under John Ashcroft, continued to work on a draft proposal to counter these procedures, but it was never finished or adopted.

As a result, when an FBI criminal investigation team discovered a link to al-Qaeda during their investigation of the U.S.S. *Cole* bombing, the CIA refused to share critical information. Khalid al-Mihdhar—a man the FBI criminal investigation team had linked with the *Cole* bombing and al-Qaeda—had been tracked by the CIA. They knew Mihdhar had obtained a U.S. visa to fly to New York with a colleague. But the CIA analyst deliberately held back crucial facts from the FBI that would have led to al-Qaeda operatives in the United States. The reason? The FBI team was made up of *criminal* investigators, so according to the CIA agents, the wall prevented them from sharing.

Later, when an FBI agent in Minneapolis learned of a suspicious man taking flying lessons, he opened an intelligence investigation to learn more. Suspicious that the man, Zacarias Moussaoui, might be planning a hijacking, the agent wanted to open a criminal investigation. Afraid of running into the wall, headquarters said no. Without proof of criminal activity, the FBI turned it over to the Immigration and Naturalization Service (INS). When the FBI agent then applied for permission to search Moussaoui's laptop and belongings, he was told that would require a FISA warrant, and that there was not enough evidence linking Moussaoui to a foreign power to get one. Fear of the wall kept anyone from testing that theory. As a result, the laptop was never searched. The al-Qaeda terrorist was simply deported.

In August 2001, an FBI analyst discovered that Mihdhar was in New York, and they realized they needed to find him. It was decided that, because of the wall, only an intelligence agent could do the job. The criminal agents could not even be told Mihdhar was there. There were many experienced criminal agents available, but instead of sending all hands on deck to locate and apprehend a possible terrorist, the job fell to one lone, and very inexperienced, intelligence agent. He failed to locate Mihdhar in time.

The wall was a bureaucratic creation that never should have existed as interpreted. It was based not on law or even decisions but on the need to avoid possible problems. The attorney general's office knew it was extremely real and solid despite its fictional nature. Yet neither Janet Reno nor John Ashcroft made any serious attempt to tear down the intelligence wall. The OIPR made it thicker and higher, and the CIA and FBI used it as an excuse to enhance their turf war. As a result, the most powerful nation in the world failed to stop a third-world terrorist plot, of which all of the parts were known, but not one person could know them all, on September 11, 2011.

Sadly, one of the original FBI investigators from the *Cole* bombing, John O'Neill, had retired from the bureau to work in the World Trade Center. He died that day trying to save others. There never was supposed to be an intelligence wall. But the conservative nature of the intelligence bureaucracy combined with the interagency rivalries turned a concern for due procedure into a hazardous information block that cost thousands of American lives.

99

UNPREPARED

The Mishandling of
Katrina

2005, U.S. GULF COAST

I n 2005, Hurricane Katrina ravaged the Gulf Coast, killing thousands and displacing many more. Kanye West, popular rapper and noted egomaniac, voiced his disapproval of federal handling of the disaster, stating baldly, "George Bush doesn't care about black people." Bush would later call that one of the worst moments of his presidency. It's a strange, somewhat disturbing statement. Bush's worst moment was not witnessing the devastation of Katrina, but rather the criticism received for his handling of the tragedy. While West's allegations of racism were over the top, he was right to lambaste the federal response to the hurricane. In a report titled "Failure of Initiative," Republican members of Congress put it curiously well: "At every level—individual, corporate, philanthropic and governmental—we failed to meet the challenge that was Katrina. In this cautionary tale, all the little pigs built houses of straw."

Hurricane Katrina, the deadliest storm of the 2005 season, ended up killing nearly two thousand people and causing $81 billion in property damage. It formed over the Bahamas on August

23, making a pit stop at Florida before hopping the Gulf of Mexico to strike southeast Louisiana. After devastating New Orleans, it crept along the coast, flooding Mississippi beachfront towns. While considered only a category 1 storm as it brushed Florida, Katrina intensified to a category 5 storm as it crossed the Gulf. It slipped back to category 3 just before hitting Louisiana on August 29. It was the costliest, most ruinous hurricane to ever strike the United States. New Orleans was left a shell of a city, flooded for weeks and reduced to anarchy, riots, and crime. Onlookers compared the metro area to Somalia for its lawless disorder. Katrina breached New Orleans's federally built levees, plunging the city under water. About 90 percent of structures within half a mile of the coastline were obliterated. What ensued was the largest displacement in American history, with hundreds of thousands forced to flee their homes.

It's easy to see why Bush incurred such criticism in the wake of the hurricane. Bush was on vacation in Texas and didn't return to Washington until two days after the hurricane struck. A picture of Bush peering out his window as *Air Force One* flew over the Gulf Coast on its return trip was criticized by some as detached and uncaring. While Bush claimed that no one anticipated the levees breaking, videos were later released showing Bush receiving such a warning just days before Katrina struck and responding, "We are fully prepared." Yet Bush also signed a $10.5 billion aid package and ordered troops to assist with relief efforts. He cannot be criticized for the failings of state and local governments and for the organizational ineptitude demonstrated by the Federal Emergency Management Agency (FEMA). As the president often is, Bush was a scapegoat for mistakes made on the ground.

As the hurricane approached, New Orleans Mayor Ray Nagin dangerously dragged his feet on implementing an evacuation plan. Emergency evacuation was not ordered until less than a day before landfall. Nagin was apparently more worried about the political costs of crying wolf if the hurricane didn't strike than the human costs of inaction if it did. Nagin's evacuation plan also included no provisions to help evacuate low-income, elderly, or ill residents, despite New Orleans's high poverty rates and the fact that 120,000 people had no private mobility. Nagin criticized Louisiana Governor Kathleen Blanco for delaying federal response efforts, as Blanco failed to ask for federal assistance with the evacuation and was slow to request federal troops for maintaining order. Perhaps most egregiously, state Representative William J. Jefferson diverted National Guard resources to check his personal property rather than help with pressing rescue efforts.

Yet local officials were disadvantaged by the paucity of federal support. New Orleans's emergency operations chief Terry Ebbert lamented, "This is not a FEMA operation. I haven't seen a single FEMA guy." Nagin also expressed frustration at the lack of federal reinforcements. Federal assistance was often patchwork and disorganized, and there was no greater culprit than FEMA.

Media coverage of the disaster relief relayed numerous anecdotes of FEMA's inadequacies and needless bureaucracy. For instance, FEMA sent hundreds of volunteer firefighters to Atlanta, where they spent their time playing cards and watching videos on the agency's history. FEMA turned away trucks loaded with water, blocked fuel deliveries, and cut emergency communications lines. FEMA failed to take advantage of offers from Amtrak to aid in relief efforts, instead using inefficient buses. CNN reported that doctors eager to assist injured evacuees "were handed mops by federal officials who expressed concern about legal liability. . . . And so they mopped, while people died around them." FEMA also confiscated relief supplies, particularly from out-of-state donors, concerned again about liability. FEMA ordered ninety-one tons of ice at a cost of $100 million for the purpose of storing emergency supplies. Yet FEMA director Michael Brown redirected the ice to federal facilities around the country, later saying, "I don't think that's a federal responsibility to provide ice to keep my hamburger meat in my freezer or refrigerator fresh."

Brown was a man in over his head. He was assigned director despite having no experience in disaster relief. He also demonstrated a lack of awareness throughout the disaster. In one incident, while being interviewed by NBC, Brown revealed that he was unaware of the thousands of starving evacuees located at the Ernest N. Morial Convention Center without power, water, medical supplies, or sanitation. Brown was axed by his superior, Secretary of Homeland Security Michael Chertoff, less than two weeks after the disaster. Before Brown was fired, Bush offered these supportive words: "Brownie, you're doing a heckuva job." The congressional report would later call Brown "clueless" and chided Chertoff as being "detached." Brown was replaced by Vice Admiral Thad W. Allen, the Coast Guard's chief of staff. Allen would receive praise for his management of the search-and-rescue efforts.

The hurricane revealed that the federal government was woefully unprepared to manage an emergency. The report said it was a case of "too many cooks in the kitchen," where overlapping bureaucracies butted heads and squabbled rather than working together to form a coherent response. Reconstruction in New Orleans and elsewhere continues to be a slow, arduous process. The Gulf itself has mostly recovered from the hurricane and is now suffering more from the 2006 BP oil spill. While there were political repercussions to the mismanagement, the greatest costs were the thousands of lost lives, the hundreds of thousands of refugees mishandled, and the billions of dollars in economic damage. Those losses will never be reclaimed. Those who were in charge of the agencies tasked with assisting and those under them almost universally failed. In an age in which terrorism remains a threat and scientists make dire predictions of environmental catastrophe caused by global warming, one can only hope that future leaders learn from these mistakes.

100

THE WORST-CASE
SCENARIO HAPPENS

Nuclear Meltdown

2011, JAPAN

On March 11, 2011, an earthquake struck off the coast of Tohoku, Japan. Prime Minister Naoto Kan called it the "toughest and most difficult crisis for Japan" since World War II. The earthquake triggered a tsunami with waves that reached heights of up to 133 feet and crept as far as six miles inland. More than fifteen hundred people died, and economic costs were estimated to be $235 billion, making it the most expensive natural disaster in world history. When the tsunami struck the Fukushima nuclear power plant and caused a meltdown, many despaired of another Chernobyl. Nuclear expert John Price lamented, "Basically, whatever can go wrong has gone wrong." Through heroic actions by plant employees, the disaster was mostly controlled, with minimal casualties. In the weeks following the meltdown, reports surfaced that government and plant officials were aware of the dangers facing the plant but neglected to act on them. The Fukushima disaster could have gone far worse, and due to gross regulatory negligence, it almost did.

When nuclear scientist Lee Furlong audited the Fukushima

Fukushima

power plant in 1984, he "threw his hands in the air" when he discovered it was built right over a minor fault. "When I asked why they did it," Furlong recalled, "they explained that they did not want to have too long a cooling pipe from the ocean." According to a diplomatic cable released by WikiLeaks after the disaster, cost-cutting measures like this were common in the industry despite jeopardizing safety. Because the public generally opposed the construction of new plants, reactors were often extended beyond their forty-year statutory limit. Such was the case with the Fukushima plant, which was given a ten-year extension for its oldest reactor just a month before it melted down. This was granted despite a history of safety mishaps at the plant. In 2000, cracks were revealed in the steel shrouds that cover reactor cores, but regulators hardly batted an eye. In 2003, operations were temporarily suspended when it was revealed that Tokyo Electric had falsified inspection records and hidden flaws for over sixteen years in an effort to save on repair costs. Just two weeks before the earthquake, the company admitted that it failed to inspect thirty-three pieces of equipment related to the plant's cooling systems, including water pumps and diesel generators.

The problem lay in the cozy relationship between the nuclear industry and the government. Before granting the extension, inspectors spent just three days assessing the reactor, a paltry amount of time when considering that assessing earthquake risks is an extremely complex problem for engineers. Regulation in Japan fell to two groups, the Nuclear and Industrial Safety Agency and the Japan Nuclear Energy Safety Organization. The former group was managed by the Ministry of Economy, Trade and Industry, whose ministers actively promoted the nuclear industry over alternative sources and were rewarded with lucrative jobs after they left government service. The latter was largely understaffed and lacked regulatory power. As former governor of the Fukushima Prefecture Eisaku Sato put it, "an organization that is inherently untrustworthy is charged with ensuring the safety of Japan's nuclear plants."

Yet despite these regulatory shortcomings, the Japanese government was well aware of the risks facing its nuclear plants. The International Atomic Energy Association (IAEA) warned Japan in 2008 that Japanese reactors were designed to withstand only a 7.0 magnitude earthquake. The Tokyo quake registered a 9.0 on the Richter scale. An IAEA official explained that it was updating its safety recommendations concerning seismic activity and informed Japan that its guidelines were outdated, but the government paid him little heed. When in 2006 a court ordered a nuclear power plant in western Japan to be shut down due to concerns that it could not withstand a powerful earthquake, the government went out of its way to overturn the ruling three years later. Perhaps most significant, the operator of the power plant ignored an internal report that suggested the Fukushima plant was susceptible to a tsunami, rejecting the dire predictions as "unrealistic." The plant was designed to withstand waves of only up to five meters in height, which the report warned may be inadequate in the event of a large tsunami. The Tokyo tsunami produced waves three times that tall, swamping the facility. This danger was not conveyed to government officials until four days before the earthquake. Had the company or government heeded any of these predictions earlier, the catastrophe could have been avoided.

Through the valor of plant employees, who devoutly worked to contain the meltdowns while exposing themselves to deadly radiation, the disaster was mitigated. Quick-witted managers injected seawater into damaged reactors, preventing fuel rods from dangerously overheating. The Japanese government was criticized for initially rating the accident Level 4 on the International Nuclear Event Scale, a rating that was later changed to 7, the highest value. The government evacuated 590,000 residents within twelve miles of the plant. A governmental report, issued in the uncertain weeks after the earthquake but kept secret for months, grimly outlined the worst-case scenario. Had the reactors completely melted down and the cooling pools failed, the government would have ordered evacuations within 155 miles. That area would have included Tokyo and affected thirty-five million people. In light of this prediction, Japan can almost be considered lucky. The meltdown made the surrounding region inhospitable and forced an economically ruinous shutdown of much of the country's energy grid, but the damage could have been far greater.

Japan is still reeling from the earthquake and the meltdown. Forced to switch to natural gas and other fossil fuels, Japan has since suffered a deep trade deficit. Though many environmentalists have used the incident as evidence that nuclear power should be abandoned, such a claim is premature. Dwindling fossil fuels, compounded by the threat of global warming, mean that nuclear power has an important place in the twenty-first-century economy. Instead of abandoning nuclear power, it is crucial that nuclear power plants adhere to safety regulations. The Japanese government was by no means at fault for pursuing nuclear power. Its mistake was to prioritize cost-cutting at the expense of safety. Having received warnings about its nuclear industry, and in particular the Fukushima plant, the Japanese government should have addressed these concerns. Its failure to do so greatly increased the cost to the environment, to its economy, and to the welfare of its citizens. Ignoring its own standards and the warnings in its reports was a mistake for which the Japanese government has no excuse. The breaches at Fukushima not only were an ecological and human disaster but also set back the future development of nuclear power unnecessarily in a world hungry for energy.

A FINAL THOUGHT

Perhaps it can be somewhat reassuring today to look at the grievous mistakes commanders and leaders have made in the past. No matter how incompetent the president or prime minister, that leader is unlikely to match Ala ad-Din Muhammed in coming close to getting nearly the entire population of the richest nation in his world killed. No matter how we think of the U.S. Congress, it cannot cause as much trouble as the Assembly in the French Revolution or as the Long Parliament did for Charles I. With modern communications and an active press, no leader can today be as out of touch as Louis XVI and Marie Antoinette. The world has progressed and the human race reached the moon, despite all the errors and stupidity of the past. A thought that, even as you look at today's headlines, can give you hope for the future.